Elections to Open Seats in the U.S. House

Elections to Open Seats in the U.S. House

Where the Action Is

Ronald Keith Gaddie and Charles S. Bullock, III

ROWMAN & LITTLEFIELD PUBLISHERS, INC.
Lanham • Boulder • New York • Oxford

ROWMAN & LITTLEFIELD PUBLISHERS, INC.

Published in the United States of America
by Rowman & Littlefield Publishers, Inc.
4720 Boston Way, Lanham, Maryland 20706
http://www.rowmanlittlefield.com

12 Hid's Copse Road, Cumnor Hill, Oxford OX2 9JJ, England

British Library Cataloguing in Publication Information Available

Library of Congress Cataloging-in-Publication Data
Gaddie, Ronald Keith.
    Elections to open seats in the U.S. House : where the action is / Ronald Keith Gaddie and Charles S. Bullock, III.
        p. cm.
    Includes bibliographical references and index.
    ISBN 0-7425-0860-9 (alk. paper) — ISBN 0-7425-0861-7 (pbk.: alk. paper)
        1. United States. Congress. House—Elections. I. Bullock, Charles S., 1942– II. Title.
JK1965 .G33 2000
324.973—dc21

00-031104

Printed in the United States of America

♾ ™The paper used in this publication meets the minimum requirements of American National Standard for Information Sciences—Permanence of Paper for Printed Library Materials ANSI/NISO Z39.48-1992.

Contents

Illustrations

FIGURES

TABLES

Acknowledgments

When we started this project in late 1993, it seemed like an interesting idea to explore the congressional elections that produced most new members of Congress. At the time, the Democrats held a solid majority in the U.S. House, and incumbent defeats continued to be rare. The 1994 election caused many congressional-election scholars to reexamine their understanding of congressional politics and the notion of the "permanent" Democratic majority. For us, it provided an opportunity to consider the indicators of political success in the absence of stifling incumbent influences and across what some have termed a "critical" election. Our conclusions will no doubt surprise some, especially as they relate to the underlying competitiveness of U.S. congressional elections both before and after the election of 1994.

A variety of professional colleagues commented on either the final book manuscript or the numerous papers and articles that preceded this study. Among those we wish to thank for their comments, criticisms, and encouragement are Alan Abramowitz, Sunil Ahuja, Hal Bass, Jim Campbell, John Clark, Gary W. Copeland, Robert Darcy, Robert England, Robert Erikson, Daniel Franklin, James K. Galbraith, James Garand, Robert Grafstein, John Hindera, Laura Junor, John Kuzenski, Brad Lockerbie, Lesli McCollum, Jonathan D. Mott, Richard Murray, David Nixon, Marvin Overby, Glenn Parker, Ronald Peters, Glenn Peterson, James L. Regens, Byron Shafer, Harold Stanley, Robert Stein, Joseph Stewart, Gregory Theilemann, Ronald Weber, Christopher Wlezien, and Mark Wrighton. Chapters 2, 4, 5, and 6 derived from prior research we published in *American Politics Quarterly, Social Science Quarterly, Political Research Quarterly*, and *Legislative Studies Quarterly*, and we thank the editors of those journals—Charles Bonjean, Robert L. Lineberry, James Garand, Melissa Collie, Lyn Ragsdale, and William J. Dixon—for their encouragement and dissemination of our work. While graduate students at the University of Oklahoma, Andrew Hicks, Kim Hoffman, Carrie Palmer, Anders Ferrington, Scott Buchanan, and Craig Williams constructed some of the various data sets used in this study. Sally Coleman Selden, now of Syracuse University, was instrumental way back in 1992 (pre-Web) in helping gain access to Federal Election Commission databases. Special thanks goes to Bridget Pilcher, who typed innumerable manuscript revisions from tape and our near-legible markups. At Rowman & Littlefield Publishers, our editor, Jennifer Knerr, kept us encouraged about this project, and the two publisher's reviewers provided critical and useful commentary. The University of Oklahoma Research Council and the Carl Albert Center for Congressional Studies provided research support that enabled us to complete the manuscript.

Mistakes are ours, the good ideas were inspired by conversations with others, and we thank all of our friends and colleagues for their continued support and indulgence. Final thanks go to our families for tolerating the late-night phone conversations and weekend research trips that typify our collaborations, especially when the Atlanta Braves are on television.

The data in tables 2.1, 3.2, 3.12, 3.14, 3.15, 3.16, 5.1, 6.1, 6.3, 6.4, and 7.7 were compiled by the authors.

This book is dedicated to the next generation that filled the open seats at our table since we started this project. For Collin, Jason, Alec, Christopher, and Cassidy Erin, with all our love, Daddy and Pawpaw.

Chapter 1

Where the Action Is: Why Open Seats Jump-Start Congressional Careers

One more article demonstrating that House incumbents tend to win reelection will induce a spontaneous primal scream among all congressional scholars across the nation.

—Charles O. Jones, 1981

Incumbency as an amulet assuring reelection has gained near universal acceptance among congressional scholars; political pundits; and, of course, frustrated congressional challengers. A forest has been sacrificed to studies that attempt to disentangle the source, magnitude, and extent of the incumbency advantage.[1] Research into the dynamics of congressional elections has beaten to death the proposition that incumbents are advantaged in seeking reelection. Despite Professor Jones's warning above, a steady output of conference papers and articles restates this finding.

Most of the focus on incumbent reelection leaves issues such as where new members of Congress come from or how they begin their congressional careers only partially explored. The bulk of congressional elections scholarship has concentrated on a place in which little has happened, is happening, and may never happen. The site where the action is, where uncertainty and change are likely, is open seat elections, but this scene remains virtually ignored. Open seats, not the defeat of incumbents, are the portal through which most legislators enter Congress. Since 1962, 58 percent of congressional freshmen came from open seats, and from 1982 to 1994, well over 70 percent of the newcomers to Congress made it there by winning open seats. They are, in fact, the people Gary Jacobson and Sam Kernell (1983) warned us about—the strategic politicians.

The route to Congress for most new members does not involve defeating an incumbent with an established record.[2] Most freshmen arrive after competing in a large field of candidates in which they have defined the cam-

1

Figure 1.1 The Electoral Avenue of Freshmen Legislators, 1954–1994

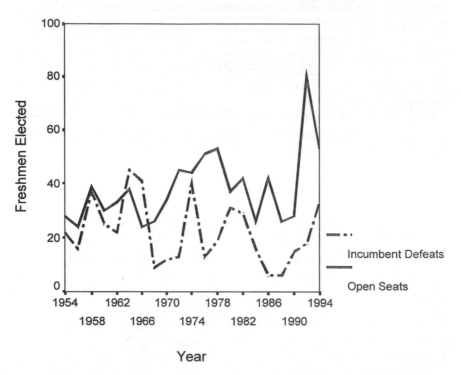

Year

paign in terms of themselves and their own political accomplishments, rather than in terms of an incumbent's record. Constituents cast ballots based on their evaluations of the promise of the contending candidates, rather than relying on retrospective evaluations framed by the incumbent's constituency service, credit claiming, or position-taking (Mayhew 1974a). Because the new contenders are not known commodities to most voters, voter judgments will be more prospective, or speculative, in nature. On this dimension alone, open seat elections differ from incumbent elections.

Recent elections illustrate this growing trend of open seats providing the predominant source of congressional freshmen. In 1993, the House welcomed 116 freshmen amid perceptions that they most often replaced incumbents who bounced checks or engaged in other misdeeds, although some departing members were induced to retire by a provision allowing them to retain leftover campaign funds.[3] In 1995, another eighty-six freshmen entered the House, boosting the total number of legislators elected during the 1990s to more than two hundred. Contrary to these perceptions, however, in these high turnover elections, most of the new blood came in open seats rather than from defeating Republicans who had served under

President Bush in 1992 or from discrediting Democratic incumbents in 1994. Open seat freshmen outnumbered successful challengers to incumbents by eighteen in 1994. In 1992, open seat winners had an even greater advantage over incumbent-beaters, outnumbering the latter by eighty to thirty-six. As figure 1.1 shows, only twice between 1954 and 1994 (1964 and 1966) did incumbent challenging prove more fruitful than open-seat seeking, and the likelihood of coming to the House via an open seat increased beginning with 1968.

From 1983 to 1995, 504 freshmen entered the U.S. House of Representatives, and of these, 314 (62.3 percent) won open seats in regular elections. Another forty-eight (9.5 percent) were elected in special open seat elections made necessary by resignation or death, so that just over one-quarter of all new legislators unhorsed incumbents.

OPEN SEAT PARTISAN SWITCHES

Not only do open seats facilitate the introduction of new personnel into Congress, they are also the basis for most partisan change. To understand why, consider figure 1.2, which shows how few incumbents lost reelection bids during the second half of the twentieth century. Even in bad years, members of the House won reelection more than 90 percent of the time.

With incumbents so difficult to dislodge, open seats are very attractive to political parties because of the opportunities they offer for change. As demonstrated in figure 1.2, even in their most virulent fits of anti-incumbency, voters cast out few incumbents. Usually the defeats that do occur are borne disproportionately by the incumbent president's party in midterm elections and by the losing party in presidential years (J. Campbell 1986, 1997; Gaddie 1997; A. Campbell 1960).

Although the retirement slump, that is, the drop in the share of the vote won by the retiring incumbent's party between the incumbent's last reelection bid and the election to fill the vacancy, does not make all open seats competitive, this slump typically increases competitiveness, thereby enhancing the likelihood of a switch in partisan control of that seat. Figure 1.3 shows how much more likely it is that there will be a change in partisan control when running for open seats than when challenging incumbents. Rarely do general elections replace even 10 percent of the incumbents, whereas 35.4 percent of the open seats changed partisan hands between 1982 and 1994. Even excluding the exceptionally high incidence of party changes in 1994, 31 percent of the open seats set up a shift in partisan control.[4] With the exception of 1992, the rate of partisan change in open seats was at least ten points higher than when an incumbent ran. The pattern of switches in open seats and incumbent races generally tracks

Figure 1.2 Incumbents Reelected to the House of Representatives, 1954–1994

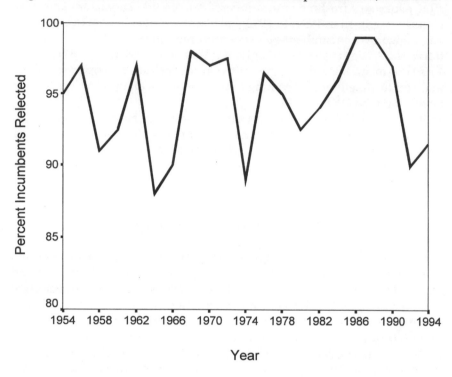

Year

together, although the relationship is moderate (r = .42), a further indication that open seats and incumbent elections are substantially different. The trend toward greater numbers of open seats in the 1990s means that more seats have been exposed to the volatility of partisan national tides. In 1994, partisan change came in more than 40 percent of the open seats, the highest incidence in forty-two years.

As a truism, open seats produce personnel turnover, but they need not trigger partisan turnover. Nonetheless, what Abramowitz has termed "seats at risk" (i.e., the number of open seats that a party defends when one of its incumbents retires) is strongly related to aggregate seat changes (Gaddie 1997). As portrayed in figure 1.4, partisan swings stemming from incumbent defeats fluctuate at less than 10 percent. And although the partisan changes from the two sources move together in years having major shifts (1958, 1974, 1980, and 1994), the vast share of the change is attributable to what happens in open seats.[5] Partisan tides leave their highest marks in open seats, when as many as 40 percent of the seats change parties, and in nine elections, the net swing to one party in open seats exceeded 10 percent; four of these occurred between 1982 and 1994.

Figure 1.3 The Proportional Partisan Shift of Open- and Incumbent-Held Seats, 1954–1994

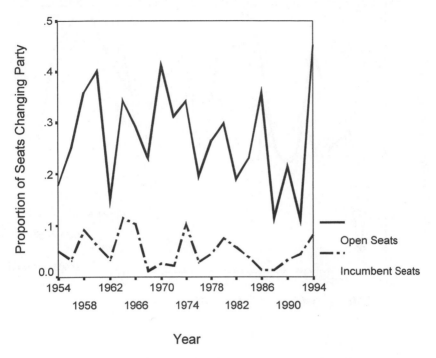

Year

OPEN SEATS CONTRASTED WITH INCUMBENT–CHALLENGER CONTESTS

The key difference between open seats and incumbent–challenger contests is the shadow an incumbent casts. Often incumbents retain office because those who might mount the most formidable challenges do not compete. Generally the most promising challengers have acquired political experience when running for lesser offices, and this may have provided them with a harsh initiation. In the course of running for lesser offices, candidates learn how to present issues, what to say, how to say it, and how to avoid statements and actions that might alienate key components of the constituency. Despite a widespread distaste for having to raise campaign funds, officeholders have typically overcome qualms associated with panhandling and have developed contacts who are likely to contribute (witness Bill Clinton and Al Gore in 1996). Those who have succeeded in winning a lesser office can use that position to develop name recognition and media skills. The officeholder also may acquire a reputation for expertise in a policy area important to the constituency and achieve a facility to

Figure 1.4　The Partisan Swing of Open- and Incumbent-Held Seats, 1954–1994

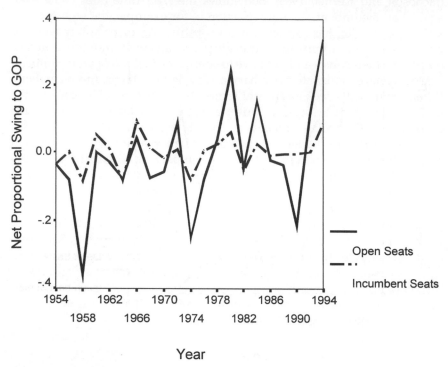

Year

respond to queries about a wide range of current issues. Elected officials can secure voter loyalty by cutting bureaucratic red tape and helping secure projects for groups and communities in the district (Mayhew 1974a). Officeholders may have learned valuable lessons in campaign organization and have skilled workers scattered about who will suit up for a new campaign.

Given the odds of beating an incumbent, it is hardly surprising that the best and brightest potential challengers usually forego contests against politically healthy members of Congress. Thomas Kazee's (1994) collection of case studies of candidate emergence in U.S. House districts reinforces the rationality of foregoing a congressional challenge. Ambition, according to Kazee's contributors, runs rampant in many constituencies, but most potential challengers are risk averse. The odds of ousting most incumbents are poor, and a failed challenge can fatally wound political prospects. A loser may be saddled with debt; may be surrounded by the stench of defeat; and will often have had to pass up reelection to the office currently held and therefore be less able to attract the media and contributors, serve constituents, and demonstrate political skills. The strategic politician awaits a propitious moment before attempting to move up the office-holding ladder (Jacobson and Kernell 1983). Sometimes the *right* time does come even against an incumbent seeking reelection if, for example, the incumbent is soiled by scandal, has lost touch with constituents, or narrowly won the previous election. More often, strategic politicians wait until they can face others like themselves and not have to confront a Goliath of an incumbent.

Most congressional elections have a well-defined focus: the incumbent. When incumbents seek additional terms, the contest revolves around the incumbent's attributes (age, seniority, race); the incumbent's activities in the chamber (committee assignments and work, legislative accomplishments, voting record); and the incumbent's constituency relations and campaign efforts (home style, pork-barrel projects, impact of redistricting) (Fenno 1978, 1991, 1996; Fowler and McClure 1989; Fowler 1993). The financing of congressional campaigns is structured by the incumbent's needs, contacts, and the financial strength and resolve of ideological or economic supporters and enemies (Grier and Munger 1991; Herrnson 1995). Contests involving incumbents tend to be retrospective, with the election being a referendum on the activities of the officeholder that the voters affirm except in extreme cases of incumbent incompetence or malfeasance. When a legislator is turned out of office, much of the postelection analysis turns to explaining "what the member did wrong" to draw a tough challenger and lose (Bauer and Hibbing 1987; Fenno 1996).

Because open seats provide a more level playing field for those wanting to go to Congress, they often attract multiple competitive contestants in one if not both party primaries (Hotelling 1929; Duverger 1954). By eliminating the advantages associated with incumbency, open seats introduce uncertainty and stimulate contests dramatically different from most incumbent reelection bids.

In open seat contests, cues that voters rely on extensively are missing, for, as Fowler and McClure (1989) observe, without an incumbent, a key linkage to the constituency has been severed. Occasionally in an open seat, a dominant candidate, such as state senator Carrie Meek (D) in Florida's Seventeenth District in 1992, emerges and overwhelms minimal opposition.[6] More commonly, even politically experienced open seat contestants lack the commanding advantage in name recognition or past favors that often renders incumbents inviolable. Even a candidate who currently or previously held public office has usually represented only a portion of the area contained in the congressional district and therefore must work to become known in other parts of the district. Except when someone such as Meek can use incumbency in one office to secure the dominance usually reserved for sitting members of Congress, voters turn to other cues when the magnetic force of incumbency is missing. When open seats attract multiple candidates, each of whom has a unique geographical base, voters may pursue what V. O. Key (1949) identified as "friends and neighbors politics," and they vote for the candidate from their city, neighborhood, or county.

Party label, which Mayhew (1974a) found could be trumped by incumbency (see also Mann and Wolfinger 1980), is more likely to structure many voters' decisions in open seats. As evidence, consider that although the margin of victory for incumbents increased after the mid-1960s, the retirement slump also increased as vote distributions return to levels uncontaminated by incumbency (Jacobson 1990). Incumbents pad their victory margins by adding some voters who identified with their opponent's party to cohesive support in their own party.

Evidence of the current strength of incumbents and subsequent large slumps upon their retirement appears in Alford and Brady's (1993) report that only twice from 1846 to 1960 did average retirement slumps approximate the *smallest* average decline registered in any year after 1960. The pattern of partisan defections concentrated among the professed loyalists of the party not holding the seat (Cover 1977; Mann and Wolfinger 1980; Bullock and Scicchitano 1982) is not repeated in the absence of an incumbent. This result is in keeping with Mayhew's (1974a) finding that open seat congressional contests and presidential voting show a greater number of competitive congressional districts than are found when analyzing incumbent-challenger elections. The presence of an incumbent distorts the picture of partisan balance found when looking at voting under other conditions. Remove the incumbent, and the voting pattern swings back to the underlying, more competitive, partisan distribution that produces the large retirement slumps.

The distortion in party loyalties produced by incumbency can enable a party supported by only a minority in a district to continue to hold a congressional seat. By discouraging serious competition while working to maintain a favorable image in a district, an incumbent can win reelection even as the district's voters support the other party's nominees for president, senator, and governor. Some have argued that the incumbency cue retarded realignment and contributed to the protracted Democratic dominance of southern House and Senate seats long after the bulk of the region's electorate began voting regularly for Republican presidential candidates.[7]

Open seats also sow uncertainty among financial contributors interested in congressional elections. Most interest groups that give to campaigns—with two notable exceptions, labor and ideological groups—want access to policymakers and therefore have little interest in providing money to people unlikely to serve in the next Congress. Losers cannot help shape public policy, and contributors to losers may face an impediment when trying to establish or maintain good relations with a legislator. The uncertainty surrounding open seat contests should prompt political action committees to hedge their bets by giving to both the Democratic and Republican nominees, or the contributor may wait until *after* the votes are counted to send a check to the winner. Therefore, money is more evenly distributed in open seat contests, rather than one candidate (the incumbent) being showered with contri-butions while the opponent starves, as usually occurs in contested House elections.

WHY STUDY OPEN SEATS?

Because most members use open seats as their launching pad to the House, to understand the dynamics of open seat elections is to understand change in the personnel and partisan composition of Congress. Despite knowledge of how occasional upsets of incumbents occur, such research tells little about the electoral origins of most contemporary members of Congress. Mayhew (1974a) and Fenno (1978) both argue that the candidates' congressional career, especially their home style, is structured by their initial electoral experience, but for most members of Congress, political science research does not speak to their formative electoral experience.

Undertaking the study of open seat elections offers the opportunity to examine explanations offered for the historic electoral frustration of the GOP. The most common reason proposed for the Republican party's inability to win a legislative majority in the 1980s was the Democratic incumbency advantage. As incumbents enjoy an electoral advantage, the absence of incumbents results in a more level playing field. Therefore, open seats should present a fortuitous opportunity for the GOP to enlarge its caucus. The lack of GOP growth through open seats prior to 1994 undercuts this hypothesis, however, and indicates that the extent of the Republican congressional malaise went beyond a simple incumbency disadvantage. If the GOP had performed no better in open seats in 1994 than it did in similar contests during the previous decade, Republicans would have won just twenty-five of fifty-two open seats and remained three seats short of a majority. The fact that in 1994 the GOP registered the largest partisan shift in open seats since 1946 merits further examination, and that examination is one of the objectives of this book.

Of course, the initial electoral experience of new incumbents structures their subsequent political behavior. Studies of incumbency advantage measure the electoral value of incumbency relative to the expected level of competition in open seats (Gelman and King 1990; Alford and Brady 1989). Winning hard-fought open seats serves as the introduction to congressional politics for two-thirds of the membership. It follows that surviving a field of experienced, well-funded candidates would induce in the new member a pattern of perpetual campaigning to stay in office or, as Representative Frank Lucas (R-OK) observed, "paranoia is why incumbents survive." This lends further cause to investigate a winning candidate's first election.

Studying the dynamics of open seats also contributes to knowledge of how electoral reform may impact congressional elections in general. Reformers have offered several options for making congressional elections more competitive. These proposals aim to offset the incumbency advantage, either by altering the system of benefits and transfers that enhance incumbent visibility or by limiting the ability of incumbents to seek reelection. The term-limit reform presumes that incumbents are essentially unbeatable, so by periodically eliminating incumbents, congressional elections will be made more competitive. The questions relevant to reform that this research must address are several. Do open seats lead to enhanced two-party competition? How are the dynamics of candidate recruitment and campaign finance related to the outcomes of open seat congressional elections? If relationships exist, how do they differ from those in incumbent elections? How will proposed reforms impact on the conduct, financing, and recruitment of open seat races?

PLAN OF THE BOOK

What is known about open seat races? What kind of candidates contest these seats? How are they financed? How do open seats contribute to the broader political changes in American politics? Those are the questions we seek to answer in this volume.

Chapter 2 discusses the initial study that laid bare the incumbent–open seat dichotomy of congressional elections. First we elaborate on the theoretic importance of open seats initially advanced by Mayhew (1974a) and present data on the continuation of marginal competition in open seats. We discuss how open seats structure changes in the composition of Congress before we shift the analysis to the district level and contemplate the existing theories of Democratic party congressional dominance in the 1980s in the context of open seats. Then, we examine the role of open seats in the shift in partisan control to the GOP in 1994, assessing the Republican triumph against the party's unsuccessful efforts in open seats during the previous decade.

Chapter 3 explores the problem of candidate recruitment and candidate emergence in open seat elections. We discuss partisan differences in candidate emergence and primary competition, modeling the emergence and quality of open seat candidates. We analyze the relationship between candidate pools and candidate development and examine the unique features of candidate recruitment and primary competition in the South in detail, using cases to illustrate the dramatic change in candidate emergence. Finally, we discuss the peculiar changes in GOP candidate emergence and competition in the 1990s, emphasizing their relevance to the Republican success in 1994.

The role of money in congressional elections is explored in depth in chapter 4. Money is thought to play a prominent part in determining election outcomes, and potential political reforms are often aimed at changing political campaign finance. In this chapter, we consider the general financial quality of candidates for open seats and ponder a variety of partisan, constituency, and candidate attributes that are thought to be related to a congressional candidate's financial quality. We then delve more deeply into the issue of campaign finance in open seats by examining the political behavior of economic interest groups and their political action committees, especially as the behavior of those groups might relate to the political changes of the 1990s.

Chapter 5 is about one of the significant electoral events of the latter twentieth century: the tremendous influx of female representatives via open seats in 1992. Direct evidence of a "Year of the Woman" effect on open seat elections is not, however, evident from this analysis. Nonetheless, women were able to command the resources needed for success in congressional elections in sufficiently large numbers to increase their representation. The underlying trends in candidate emergence and campaign finance worked to the advantage of women. The large number of open seats afforded women expanded opportunities for advancement. The Year of the Woman had a decidedly partisan overtone, as gender benefits accrued to Democratic, but not Republican, female candidates. We note how the disproportionate presence of women among Democratic candidates exaggerated female losses in 1994. The potential for female advancement appears to be substantial, but only to the extent that politically experienced women continue to mobilize campaign resources in both parties.

Chapter 6 considers a particular type of open seat—special elections. We examine the emergence of candidates in special open seat races and then test a series of models on special election outcomes. Despite being inoculated from contests for other offices, there appears to be little that is unique to special elections other than their timing. Candidate spending and constituency characteristics play important roles in election outcomes. The one major difference is that candidate experience is less important in special elections than in other open seat contests.

In chapter 7, we attempt to place the findings from chapters 2 through 6 into broader contexts of representation, competition, and political reform. In particular, we consider recent developments in open seats, especially the competitiveness of open seats in 1996 and 1998, and use those elections to place the 1994 election into a more proper context. The predictive validity of the open seat model is then demonstrated, and we apply the model to forecast the outcome in open seat contests for the 2000 election. Finally, we use the results of our analysis to paint a hypothetical picture of congressional elections in 2000 if every seat were open, and we use a variety of scenarios to demonstrate the responsiveness of American congressional elections to partisan tides in the absence of incumbency.

It is our intent that this study do more than simply fill in the gap left in the tapestry of congressional elections research. This analysis opens a window to the dynamics of the most competitive of congressional elections while also offering insights on questions of partisan competition, electoral realignment, and interest group influence that continue to hold the fascination of students of American politics.

NOTES

1. See Gary C. Jacobson (1990), *The Electoral Origins of Divided Government,* for an excellent discussion of the incumbency advantage and the debate surrounding its effects.

2. Of House members reelected in 1972, 41 percent had beaten an incumbent to get to Congress. Over the next two decades, 25 percent of the class elected to the House in 1952 lost general elections, and another 10 percent was felled in a primary (Erikson 1976).

3. Incumbent House members elected prior to 1982 could take advantage of a grandfather clause in the campaign finance laws that allowed them to retire and convert their leftover campaign funds to personal or charitable use. Incumbents who wished to retain those funds had to retire before January 3, 1993. A logistic regression of factors related to retirements in 1992 found eligibility under the grandfather clause to be significantly and positively related to the decision to leave office voluntarily (Regens, Gaddie, and Lockerbie 1995).

4. In 1996, 24 percent of open seats changed party.

5. We should note that these analyses exclude seats created through reapportionment, where partisan switches by definition cannot occur.

6. Meek, who was initially elected to the House at age sixty-eight, is a Miami political institution. She was the first black woman elected to the Florida legislature and the first black ever elected to the Florida Senate. She served a total of fourteen years before moving on to Congress.

7. Although a factor, incumbency alone did not account for Democratic success in House contests long after the region shifted parties at the presidential level (Aistrup 1996), because even in special elections, the GOP often failed to capitalize on the opportunity provided by an open seat (Glaser 1996).

Chapter 2

Open Seat Congressional Elections: Are These Influenced by the Same Factors as Incumbent Elections?

The extensive research into elections that involve incumbents has identified candidate spending, challenger attributes, partisan tides, and constituency factors as elements that can influence outcomes. The impact of these factors is often diluted, sometimes largely eliminated, by the dominance of incumbency. A few sitting members of Congress appear so secure that no one ventures forth to mount a challenge, whereas in many other districts, the challengers are woefully lacking in political experience. When unable to stimulate contributions from parties and political action committees (PACs), challengers are reduced to running shoe-string campaigns funded out of their own savings and a second mortgage on the family home. In contrast, incumbents can tap into seemingly unlimited interest group money. The strategic-politician literature reports that the best potential opponents frequently sit on the sidelines rather than risk fortune and reputation challenging incumbents who regularly win more than 90 percent of the time (Jacobson and Kernell 1983).

Put simply, there is more of the "stuff" that makes for competitive elections when the incumbent is removed from the equation. Jacobson's summary treatment of open seats reflects this perspective:

> [In open seats] both candidates are likely to have some experience in elective office, and, therefore, some familiarity with at least a part of the constituency. . . . Both are likely to have adequate campaign resources because contests for open seats are notoriously competitive; the best chance by far to take a seat from the opposing party occurs when no incumbent is involved. . . . When incumbency is not a factor, local partisan habits and national politics do more to shape campaigns and therefore election results. Party affiliation, national tides, and presidential coattails become a bigger part of the story. (1997, 77a)

13

This chapter examines open seat elections using knowledge gained about congressional elections in general. The objective here is to examine major features of congressional elections and determine whether results for open seats are influenced by the same factors that impact contests with an incumbent.

The first topic we examine is the rate of marginality in open seats. As indicated in chapter 1, a major emphasis of congressional elections research has been on the security incumbents enjoy, with very few pushed into serious competitive efforts in any given year.

The second topic is an analysis of three factors derived from the literature on incumbent reelections in the context of open seat contests. First, access to funds and political experience will likely promote the chances of a candidate for an open seat just as they help challengers draw votes away from incumbents. Second, the racial makeup of districts has been important in determining partisan outcomes, especially in the South. Therefore, we examine racial composition of the district and the changes brought by redistricting. Presidential coattails, which can be strong enough to topple even seemingly safe incumbents, is the third factor. These three elements are then combined in multivariate models. We conclude by placing 1994 in context. Were the results of that year simply business as usual in open seats or was it a break from tradition?

MARGINALITY AND OPEN SEATS

Political scientist David Mayhew (1974a) observed that, starting in the 1960s, fewer and fewer incumbents had competitive elections. Histograms displaying vote shares of a party's candidates, similar to those in figure 2.1, show a shift away from a normally distributed vote and toward a bimodal distribution of competition with increasing vote shares won by incumbents of both parties. In each election from 1982 to 1992, at least two-thirds of the House incumbents won more than 60 percent of the vote, and in 1988, almost nine of every ten incumbents sailed through with 60 percent support (Ornstein, Mann, and Malbin 1998, 68).

Unlike incumbent elections, Mayhew found that open seats continued to demonstrate the unimodal pattern in which great numbers of districts are competitive, much as had been observed in elections involving incumbents as recently as the 1950s. This unimodal pattern resembles the pattern of presidential competition in the districts. As incumbents increased their electoral security and insulated themselves from changes in partisan political tides, partisan seat changes became largely confined to districts without incumbents, and overall seat swings were structured by both the frequency of open seats and the vulnerability of the respective parties as a result of retirements (cf., Hibbing 1982; Fowler 1993).

Mayhew suggests that national tides and open seats are related. He links incumbent and open seat elections, noting, "If fewer House members are winning elections narrowly, and if the proportion of 'open seats' per election is not rising, it ought to follow that congressional seat swings are declining in amplitude" (1974a, 30). Goidel and Shields (1994) speculate that the different patterns of competition for incumbents and open seats may not persist because open seats might not be especially competitive over time. If they are correct, vote distributions in open seats should develop the bimodal trough of low competitiveness that Mayhew observes in incumbent contests.

If competition is disappearing from open seats, much like its typical absence when incumbents seek reelection, there will be long-term implications for congressional elections. Collie (1981) reports that the initial election of a candidate in an open seat has repercussions for that person's subsequent reelections. Her analysis of incumbents who entered Congress between 1952 and 1972 finds that those initially elected with comfortable margins won reelection at a rate roughly ten points higher than incumbents who narrowly won their open seat. The initial advantage persisted as legislators who had large first-victory margins won at least three more terms at a rate twenty points higher than other incumbents. If initial elections are not competitive, then there may be less subsequent competition in those districts.

As indicated in figure 2.1, the distribution of marginal open seats since 1982 resembles the patterns for open seats noted by Mayhew in the 1960s and 1970s. There is some variation in the year-to-year placement of the mode and in the average level of support for Republican nominees, although the means, medians, and modes are consistently near 50 percent. The high level of competitiveness in open seats has continued.

How stable are patterns of open seat competition? Except for 1982 and 1994, the modal category of open seat elections is the competitive 45 to 55 percent range. The most common outcome is for the Republican to win with 50 to 55 percent of the vote or to lose to a Democrat who has polled 50 to 55 percent of the vote. In 1982, the mode for open seat outcomes was the 35 to 45 percent Republican vote; in 1994, it was the 55 to 65 percent Republican vote. The range of competition resembles a normal distribution, although the tail of Republican votes below 50 percent is longer and indicates some very weak districts for the GOP. In only one contested open seat has a Republican garnered more than 75 percent of the vote.[1]

Marginal contests continue to be more common in open seat than incumbent elections, but open seats are not always competitive. Figure 2.1 indicates that never do more than half the open seats fall in the 45 to 55 percent range, and the number of hotly contested open seats fell to 29 percent in 1982. Since 1982, 36 percent of all open seats fell into the marginal range. A deeper examination of the dynamics of open seat congressional elections is needed to understand the variation in competition across constituencies.

Figure 2.1   The Marginals in Open Seat Elections, 1982–1994

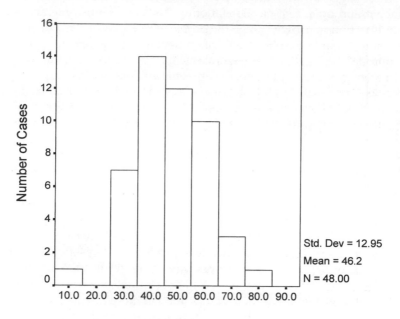

1982

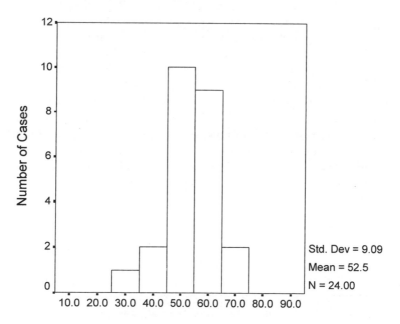

1984

Figure 2.1   Continued

1986

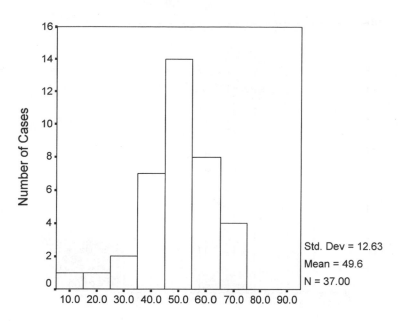

Std. Dev = 12.63
Mean = 49.6
N = 37.00

Republican Vote Share

1988

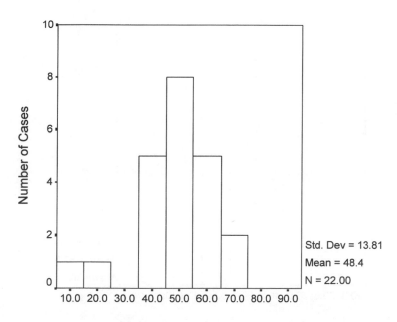

Std. Dev = 13.81
Mean = 48.4
N = 22.00

Republican Vote Share

Figure 2.1   Continued

1990

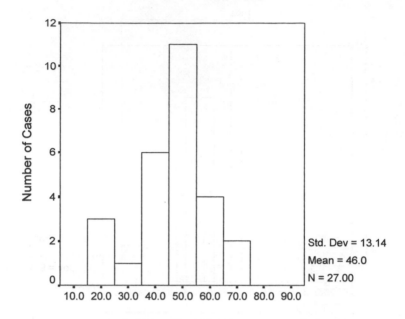

Std. Dev = 13.14
Mean = 46.0
N = 27.00

Republican Vote Share

1992

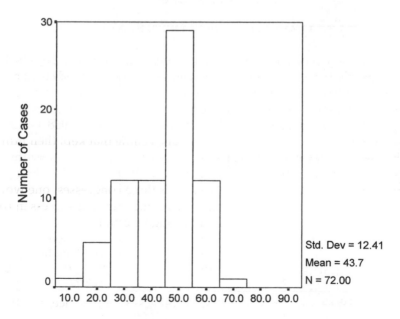

Std. Dev = 12.41
Mean = 43.7
N = 72.00

Republican Vote Share

Figure 2.1   Continued
1994

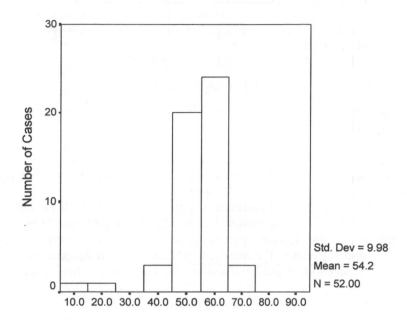

Republican Vote Share

COMPETITION FOR OPEN SEATS

Given the infrequency with which incumbents lose, open seat results are the most promising tea leaves for those who seek to understand change (or its absence) in partisan control of the House. A persistent mystery prior to 1994 centered on the inability of the GOP to come close to a majority in the House even as it dominated presidential elections from 1968 to 1992. House Republicans seemed to confront a glass ceiling that kept their numbers below 192, a level that they attained in the Ninety-first, Ninety-third, and Ninety-seventh Congresses. Now that the GOP has shattered the glass ceiling and retained control of the House for three congresses, one wonders whether the same factors associated with their limited success in the past continued to impact the 1994 breakthrough election.

Republicans frequently offered three explanations for their decades locked in the minority: (1) entrenched Democratic incumbents held seats that were "natural" Republican constituencies, especially in the South; (2) mapmakers created districts friendly to Democratic candidates; and (3) Democrats ran candidates who had advantages in experience, funding, and message (Jacobson 1990). Another explanation proffered by former Democratic House Speaker Tom Foley, in 1997, attributed the sustained Democratic majority to being in the majority when the era of safe incumbents started. If the Republican problems were incumbent-oriented, then the retirements of Democrats, especially in the South, should open the way for Republican gains.

Natural Constituencies: Split-Level Partisanship

Were Republican congressional candidates penalized by American voters in the 1980s? Were Democrats the beneficiaries of voting behavior that supported Republicans for president but Democrats for Congress? Did the incongruence so often observed in incumbent elections—out-party identifiers defecting to support the incumbent's party (Mann and Wolfinger 1980)—carry over to open seat elections?

Throughout the 1980s, Republicans argued that Democratic incumbents were the problem in congressional elections. If not for those Democratic incumbents, so the argument ran, congressional Republicans would have pulled broad support in the same manner that Ronald Reagan did at the top of the ticket and would have become the House majority party in 1980 or 1984 instead of waiting until 1994. Democratic legislators sat on "natural" Republican constituencies, especially in the South, where Reagan and Bush ran ahead of their national showings, while Republicans languished with less than 40 percent of congressional seats. *Get rid of the Democratic incumbents,* went this argument, *and obtain a Republican Congress.*

Alan Abramowitz (1991a) was among the first to challenge this argument, noting that if the Republican problem was Democratic incumbents, then open seats should be trending Republican. In fact, his analysis indicates that in the 1980s, the GOP lost a net of six open seats, just the opposite of the presidential trend. Of course, it is possible that those lost districts were held by Republicans as a result of a GOP incumbent advantage and that the natural partisanship of those districts was Democratic. To test this possibility, we examine the difference between the district's normal vote and the open seat candidate's performance, thereby taking the incumbent out of the equation.

Normal vote measures are often used to assess the equilibrium level of partisan competition in constituencies. The normal vote is typically calculated by averaging a party's share of the vote in several elections in a constituency. Because we are concerned with a very specific argument—that incumbents stifled presidential Republicanism from moving down ticket—we use the average GOP share of the two-party vote for president in the previous two elections.

Table 2.1 reports the Republican normal presidential vote by region from 1982 to 1994. For the decade of the 1980s (1982 to 1990), the Republican normal vote in open seats was substantial. In the South, the average normal vote was more than 57 percent, which many would consider a landslide. Outside the South, the Republican normal vote was almost 56 percent. In 1992, the GOP normal vote in the open seats slipped to 53.13 percent in the South and 51.45 percent in the nonsouth. The districts that came open in 1994 were even weaker in terms of GOP presidential partisanship. In the South, the GOP normal vote was off slightly from districts in 1992, at 51.72 percent. But in the nonsouth, the falloff was substantial, with districts that came open having an average Republican normal vote of only 46.68 percent, nine points lower than the normal vote of the 1980s.

To illustrate the nature of the Republican problem, figures 2.2 through 2.4 plot the percent vote for the Republican candidate (Y-axis) against the Republican presidential normal vote (X-axis) for the elections from 1982 to 1990 (collectively) (figure 2.2), the 1992 election (figure 2.3), and the 1994 election (figure 2.4). In each figure, a 45-degree reference line is plotted running out of the origin. When cases fall below the line (to the southeast), the Republican candidate ran behind the Republican presidential normal vote; when cases fall above the line (to the northwest), the Republican candidate ran ahead of the district normal vote.

In the 1980s, Republican open seat candidates typically ran behind the normal vote in their districts. More than 75 percent of cases fall below the 45-degree line, and the cases below the line are disproportionately southern. Of particular interest is the large cluster of cases in which the GOP normal vote is greater than 50 percent but the Republican nominee failed to win. The robust presidential support in those districts indicates support for the GOP, but the anemic showings of Republican congressional candidates suggest the presence of split-level partisanship, especially in the South. Figure 2.2 shows that the bias against Republicans in the South was not just a product of incumbency but involved other factors, which we will discuss further.

Table 2.1   "Natural Constituencies?" The Republican Presidential Normal Vote, 1982–1994

Year	Region	N	Mean	Standard Deviation
1982–1990	South	45	57.33	10.40
	Nonsouth	113	55.76	11.43
1992	South	23	53.13	13.72
	Nonsouth	49	51.45	11.69
1994	South	16	51.72	10.03
	Nonsouth	36	46.68	8.91

Note: Contested seats only.

Figure 2.2   Presidential Partisanship and Republican Performance in Open Seats, 1982–1990

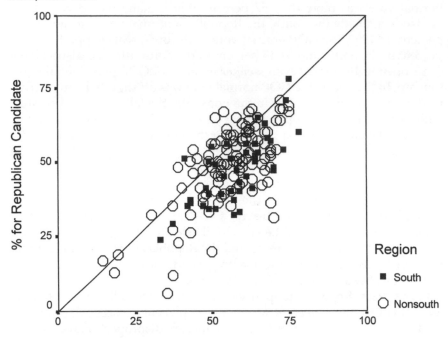

% Republican Presidential Normal Vote

As poor as the Republican showing was in the 1980s, the 1992 election marked the depth of Republican frustrations with split-decisions (figure 2.3). Fewer open seats had a pro-Republican normal vote than in the 1980s, in part because redistricting created heavily minority open seats in which voters gave strong support to Democrats. Despite fewer districts that supported GOP presidential nominees, Republican congressional candidates continued to lag behind the top of their ticket. Proportionally more Republican candidates ran behind the district normal vote in 1992 than in the previous decade, and in every southern district, the Republican candidate ran behind the normal vote, often by a large margin. Unlike in the 1980s, there is little to distinguish the South from the rest of the nation. The five cases in which a Republican ran ahead of the district normal vote did come from the nonsouth, but those cases represent 10 percent of all nonsouthern open seats.

The 1994 election can only be considered a reversal of fortune. Whereas in the past six elections open seat Republicans ran consistently behind their party's normal vote, in 1994, GOP congressional candidates consistently outperformed the normal vote. As indicated in figure 2.4, only four

Figure 2.3 Presidential Partisanship and Republican Performance in Open Seats, 1992

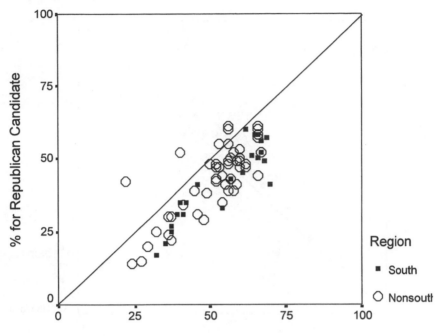

% Republican Presidential Normal Vote

GOP candidates ran behind the district normal vote. The fit between the normal vote and the congressional vote is tighter than for any other election and indicates relative consistency in the degree to which open seat GOP candidates improved on the normal Republican vote. On one hand, this pattern results from Bush's smaller vote shares in 1992 than GOP presidential nominees achieved during the 1980s, and this depressed the normal vote. On the other hand, GOP congressional candidates turned in extraordinary performances in 1994. The consistency with which Republican open seat candidates exceeded the normal vote may be a product of their efforts to nationalize the 1994 campaign.

Until 1994, Republican congressional candidates consistently ran behind the GOP presidential vote, especially in the South, where the GOP national ticket is strongest but the congruence of partisanship is weak. From 1982 to 1992, only three southern Republican open seat candidates ran ahead of their districts' normal vote. This disconnect between support for Republican presidential and congressional candidates helps explain the GOP's prolonged status as the House minority party.

Figure 2.4   **Presidential Partisanship and Republican Performance in Open Seats, 1994**

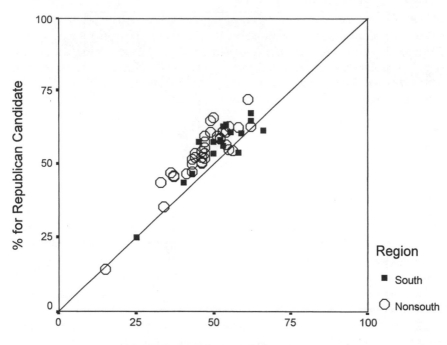

% Republican Presidential Normal Vote

The election of 1994 represented a significant departure. Only two southerners turned in weaker performances than the normal vote in their districts. For the first time in recent elections, Democrats—not Republicans—failed to match the strength of their presidential nominees. The GOP success in 1994 is *not* the result of a set of seats coming open in which Republican presidential nominees had established a base of support for the party. Instead, 1994 Republican open seat candidates were over-achievers; in previous elections, they failed to live up to their potential.

What is not evident from this analysis is why that shift occurred. Was it realignment, as has been argued, or was the 1994 election a product of other forces embedded in constituencies, candidates, and the financing of elections? In the following sections, we explore the relationships between these factors and the outcomes of open seats.

District Drawing: "Mapmaker, Mapmaker, Make Me a Map"

Among the major factors related to election outcomes, constituency characteristics are the most difficult for parties or candidates to alter. Once a decade, however, incumbents, parties, state legislators, and others have the opportunity to reshape constituencies in the course of drawing new districts to reflect population shifts.

One of the most common traits of bad sportsmanship is to blame the rules for the failure of a team or an individual to perform successfully. Sometimes, however, complaints of an unfair playing field are valid, which necessitates a reexamination of the rules by which various games in life are played. Whether in finance, the distribution of social benefits, or the conduct of elections, the government has periodically acted to assure that the rules treat all players fairly. At times, electoral rules have favored one group over the other. Does the design of legislative constituencies compose such an inequity?

The most sustained debate of the last half of the twentieth century regarding the rules of elections concerns the crafting of electoral constituencies. Designing legislative districts has traditionally been a spoil of the legislative majority. At the end of the eighteenth century, Elbridge Gerry, governor of Massachusetts, drew legislative districts to the disadvantage of his political opponents that led to the coining of the "gerrymander" (after a lizard-like district drawn by the honorable Mr. Gerry).

Until 1962, courts stayed out of redistricting issues and instead heeded Justice Felix Frankfurter's warning in 1946 that the whole topic was a "political thicket" best left to the legislature. Then, in 1962, in a Tennessee case, *Baker v. Carr*, the U.S. Supreme Court ruled that state legislative districts could not deviate substantially in terms of population. Before *Baker*, Tennessee had apportioned the state legislature to ensure that every county had at least one state legislator. This pre-*Baker* process led to dramatic variations in the populations of legislative districts and resulted in severe under-representation of urban and suburban communities. The Court extended the *Baker* precedent to congressional districts two years later in *Wesberry v. Sanders*.

By addressing the question of proportionality of representation in redistricting, the Court opened the way for litigation regarding other aspects of district design, including partisan and racially biased districting. The Voting Rights Act of 1965 seeks to ensure that in covered jurisdictions, election laws are not altered so as to impede or dilute electoral participation by minorities. Section 5 of this act requires that jurisdictions subject to preclearance secure approval of the Department of Justice or the district court of the District of Columbia before implementing new districting plans.[2] The preclearance provision was used to great effect in shaping congressional districts in the early 1990s, especially in the South, where all but two states must have districting plans precleared.

Litigation challenging alleged partisan gerrymandering has met with far less success. The best-known effort to litigate the product of a district plan on partisan grounds came in 1982, when the Democratic party of Indi-

Figure 2.5A   Partisan Gerrymandering in Indiana, 1982, before Redistricting

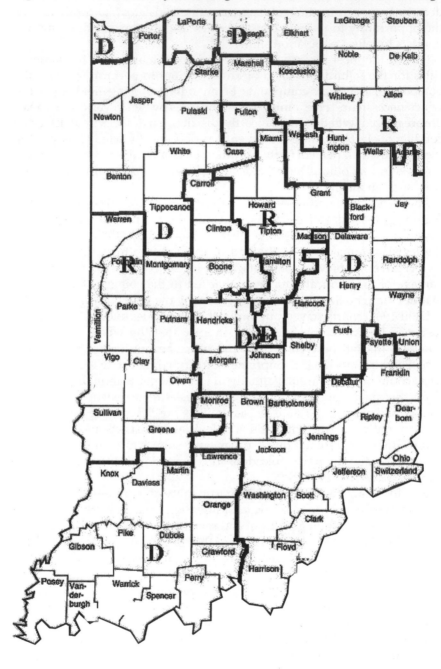

A

Figure 2.5B   Partisan Gerrymandering in Indiana, 1982, after Redistricting

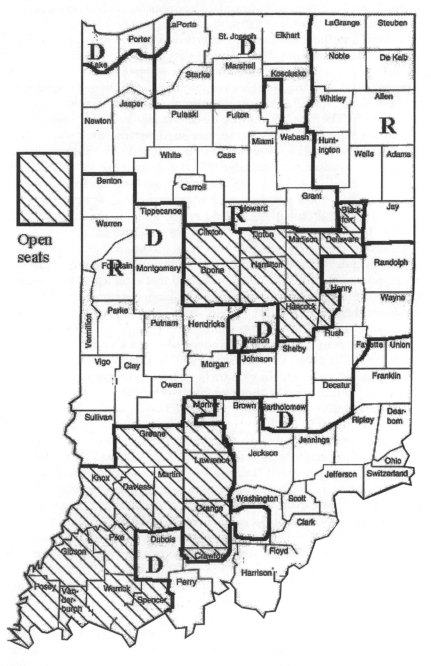

B

ana brought suit against the state and its Republican-controlled legislature over the post-1980 census redistricting. Indiana lost a congressional district in 1980 and therefore had to carry out extensive remapping. In the process, the legislature produced a map that protected the districts of all but one Republican incumbent and created two open seats, while placing six incumbents (including five Democrats) in three districts. This map also displaced four incumbent Democrats from most of their previous districts (see figure 2.5). The Republicans also devised plans to disadvantage Democrats in the state legislature. Democrats sued because their share of the seats was far less than their share of the vote statewide. The Supreme Court held that this partisan gerrymander was not so extreme as to violate the Equal Protection Clause of the U.S. Constitution. More recently, Virginia Republicans brought a partisan gerrymandering suit against the commonwealth in the aftermath of the 1991 redistricting. The suit was unsuccessful, as have been challenges in California and Texas.

Republicans repeatedly charged that redistricting prior to 1990 advantaged Democrats. The gerrymandering explanation for continued Democratic hegemony during the 1980s contended that state legislatures—most of which were then in Democratic hands—fashioned congressional districts favorable to their party. Central to the district-mapping argument are three assumptions: (1) redistricting was controlled by Democrats in most states, (2) Democrats created districts predisposed to elect Democrats (Niemi and Winsky 1992; Campagna and Grofman 1990; Abramowitz 1983), and (3) a principal component of creating districts was spreading around or "cracking" minority populations to shore up support for Democrats.

One example offered to support the districting explanation is the "Burton Plan" in California, implemented in 1982, which produced a net Democratic gain of six seats although the state added only two seats in 1982. The Burton Plan gets its name from then-Representative Phil Burton (D), who took advantage of what was relatively new computing technologies in data management and mapping to create ingeniously shaped congressional districts that maximized the advantages of Democratic constituencies and Democratic incumbency. The impact of the Burton Plan was long lived. Democrats retained all but two of the twenty-eight seats won in 1982 for the entire decade. Bruce Cain (1984) detects a Democratic bias in this 1982 California redistricting. California is not the only state subject to this charge; Abramowitz (1983) notes a doubling in the size of the Democratic swing ratio in the seventeen states in which Democrats controlled the entire redistricting process.[3]

Jacobson (1990) dissents from the gerrymandering explanation for Democratic dominance throughout the 1970s and 1980s. He contends that district drawing did not produce significant benefits for either party before 1990. Other work indicates historical variation in the impact of redistricting on partisan competition. Erikson (1972) notes that redistricting in the thirty-nine nonsouthern states was biased toward the GOP in the 1960s, and Bullock (1975) observed no effect of redistricting on incumbent success in the 1960s and 1970s. Ferejohn (1977) likewise found no relationship between redistricting and the general decline of electoral competition. Aistrup (1990,1995,1996) indicates that much of the Republican frustration in state legislative districts in the South had less to do with population distributions across districts and more to do with the long-standing allegiance to the Democratic party among rural whites and the unified support offered to Democrats by black voters in general elections (see also Aistrup and Gaddie 1999).

The impact of Democratic party control of the 1980s redistricting process was most evident in the Sun Belt states—the crescent of southern and southwestern states that runs from North Carolina to California. Although growth rates have not been even in this area, this is the portion of the country that has added congressional seats in recent decades at the expense of the Northeast and Midwest, where Democrats do better. Much of the growth in the Sun Belt has occurred in upscale suburbs, in which support for the GOP often runs high, leading to an expectation that Republicans would be elected from many of the newly drawn seats. Contrary to these expectations, Schwab (1985) found no GOP gains among the seats that shifted from the Frost Belt to the Sun Belt in 1982. Democrats more than held their own in the Sun Belt's biggest gainers, adding six seats in California, which was a result of the Burton Plan. In Texas, which got three more seats, Democrats had a net gain of two, while Florida Democrats added a net of two seats out of a total of four newly allocated to the Sunshine State.

The distribution of minority voters was often critical if Democratic legislatures were to limit Republican numbers in newly drawn districts. Prior to 1990, the main constraint on the distribution of minorities among legislative districts was a prohibition on retrogression, which barred mapmakers from reducing the numbers of African Americans or Hispanics in districts in which they already constituted a majority or a near majority. However, where minorities were not at or near majority status in a district, they could be used to bolster Democratic strength, because, except for Cuban Americans in south Florida (who usually support the Republican party), blacks and Hispanics are among the strongest supporters of the Democratic party. In statewide elections in the South, Democrats often combine a solid black vote with 40 to 45 percent of the white vote to create a moderate Democratic coalition that in the past has elected white Democrats (Black and Black 1987; Lamis 1988). When districts were being redrawn in the early 1980s, minority votes often provided the balance of power that secured Democrats' elections.

Concentrating or dispersing black populations impacts Republican electoral performance. For example, breaking up multimember North Carolina state legislative districts created several majority black districts. The residual districts surrounding the new black majority districts were overwhelmingly white, and in the next three elections, they switched from being held primarily by Democrats to electing mainly Republicans (Bullock and Gaddie 1993). If black populations are physically fractured, they can be paired with a Democratic minority among white voters to hinder the election of Republicans (Black and Black 1987). As little as 35 percent of the white vote may suffice to elect Democrats in many southern congressional districts (Petrocik and Desposato 1998). In the long run, continued defeats could dry up Republican candidate pools and discourage quality candidates from running.

The critical role of the racial composition of districts in determining partisan outcomes can be seen in table 2.2, which presents the relationship between racial composition and Republican electoral success in the South, the most heavily black region of the United States. The likelihood of GOP representation declines as black population in a district increases. Of the 195 southern congressional elections won by Republicans in the decade 1982 to 1990, 142 (72.8 percent) came in constituencies that were less than 20 percent black. The GOP won 46.7 percent of all races in districts that were less than 10 percent black and 49.4 percent in districts between 10 and 20 percent black, but they won only one in six elections in districts with black populations in excess of 20 percent. To the extent that Democrats could create districts that had a black population greater than 20 percent, it gave them a headstart toward holding the seats.

Table 2.2   Numbers of Districts by Black Population and Republican Success in the South

	District Percent Black					
Year	<10	10–20	20–30	30–40	40+	Total
1982	27	32	30	20	9	116
1992	53	32	19	3	18	125
1996	47	28	24	11	15	125
	Percent Republican Representatives					
1982	33.3	40.6	16.7	25.0	22.2	29.3
1984	55.5	50.0	16.7	25.0	22.2	37.1
1986	48.1	51.5	13.3	25.0	0	33.6
1988	48.1	51.5	16.7	25.0	0	34.5
1990	48.1	50.0	16.7	25.0	0	33.6
1992	62.2	28.1	31.6	0	0	38.4
1994	70.0	48.3	60.0	0	0	48.8
1996	76.6	53.6	50.0	63.6	6.7	56.8

Source: Barone and Ujifusa 1983, 1985, 1987, 1989, 1991, 1993, 1995, 1997; Bullock and Rozell 1998.

After the 1992 redistricting, the relationship between a district's percentage of blacks and GOP electoral success became stronger. In the course of adjusting to new census figures, eight southern states had to draw new majority black districts before the Department of Justice or the courts would approve their plans.[4] Aggregating black concentrations to draw the majority black districts resulted in much whiter adjacent districts. The whiter districts that bordered the twelve new black districts proved to be a boon to Republicans who, in the next two elections, won open seats in Florida, Alabama, Georgia, Louisiana, North Carolina, South Carolina, Texas, and Virginia. The impact on adjacent districts is most clearly evident in Georgia. Of the eleven congressional districts drawn in Georgia in 1992, three had black majorities—the compact, Atlanta-based Fifth District, which was created in 1982, and Congressional Districts Two and Eleven (shaded in gray). The other eight districts were less than 23 percent black by population. All three majority-black districts elected African Americans in 1992. In 1992 and 1994, Republicans defeated three Democratic incumbents in districts adjacent to newly created black districts and picked up three other adjacent districts that came open as a result of Democratic incumbent retirements.

Following the 1992 election, more than 70 percent of the GOP representatives came from districts with less than 10 percent black population, and more than 60 percent of the districts that were less than 10 percent black elected Republicans. No Republican won a district that was more than 27 percent black. The 1994 elections saw Republicans' share of seats rise further in districts that were less than 10 percent black and double in districts 20 to 30 percent black. Although Republicans had done equally well during the 1980s in the two most heavily white sets of districts in table 2.2, 1994 marked the first time that the GOP had strong showings in districts that were 20 to 30 percent black to accompany the successes registered in whiter districts.

After 1996, table 2.2 shows that Republicans did well under a wider range of racial concentrations. Fully three-quarters of districts that were less that 10 percent black were in Republican hands. Republicans also held most seats in districts that were between 10 and 30 percent black, and, curiously, 63.6 percent of the eleven seats from districts that were between 30 and 40 percent black. A major factor in 1996 was the redrawing of districts in Florida, Georgia, Louisiana, and Texas in the wake of Supreme Court decisions invalidating plans drawn primarily on the basis of race (Bullock and Rozell 1998). Four of the seven Republican districts were greater than 30 percent black by population and the one district that was more than 40 percent black had been held by Republicans before having its black population increased through court-ordered redistricting.

The role of race is especially evident in southern open seat contests.

Figure 2.6 Drawing Majority-Black Congressional Districts in Georgia, 1992

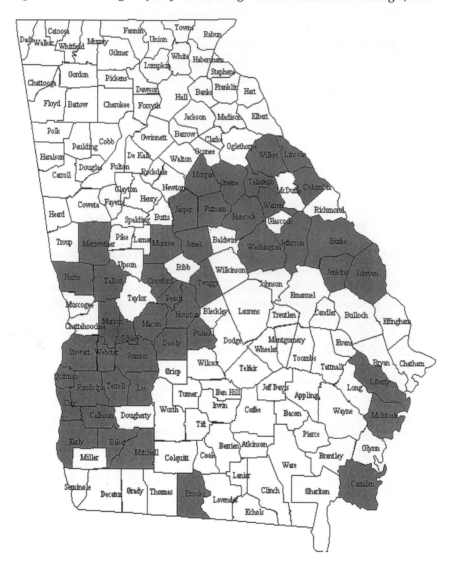

A

Figure 2.6   Continued

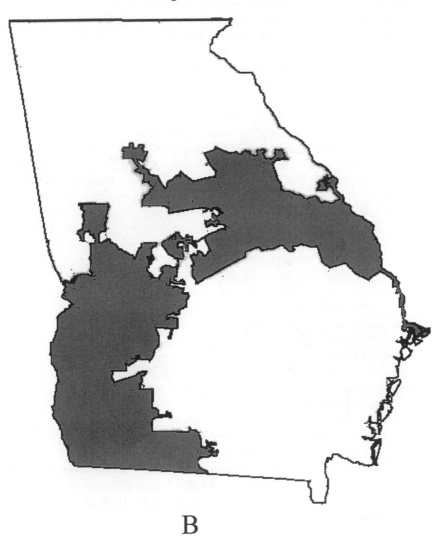

B

From 1982 to 1992, fourteen of thirty southern Republican victories came in districts less than 10 percent black, another nine occurred in districts 10 to 20 percent black, and only seven were in districts more than 20 percent black. These account for 53.5 percent of all open southern seats with less than 20 percent black population and 77 percent of Republican open seat victories overall in the South. By contrast, of the twenty-five southern open seats with black populations of more than 20 percent, Republicans won just seven (28 percent). The disparity is more pronounced in the nonsouth, where Republicans won 79 of 149 open seat contests in districts less than 20 percent black (53 percent of cases) but prevailed in none of the 13 open seats with more than 20 percent black population.

Redistricting can affect competition first by separating incumbents from their constituents and second by altering the distribution of partisans. The early 1990s redistricting produced districts designed to enhance minority representation by removing core Democratic partisans from some existing Democratic districts and recombining them in districts in which blacks or Hispanics constituted the majority. Adjacent districts made whiter also became more Republican. In effect, a partisan gerrymander was nested inside a racial gerrymander. The most pronounced consequences showed up in the South, where a dozen new black districts were created in 1992. After pointing up problems with analyses purporting to show a modest effect, David Lublin (1998, 114) concludes that "the Democrats minimally lost seven seats due to racial redistricting," and he identifies at least four more that Democrats could have retained had the black population not been reduced. Carol Swain saw Democrats losing seventeen seats in the first two elections after racial redistricting (1995), whereas applying Bullock's (1995) criteria sets a minimum Democratic loss of nine seats. At least five of the GOP gains came in open seats. In perhaps the most clear-cut example, John Linder (R) won Georgia's open Fourth District by 2,676 votes after its black population was pared down to 12 percent; this in turn created a 64 percent black Eleventh District that Cynthia McKinney (D) won with 73 percent of the vote.

Petrocik and Desposato (1998) believe redistricting had an indirect impact, at least when it came to the defeat of Democratic incumbents. They argue that the new districts, and especially the crafting of majority black constituencies, made Democrats potentially vulnerable by giving them new constituents who had less awareness of the incumbent or appreciation of the service provided the district by the member.

District reconfiguration—and it need not be restricted to replacing blacks with whites—can create open seats in two ways. States that get additional seats will have some seats that lack an incumbent. As described above, even in the absence of a state gaining one or more seats, open seats may be created by placing multiple incumbents in a single district, effectively taking away their seats and forcing them to chose whether to run for the open seat. A second way in which to get an open seat is for the incumbent to retire rather than campaign in a transformed district.

In the 1990s, Republicans capitalized on new Department of Justice standards that forced the maximization of majority-minority districts to disrupt the status quo. In some southern districts, enough black voters were removed to tip the balance to the GOP. Elsewhere, the swapping of blacks for whites brought in so many new Republican voters that Democratic incumbents foundered or retired.

Money, Experience, and Candidates

A resource-based explanation for election outcomes suggests that each party performs better when its nominee has an advantage in fund-raising, political experience, or both. Whether one assumes that the dissemination of information in political campaigns requires money or that candidates who raise and spend more money are implicitly better connected than other candidates, spending coincides with other candidate characteristics to influence electoral fortunes (Fowler and McClure 1989). Incumbents can almost always raise more money than challengers, with the incumbent's advantage particularly great when prospecting among PACs. PACs know that few incumbents lose, and because only sitting legislators can help organizations achieve their public policy objectives, incumbents feast on PAC money while challengers get less than a Slim Fast diet. Differences in the money available go a long way toward explaining why viable opponents to incumbents often fail to materialize. It simply costs too much to achieve the kinds of visibility that the incumbent already enjoys. Challengers who succeed in raising substantial sums can become formidable opponents (Jacobson 1980).

Other research has sought to measure political experience. Jacobson (1990) limits what he recognizes as politically relevant experience to a candidate's having held office. Two University of California-Berkeley-trained scholars (Krasno and Green 1988; Green and Krasno 1988) advance an alternative, arguing that the specification of political experience needs to be expanded to encompass more than the dichotomy advanced by Jacobson. The Krasno-Green index of candidate experience incorporates professional, celebrity, and elective activities into one measure, ranging in value from 0 to 8. Candidates who had held office are coded 4, and their score increases by +1 for the following factors: incumbency in an elective office, holding high office, prior run for the House, and celebrity status. Candidates who have not held office start at a score of 0, and their score increases by +1 for the following factors: party activism; having run for office; having run for high office; having run for the House before; professional status, such as a lawyer, professor, or other profession that involves public speaking; holding an appointive office; and having celebrity status.

When the Krasno-Green index was included in a two-stage regression estimation of incumbent election outcomes, it enhanced the results of the analysis compared with a similar analysis using Jacobson's dichotomous measure of candidate experience. There is controversy regarding the applicability of the Krasno-Green index to continuous data. As a count of attributes, the index assumes a level of equality among many previous candidate experiences, and it also imposes a cardinal order on attributes by placing prior office-holding above other experiences. But because the Krasno-Green index produces a better fit to election outcomes than the dichotomous measure of experience, we use it in our analysis.

Money and experience are important factors in elections involving incumbents. How important are they in open seats? In the decade 1982 to 1990, nonsouthern Republicans won 88.6 percent of open seat contests in which they had more money and experience than their Democratic foes; Democrats had equally impressive margins of success when holding both advantages. The data in table 2.3 further show that when the spending and experience advantages are split between the parties, each party wins half the time. During the 1980s, success rates when controlling for advantages in spending and experience are similar for both regions.

In 1992 open seat elections, these patterns remained largely unaltered: nominees holding both the spending and experience advantages won more than 80 percent of the time. When the resource advantages were split, Republicans won 55.6 percent of nonsouthern open seats and four of five southern open seats. Table 2.3 shows that in an inordinately large share of the contests, Democrats held both advantages, and this accounts for the ten point decline in GOP open seat success in 1992 compared with the previous decade. The 1992 pattern is not the product of Republicans' inability to exploit their advantages, because they continued to win more than 80 percent of the time when their candidates held the advantage on the two dimensions. But whereas Democrats held both advantages from 1982 to 1990 in 29 percent of the nonsouth and 38 percent of the southern seats, in 1992 they scored double advantages in 49 percent of the nonsouthern and 47 percent of the southern districts. The backgrounds of the candidates and the balance of resources structured the extent of Democratic success, rather than a fundamental change in the way in which electoral assets translated into votes.

In 1994, Republicans continued to win at an overwhelming rate in contests in which they had the advantage in both types of resources. What is different is that they did much better than in the past when they lacked the dual advantage. When the two parties each had the advantage with one type of resource, Republican success exceeded 80 percent, far higher than during the 1980s. Even when Republicans had the advantage on neither

Table 2.3   Experience, Spending, and Republican Electoral Success in Open Seats, 1982–1994

	Nonsouthern Seats		Southern Seats	
Republican Advantages	*Seats*	*GOP Win (%)*	*Seats*	*GOP Win (%)*
1982–1990				
Spending and Experience	35	31 (88.6)	12	10 (83.3)
Spending or Experience	45	22 (48.9)	16	8 (50.0)
Neither Advantage	33	6 (18.2)	17	3 (17.6)
1992				
Spending and Experience	7	6 (85.7)	12	10 (83.3)
Spending or Experience	18	10 (55.6)	5	4 (80.0)
Neither Advantage	24	4 (16.7)	15	2 (13.3)
1994				
Spending and Experience	11	10 (90.0)	2	2 (100.0)
Spending or Experience	12	11 (91.7)	6	5 (83.3)
Neither Advantage	13	5 (38.5)	8	6 (75.0)

dimension, their success rates were far higher in 1994. This success even in the absence of cornering the market on resources is particularly pronounced in the South, where disadvantaged Republicans nonetheless won six of eight open seats. The tidal wave of 1994 managed to lift to victory several Republicans who in previous years would probably have lost to better financed or more experienced Democrats. Indeed in the South in 1994, GOP success was not linked to resources!

Throughout the period under study, if Republicans held only one advantage, it was likely to be money. As indicated in table 2.4, the average Republican spent about $70,000 more than the average Democrat outside the South from 1982 to 1990. Republicans in the South were outspent by an average of $30,000 during this period, but in 1992, Republicans found themselves substantially outspent in both regions.[5] The magnitude of the Democratic spending advantage in 1992 resulted largely from a falloff in Republican funding. In constant dollars, average spending by Republicans was off by more than 40 percent from the average for the preceding decade. Democratic spending was also off in the South but not nearly as precipitously as for Republicans. In 1994, although Republican spending largely recovered from the low level of 1992, in neither region did the average Republican spend as much as the average opponent. The disparity is particularly pronounced in the South. Nonetheless, as shown in table 2.3, being underfinanced in 1994 often did not prove fatal to Republicans.

In none of the comparisons in table 2.4 do Republicans have, on average, greater experience than that accumulated by Democrats. Disparities are greatest in 1992 when the Democratic team had an especially impressive

Table 2.4   Experience and Financial Quality of Open Seat Candidates, 1982–1994

		Spending (in $1,000)		Experience	
		Republican	Democrat	Republican	Democrat
1982–1990	South	593 (378)	624 (354)	3.20 (1.66)	3.29 (1.97)
	Nonsouth	542 (328)	473 (402)	3.34 (1.90)	3.62 (1.70)
1992	South	298 (243)	486 (171)	2.09 (1.93)	4.48 (1.20)
	Nonsouth	381 (255)	527 (863)	3.49 (2.04)	4.20 (1.63)
1994	South	560 (319)	708 (670)	2.31 (1.61)	3.75 (1.74)
	Nonsouth	501 (232)	551 (395)	3.67 (1.90)	3.81 (1.79)

Note: Campaign finance data are expressed in constant 1994 dollars. Experience is measured on the Krasno-Green index (see page 35). Figures in parentheses are standard deviations.

set of resumes and an inordinate number of southern Republicans were novices. Southern Republicans continued to include several rookies in 1994, whereas their nonsouthern cousins offered their most experienced cohort, a group that almost matched the average for Democrats.

As was shown above, money and experience structure open seat election outcomes, much as the challenger's money and experience affect incumbent elections. Open seat candidates who dominate on the money and experience dimensions typically win at least 80 percent of the time—a level of success not too dissimilar from that of incumbents.

As a test of the degree to which incumbent and open seat contests are influenced by money and experience, we specified a regression model of the open seat vote that is similar to Jacobson's incumbent model. To use the experience/spending model in open seats necessitated coding experience and spending separately for each candidate in the contest. In table 2.5, we present four regression models of open seat elections from 1982 to 1992. In the first and third models, we test the relationship between the dichotomous measure of experience advocated by Jacobson, whereas models II and IV use the Krasno-Green measure of experience. Because the dependent variable in table 2.5 is the Republican share of the vote, the measures of GOP experience and funding should relate positively to the dependent variable, whereas measures of Democratic experience and money should be signed negative.

Political experience by Democratic and Republican candidates affects GOP vote shares, and when experience is measured with the Krasno-Green index, the Republican and Democratic slopes are almost identical. Without other controls, the Krasno-Green index (Model I) provides a much better fit to the open seat vote than the dichotomy for office-holding and explains 12 percentage points more of the variance (adjusted-R^2 = .42 for the Krasno-Green index versus .30 for the dichotomy). The intercept is relatively stable across both equations.

Table 2.5   Experience, Spending, and Open Seat Elections, 1982–1992

Variable	I	II	III	IV
Constant	46.20	47.61	34.32	38.04
Republican's Experience	10.93	3.13	4.89	1.41
	(7.71)***	(9.37)***	(4.63)***	(5.03)***
Democrat's Experience	−9.13	−3.00	−3.86	−1.57
	(−6.16)***	(−8.12)***	(−3.54)***	(−5.28)***
Republican's Spending (ln$)	—	—	12.58	11.32
			(13.06)***	(11.42)***
Democrat's Spending (ln$)	—	—	−10.22	−9.35
			(−7.93)***	(−7.93)***
Adjusted-R^2	.30	.42	.62	.65
$N = 230$				

Note: Dependent variable is the GOP candidate's share of the two-party vote. I and III use Jacobson's dichotomous measure of experience. II and IV use the Krasno-Green experience index.

*** $p < .001$, one-tailed test.

In the third and fourth columns, measures of campaign spending for Democrats and Republicans have been added to accompany the respective specifications of experience. The spending variables have the expected effect. Both Republicans and Democrats benefit by spending more money, but the positive slopes for Republicans exceed the negative slopes for Democrats. In both models, the slopes of experience drop to about half of their previous magnitude but remain significant. The advantage in explanatory power of the Krasno-Green index largely disappears when spending controls are added. For the balance of our analysis, we use the Krasno-Green index when testing multivariate models that require controls for experience.

The Presidential Pulse in District-Level Elections

One of the most prominent predictors of partisan seat change is the presidential pulse—the enhancing effect of coattails in presidential election years and the president's party's decline in the subsequent midterm election. Erikson (1972), Born (1984), and Campbell (1997) find evidence of a coattail effect in congressional elections at the district level, whereas Campbell and Sumners (1990) and Chubb (1988) see evidence of presidential coattails in state-level analyses of U.S. Senate elections.

The consequences of coattails have also been examined in open seat House elections. Mondak's (1994) comparison of open seat and incumbent elections shows that presidential coattails had greater effect in open seats. According to Mondak, removing the dampening effects of incumbency enhances the impact of national forces. Flemming (1995) too finds coattails to be important in open seats from 1976 to 1990, although he concludes that coattails affect far fewer district outcomes than Mondak claims and that coattails were predominantly a Republican phenomenon. The Republican dominance in presidential elections, combined with the almost perpetual Democratic control of the House, reflects this finding: Republican presidents ran ahead of Republican congressional candidates in general, thereby affording more opportunities for coattails to be exerted.

Table 2.6 shows how often Republican candidates ran ahead of their presidential ticket. In the three presidential election years, only 9 of 118 Republicans contesting open seats finished ahead to the national ticket. The lower portion of the table examines the frequency with which Republicans at midterm ran ahead of the last national ticket. A greater proportion of open seat Republicans ran ahead of the national ticket's most recent performance in 1982 and 1990 than in presidential elections. In 1994, Republican congressional candidates staggered all expectations by eclipsing Bush's level of support in 88.5 percent of cases. The pull of the Republican party has been greatest at the top of the ticket; until 1994, down-ticket Republicans were not replicating their presidential performance in the absence of incumbency.

Table 2.7 presents a simple test of the presence of presidential coattails in open seats. The first column reports the bivariate regression coefficient when the Republican candidate's share of the two-party vote is the dependent variable and the independent variable is the Republican presidential vote in the district. For the presidential election years 1984,1988, and1992,

Table 2.6   Running Behind: Republican Candidates Usually Ran Behind Their President

Year	No	Yes	% Running Ahead
	Did Republican Candidate Run Ahead of President's Two-Party Vote This Election?		
1984	22	2	8.3
1988	18	4	18.2
1992	69	3	4.2
	Did Republican Candidate Run Ahead of President's Two-Party Vote Last Election?		
Year	No	Yes	% Running Ahead
1982	34	14	29.2
1986	31	6	16.2
1990	19	8	29.6
1994	6	46	88.5

the presidential coattails explain 73 percent of the variance in Republican candidate's vote. This analysis also indicates the fundamental problem of split-level partisanship for the GOP: Every percentage point of support for the Republican presidential candidate translated into .93 of a point for the congressional candidate. The negative intercept expands the gap between presidential Republican voting and congressional Republican voting. To illustrate: A Republican presidential candidate could carry a district with 55 percent of the vote, but a Republican open seat candidate in the district should only expect about 46.8 percent of the vote. The model predicts that for a Republican to win a majority in a congressional contest, the presidential nominee needs at least 58.5 percent of the vote in the district.

The second column illustrates the impact of coattails when presidential election years and midterm years are pooled together. According to Chubb (1988), presidential and midterm years can be pooled, provided that there are sufficient controls for the influence of coattails in election years and year-control variables to offset the large number of 0 values that the coattails variable takes on in midterm years when coattails are absent. To implement Chubb's approach, we coded presidential coattails as the value of coattails in the presidential election year and as 0 in midterms. Three presidential election year dummy variables for 1984, 1988, and 1992, are included to control for possible variation in the impact of coattails in different presidential years and the effect of the large number of 0 values in the midterm years (Gaddie 1995a). The results are not as robust as when only presidential years were analyzed, but the presidential coattail slope is virtually unchanged. The year-shift coefficients indicate that the threshold for coattails to affect open seat candidates varies by year. Republican open seat candidates received a positive coattail benefit from Reagan in 1984 when their district vote share reached approximately 56 percent of the vote. In 1988, Bush's coattails affected open seats sooner, at 53.4 percent of the vote. Bush's coattails were far weaker in 1992. For a Republican to obtain a positive benefit from Bush's performance required 58.4 percent of the vote on the part of the incumbent president. In the absence of a national election, Republican candidates are highly competitive for open seats, although the intercept (49.15) was less than a majority for Republicans.

The presidential pulse is in evidence in the open seat results. Open seat outcomes are significantly and positively related to the performance of presidential candidates. There is variation in the impact of coattails over time. Republicans appear to be especially reliant on strong mobilization of Republican partisans. Open seat Republicans traditionally run behind their national party ticket so that even districts that consistently give Republican presidential candidates comfortable majorities may be competitive in open seat elections.

To assess fully the impact of coattails will require an examination of

Table 2.7   Presidential Coattails and Open Seat Congressional Elections, 1984–1992

Variable	Presidential Years		All Years	
	b	*t*	*b*	*t*
Constant	−4.39		49.15	
Presidential Coattails	0.93	17.82***	0.92	2.07***
Year 1984	—		−51.708	−9.01
Year 1988	—		−49.121	−9.45***
Year 1992	—		−53.805	−11.34***
Adjusted R²	.73		.38	
N	118		230	

Note: Dependent variable is the Republican candidate's share of the two-party vote ***p < .001, one-tailed test.

other predictors that influence open seat outcomes. The next section contains an integrated model that considers presidential coattails and other variables such as constituency attributes and candidate experience and spending, which also are related to the success and failure of congressional Republicans.

PUTTING IT ALL TOGETHER: THE OPEN SEAT ELECTION MODEL

Table 2.8 combines the elements discussed above in a district-level model of open seat congressional elections from 1982 to 1992. This model estimates the impact of candidate experience,[6] spending,[7] district racial and ethnic composition,[8] and presidential coattails[9] on the Republican vote in 230 contested open districts.

The model explains more than 70 percent of the variation in the Republican share of the two-party vote in open seats, and the regression coefficients support the conventional hypotheses about how candidate attributes affect congressional competition.[10] Experienced and well-funded candidates of both parties did better in open seat elections, although as expected from the examination of prior research, national political tides also had an effect on election outcomes. Democrats obtained slightly larger benefits from experience than Republicans, whereas Republicans reaped greater advantages from spending than Democrats, indicating that the relative strengths possessed by each party served it well in open seat contests.

Observers have long treated the South as an anomaly in American politics, to the extent of often excluding southern contests from their analyses. Some of the evidence above indicated possible differences in open seat outcomes on the basis of region, so table 2.8 included a dummy variable for

Table 2.8   Open Seat Congressional Elections, 1984–1992

Variable	b	t
Constant	49.54	
Republican's Experience	1.43	5.43***
Democrat's Experience	−1.77	−6.48***
Republican's Spending ($100K)	1.11	6.51***
Democrat's Spending ($100K)	−0.79	−6.43
Black Population	−0.22	−6.49***
Hispanic Population	−0.10	−2.90***
South	1.09	0.99
Presidential Coattails	0.40	4.98***
Year 1984	−21.36	−4.10
Year 1988	−20.95	−4.47***
Year 1992	−13.74	−4.37***
R^2	.74	
Adjusted-R^2	.73	
N	230	

Note: The dependent variable is the Republican candidate's share of the major two-party vote.
***p < .001, one-tailed test.

the South. The variable was insignificant, indicating no partisan bias in southern seats before 1992. In other words, the same factors influenced candidate performance in open seats in the two regions. Minority populations were significantly and negatively related to the Republican vote, which reinforces earlier observations about the role of racial voting blocs in congressional elections. The presence of sizeable blocs of blacks or Hispanics in a district harmed GOP prospects and decreased the share of the white vote necessary for Democratic success. The positive sign for presidential coattails indicates that Republicans ran better in districts where Reagan and Bush showed strength.

OPEN SEATS IN 1994: REALIGNMENT OR ELECTIONS AS USUAL?

When compared with the middling performance of Republican candidates for open seats in the preceding six election years, the GOP breakthrough of 1994 goes beyond stunning. The overall level of Republican success was also affected by fundamental departures from expected behavior in congressional elections that we will describe and explain below.

Outside of the South, Republicans in 1994 recruited their most experienced team since 1982. Two-thirds of the Republican nominees in the fifty-two open seats had held elective office, sought statewide office, or previously ran for Congress. Despite a well-prepared set of open seat candidates, Republicans did not corner the experience market; Democrats offered a set of competing candidates who had, on balance, even more impressive credentials than their opponents. For example, in Mississippi's First Congressional District, the Republican nominee had served as a state legislator but was trumped by his Democratic opponent who had not only been a member of the state house but was its presiding officer. Overall, Democrats averaged half a point more experience on the Krasno-Green index than did Republicans, and 13.5 percent more Democrats than Republicans were highly experienced, either having held office or having a set of experiences that placed them above 4 on the 8-point scale.

One of the critical changes in the dynamic of open seats was the negation of experience as a source of Democratic advantage. This was partially a function of Republican efforts in campaign finance. Republicans held a financial advantage in 54 percent of the open seats. Republicans won almost 90 percent of races when they held the spending advantage. When Democrats held the spending advantage, GOP candidates still won 75 percent of southern races but only half of nonsouthern contests.

When spending and experience are considered simultaneously, table 2.3 shows Republicans enjoyed a higher incidence of success at each of several combinations of election attributes. Republicans won twelve of thirteen open seats in 1994 when their nominee had more money and experience than the opponent. Among Republican nominees who had the edge on only one dimension, 88.9 percent won election, which far outstrips the GOP's performance under similar circumstances during the previous decade. Even when Democrats held both the spending and experience advantages, Republicans won eleven of twenty-one contests as a result of their strong showing in the South. Over the previous six elections, Democrats won 83.1 percent of the times when they held both advantages. Had Republicans seeking open seats in 1994 fared as they had done from 1982 to 1992, controlling for region, experience, and spending, they would have chalked up just twenty-four wins instead of thirty-nine. With only twenty-four open seat triumphs, Republicans would have come up three seats short of a majority.[11]

The 1992 redistricting continued to be a factor in 1994, although the impact was not as dramatic or obvious initially. In 1992, several minority candidates won constituencies redrawn so that their race or ethnic group constituted a majority of the district population. The only minority candidate to lose a majority–minority open seat was Ben Reyes, who fell in the Democratic runoff in the Texas Twenty-ninth District (Abel and Oppenheimer 1994). The architects of this Rorschach ink blot of a district went block-by-block assembling Hispanics so they would constitute 61 percent of the population. Despite an advantage in population, less than a third of the voters had Spanish surnames, and Hispanics in this district turned out at lower rates than their Caucasian neighbors, which enabled Gene Green to win by 180 votes after trailing by 6 percentage points in a five-candidate primary.[12]

As explained previously, a residual of drawing majority–minority districts was the creation of adjacent, heavily white districts more hospitable to Republicans. The trend of Republicans winning districts with reduced-minority populations continued into 1994 as Republicans picked up previously Democratic southern open seats. Republicans retained four other open seats in which black votes were siphoned off to create majority-black districts and, in three cases, Republicans captured previously Democratic seats that had black populations reduced to create adjacent majority-black districts. For example, in Georgia, Saxby Chambliss, who had failed to win the GOP nomination in 1992, swept up more than 60 percent of the vote to succeed retiring Democrat Roy Rowland in a district that had plummeted from 36 to 21 percent black.

Taking advantage of reduced black populations in open seats is a consequence of the growing tendency of southern whites to vote for Republicans. As reported in table 2.9, Republicans carried an overwhelming number of predominantly white districts. The only Republican losses in the South came in the three open seats in which blacks or Hispanics constituted more than 30 percent of the population. Republican victories in all nine overwhelmingly white districts with retiring Democratic incumbents offer evidence that the long-term impact of affirmative-action redistricting advantaged the GOP. Since 1992, black representation in the South increased by twelve seats as a result of redistricting; Republicans made net gains of seventeen seats in the region through open seats in 1992 to 1994. Outside the South, Republicans carried almost 80 percent of districts that were less than 10 percent black.

Table 2.10 applies the model from table 2.8 to open seats in 1994. For obvious reasons, there can be no impact of presidential coattails in table 2.10, so the related variables are absent. Otherwise the models in the two tables have similar specifications. The multivariate analysis for 1994 confirms the indications of previously presented descriptive materials showing that the dynamics of open seat elections changed that year. The experience of the Democratic nominee ceased to be a useful predictor in 1994,

Table 2.9   **Minority Population and Republican Success in Open Seats, 1994**

% Minority Population	Nonsouthern Seats		Southern Seats	
	N	GOP Win(%)	N	GOP Win(%)
< 10	24	19 (79.2)	4	4 (100.0)
10–20	6	4 (66.7)	4	4 (100.0)
20–30	3	2 (66.7)	5	5 (100.0)
30+	3	1 (33.3)	3	0 (0)

Table 2.10   Open Seat Congressional Elections, 1994

Variable	b	t
Constant	55.42	
Republican's Experience	1.45	2.71***
Democrat's Experience	−0.53	−0.94
Republican's Spending ($100K)	0.48	1.79*
Democrat's Spending ($100K)	−0.55	−1.85*
Black Population	−0.49	−5.36***
Hispanic Population	−0.28	−2.18***
South	8.37	3.64***
R^2	.62	
Adjusted-R^2	.56	
N	52	

Note: The dependent variable is the Republican candidate's share of the major two-party vote.

*p < .05, one-tailed test; **p < .01, one-tailed test; ***p < .001, one-tailed test.

whereas Republican spending and Democratic spending, although still significantly related to electoral performance, played smaller roles than in the past. In contrast, each point of experience possessed by a Republican had the same impact in 1994 as in previous years. Three variables (black population, Hispanic population, and the regional variable) point up the impact of redistricting in 1994 when the Department of Justice pressured states—primarily in the South—to devise majority–minority districts whenever possible. The coefficients for each of these variables becomes larger in 1994, with Republicans faring more poorly in heavily black and heavily Hispanic districts but, when other factors are held constant, doing eight points better in the South where minorities had been reduced in many districts, thereby improving GOP prospects.

There are two explanations for the failure of Democrats in the South in 1994. First, voters rejected President Clinton and his policies and registered that protest by voting against congressional Democrats. Cable News Network pollster William Schneider concluded that protest voting was greater in the South than elsewhere. At the anecdotal level, a GOP operative working in the South noted that conservatives in the region who wanted to show their displeasure with the president took it out on his party's congressional nominees (Austin 1999). Logistic regression analysis of ANES (American National Election Study) data on voters in open seats in 1994 indicated that voter disapproval was such an overwhelming predictor of Republican voting in open seat contests that other variables such as region were not significant. When one considers that polling data showed that Clinton's approval rating was only in the 30 percent range in the South before the election, it is not surprising that open seat Democrats ran poorly. This, however, does not explain the randomized effect of experience.

The second explanation is that southern voters not only rejected President Clinton but also turned against professional politicians and incumbents. With regard to this hypothesis, the significant positive coefficient of Republican experience indicates that negative feelings about professional politicians were directed only at Democrats. This fits with the evidence that nullification of Democratic experience was most pronounced in the South. Is it possible that *outside the South*, experienced Democratic nominees cut into the GOP share of the vote? To test for this possibility, we re-specified the regression equation to include an interaction between the southern dummy variable and Democratic experience. Including the interaction term in table 2.11 reveals that open seat elections in 1994 conformed to the pattern observed in previous years. The slope of Democratic experience is significantly and negatively related to Republican election performance.

Except for the South variable, other predictors are not substantially altered by the inclusion of the interaction term. The Democratic party suffered a wholesale rejection of the historically most-successful candidates in southern congressional elections: officeholders. Combining the effect of Democratic experience (b = −1.13) and the interaction term (b = 2.57) suggests a net gain in the Republican vote share in the South of 1.44 for every point of Democratic candidate's experience over 1. Southerners voted against Democratic candidates who had more political experience. Republicans won under essentially "normal" conditions outside the South but prevailed in the South because voters punished experienced Democrats.

So what to make of 1994? Certainly open seats played a critical role in

Table 2.11   Disentangling the Different Effects of Experience in 1994

Variable	b	t
Constant	58.17	
Republican's Experience	1.49	2.88***
Democrat's Experience	−1.13	−1.84*
Republican's Spending ($100K)	0.50	1.96**
Democrat's Spending ($100K)	−0.65	−2.21**
Black Population	−0.52	−5.82***
Hispanic Population	−0.29	−2.37***
South	−0.98	−0.20
Democratic Experience × South	2.57	2.10**
R^2	.66	
Adjusted-R^2	.60	
N	52	

Note: The dependent variable is the Republican candidate's share of the major two-party vote.

*p < .05, one-tailed test; **p < .01, one-tailed test; ***p < .001, one-tailed test.

the Republicans' disruption of forty years of Democratic control. Without the exceptional performance witnessed in open seats, the House would have remained in Democratic hands, and in a closely divided partisan House, the GOP initiatives under the Contract with America would have languished in committee. There is also reason to believe that the 1994 election constituted more than a momentary aberration in political behavior, especially in the South. The rejection of Democratic candidates by southern voters ended forty years of split partisanship. Constituencies that had elected Democratic representatives while supporting Republican presidents purged themselves of electoral schizophrenia. Outside the South, the GOP won on the basis of business as usual: They won by running well-financed, quality candidates in favorable constituencies.

CONCLUSION

When we removed the incumbency constraint and looked at open seats, powerful patterns emerged in the outcomes of open seat congressional elections.

Open Seat Contests Are Partisan but Not Rigidly So

Outcomes in open seat contests followed the contours of national partisanship. Generally, Republicans did well in congressional districts in which their presidential ticket traditionally ran strong, although presidential partisanship does not translate into one-to-one support for congressional candidates. Republicans run behind the presidential ticket in presidential years and behind the normal vote in most districts. Only in 1994 did most Republicans outperform the normal vote.

The GOP complaint that Democrats were holding on to districts that supported Republicans for president was accurate from 1982 to 1992. The Republican claim that this denied them a majority falls apart, however, because even when Democratic incumbents stepped aside, many Republicans competing for open seats failed to match the performance of their party's presidential nominees. In 1994, this changed dramatically, as almost all Republican open seat candidates performed better than the normal vote.

Altering Constituency Boundaries Influenced Republican Prospects in Open Seats

The implementation of the 1982 Voting Rights Act in the early 1990s resulted in the separation of many black and Hispanic voters from whites, especially in the South. The significant, direct impact of race on open seat outcomes, even in the presence of other predictor variables, supports the contention that packing black voters into majority-black constituencies benefited Republicans. According to the regression analysis in table 2.8, a ten-point reduction in the black population of a district would produce a shift of more than two points to the GOP. The influence of race was more pronounced in 1994, when a ten-point reduction in the black population indicated a five-point increase in the Republican vote, whereas a ten-point reduction in the Hispanic population was linked to 3 percent more of the vote going Republican. The political impact of drawing majority–minority districts clearly influenced the partisan makeup of congressional districts and afforded opportunities for Republicans in 1992 and 1994. GOP gains in whiter districts offset the new majority–minority districts that ended up in the Democratic column.

The Candidate Attributes That Help Make Incumbents Secure Are Important in Open Seat Elections

Incumbent House members win more than 90 percent of the time in large part because they dominate fund-raising and are far more experienced than their challengers. The amount of money raised by those vying for an open seat and the length of their political resumes are also strongly related to the vote shares that they win. Candidates who have the advantage in both spending and experience win open seats at rates not much lower than the reelection rates of incumbents.

The Conditions That Promote Greater Competition Are More Widespread in Open Seat Contests, but Even Many of These Elections Are Not Hotly Contested

Experienced and generously financed candidates are far more common in open seats than among the ranks of those who challenge incumbents (Fowler 1993; Jacobson 1990). Being politically experienced and well financed is important to the success of open seat candidates. All of the experience and money floating around indicates that open seats are viewed as more competitive, with the outcomes less certain than when an incumbent is on the ballot.

Although more often competitive than incumbent-challenger faceoffs, open seats are not as competitive as might be expected. Even with more widespread experience and money and a lack of incumbency, more than 60 percent of open seats are outside the marginal range. In light of the Republican tendency to run behind the national normal vote, it is not surprising that open seats that are won by very large margins (75 to 25 percent) are most often won by Democrats.

Was 1994 Realignment or Politics as Usual?

There are a variety of indications that the 1994 election represented a significant departure from the past. Republicans overwhelmed Democrats in the open seats, especially in the South, where in the absence of incumbents, they reversed more than a decade of decline. Republicans who ran in open seats usually exceeded the normal Republican vote for the district, thereby eliminating, at least for the moment, the pesky problem of split-level partisanship. So strong was the GOP tide that half the Republicans who were under-financed and less experienced than their opponents won. The GOP surge occurred even though, overall, 1994 open seats were less hospitable to Republicans than in previous elections. On an institutional level, the improvement of Republicans in open seats was the basis for the Republican majority in the 104th Congress, which facilitated the shift in policy priorities at the national level. The most pronounced mark left by the 1994 election came in the South, where even experience was of no help to Democrats. In the region where for generations the politically ambitious paid their dues in the state legislature or local office awaiting the retirement of the member of Congress, the old formula lost its magic. Rather than paving the way to Congress, political activities actually seemed to cost southern Democrats votes in 1994.

The next two chapters deal with the emergence of open seat candidates (chapter 3) and the financing of their campaigns (chapter 4) to better inform the initial results reported here.

NOTES

1. The analysis includes only contested open seats, that is, those that had at least two candidates.

2. States subject to preclearance were initially those that employed devices as prerequisites to registration, such as literacy tests, and in which turnout in the 1964 presidential election fell below 50 percent of the voting age population. Amendments to the Voting Rights Act approved in 1970 and 1975 set forth new criteria that brought additional states under the preclearance umbrella. Currently, nine states (seven in the South) are wholly covered by the preclearance requirement, as are portions of another seven states.

3. The swing-ratio measures the extent to which shifts in popular vote are reflected in the change in the proportion of legislative seats held by a party. Bias in the Burton Plan meant that a small shift in the vote toward the Democratic party results in a larger seat gain by the Democrats than Republicans would achieve if they managed to win the same share of the vote as Democrats received.

4. By 1990, the U.S. Department of Justice had redefined its role from passive to active. Whereas previously it had used a rule banning retrogression to ensure that districts with preexisting concentrations of blacks not be divided so as to split

up those populations, the department now demanded that when possible, districts having black majorities be cobbled together. This resulted in stringing together black populations that had been distributed across multiple districts.

5. Campaign finance data are obtained from Federal Election Commission releases of campaign finance reports and are expressed in constant 1994 dollars to control for inflation.

6. Experience is coded on the Krasno-Green index for each candidate.

7. Spending data were obtained from the Federal Election Commission and are expressed in constant 1994 dollars.

8. District demographic data were obtained from appropriate editions of Barone and Ujifusa.

9. The effect of presidential coattails is estimated as follows: The coefficient of the presidential election year dummy variable is a constant for particular election years. The coattails coefficient indicates the impact of a one-percentage-point change in the presidential vote at the congressional district level. The coefficient of the presidential election year is divided by the coattails coefficient, multiplied by -1, to yield the percent presidential vote needed to create a coattail benefit. District presidential vote data were obtained from appropriate editions of Barone and Ujifusa.

10. We also estimated the model using the ln\$ measure advanced by Jacobson and used in the analysis in table 2.5. The slopes of the other coefficients were essentially unchanged in the analysis, but the use of the logged spending variables produced a weaker fit to the data. We also used the dichotomous experience variables in a version of the analysis. Again the other significant predictors were unchanged, but the fit to the model was not as good as presented in table 2.8.

11. Figures from table 2.3 showed nonsouthern Republicans winning 88.1 percent of the 1982 to 1992 open seats when they had both the spending and experience advantages. Had Republicans won 88.1 percent of the seats in this category, they would have won 9.7 seats, which rounds up to 10. The table below shows how the estimate of twenty-four open seat wins based on 1982 to 1992 success rate was derived:

Nonsouth			*South*			*Total*
(% success) × *(1994 seats)* = *Wins*			*(% success)* × *(1994 seats)* = *Wins*			*Wins*
.881	11	10	.867	2	2	12
.508	12	6	.573	6	3	9
.175	13	2	.156	8	1	3
						= 24

12. Reyes lodged a successful challenge to his narrow loss by convincing a court that several Republicans illegally voted in the runoff and this might account for the result. Green proved more successful than Reyes in getting his voters back to the polls and won the second runoff by more than 110 votes.

Chapter 3

Candidates and Competition: Who Are They? Where Do They Come From?

Open seats afford the "last, best" opportunity for many potential candidates, and because of the infrequency with which open seats occur, they often set off free-for-alls in at least one party. Although uncontested primaries are not unheard of in open seats, in most instances, party nominees must fight their way through a crowded primary. In this chapter, we analyze the experience of candidates for open seats at two stages: as they compete for their party's nomination and as they compete in the general election.

With the exception of the work of Canon (1993) and case studies by Kazee (1994) and the brief works of Robeck (1982), Bianco (1984), Wilcox (1987), and Wilcox and Biersack (1990), there is little research on the political experience and quality of candidates in congressional primaries. We expect that experienced candidates in primaries probably enjoy the same advantages that they have in general elections; however, this notion has yet to be tested.

The electoral dominance demonstrated so often by incumbents who already have extensive name recognition (Mann and Wolfinger 1980), finely tuned campaign skills, and the inside track to funding sources dissuades many of those best positioned to mount a challenge (Kazee 1994). State legislators and other local officials not only shy away from confronting the seasoned Goliaths of the House, but they give wide berth to sophomores, who usually increase their vote share from the initial election (Erikson 1972; Alford and Hibbing 1981). That is why the exit of an incumbent, with no clear heir apparent or candidate with overwhelming resources on the horizon, attracts such a surfeit of candidates eager to pursue their opportunity for advancing to the House while they are at the right age. Most new members of the House arrive in the chamber between the ages of thirty-five and fifty-five, so there is a relatively narrow window in each prospective candidate's life when he or she will be "ripe" for a congressional campaign

(Canon 1990). In some especially stable constituencies, many potential candidates will see an open seat occur only once in their political generation. Even in a more fluid environment, open seats are not that common. Missouri's Fifth Congressional District, discussed below, has undergone this type of competition twice in recent years; this situation illustrates the blossoming of ambition when the sun of opportunity shines through, free of the clouds of incumbency.

MISSOURI'S FIFTH CONGRESSIONAL DISTRICT

Missouri's Fifth Congressional District lies in Jackson County and includes Kansas City and Independence; it is an area with a rich political history. Harry Truman's political career started here as a candidate for county judge (executive) in the Pendergast machine, a powerful force in the 1920s and 1930s.[1] Truman would not have won the 1940 Senate primary but for the solid vote delivered by the Pendergast machine.

Democrat Richard Bolling represented this district for thirty-four years after World War II. When Bolling first ran in 1948, the thirty-two-year-old World War II veteran had only lived in the area for a couple of years; he went on to poll consistently 55 to 70 percent of the vote during his long career. Fondly recalled in academic circles for his books on Congress, Bolling pushed congressional reform from his position on the Rules Committee, which he chaired during his last three terms.

Bolling's retirement in 1982 touched off tumultuous primary and general election competition. Fifteen candidates sought major party nominations: eight Democrats and seven Republicans. Unlike in some instances in which a retiring incumbent endorses a candidate before the primary, Bolling purposely withheld his mark, adding to the uncertainty. The primary was characterized by both historic and contemporary elements of open seat politics, with intense primary competition; savvy media advice and strategic planning; and, interestingly, machine politics and maneuvering for postprimary support. The primary field on the Democratic side included two state legislators, two local elected officials, and two attorneys. On the GOP side, the chance to pick up Bolling's seat attracted three local Jackson county officials (one female) and two state legislators. Applying Gary Jacobson's criterion of a quality candidate (i.e., having held elective office), then no fewer than nine quality candidates emerged here.

The outcome of the Democratic primary ultimately hinged on the innovative campaign strategy and hard work of the winner, Alan Wheat, and his ability to command the local black political machine, Freedom Incorporated.[2] Virtually everyone around him, including his family, discouraged the thirty-year-old black state legislator from seeking Bolling's seat.

As a candidate in this 20 percent black district, most consultants advised Wheat to run a dual campaign, actively campaigning in the black community and relying on direct mail (sans photograph) to garner votes in the white community. Wheat rejected this advice and took his campaign to the white community. His active campaigning, combined with solid support from Freedom Incorporated, netted 29 percent of the vote and the nomination (see table 3.1). A third of Wheat's vote came from the white southwest Kansas City suburbs and provided his margin of victory. A member of the Independence city council ran a close second, finishing 1,004 votes behind, with a second state legislator in the race slightly further back. Wheat ascribed his victory to the gentle treatment he received from the other candidates, who believing Wheat could not win, did not want to alienate the black vote that would be critical for the Democratic nominee in the November general election.

The primary was just as fractured on the Republican side. The race for the nomination came down to the two state legislators and the former president of the Kansas City School Board. The winner, a veteran state legislator, had a pro-labor record. Later, in the general election campaign, the Republican turned right and tried to make school busing an issue, which some perceived as a code word to exploit racial fears among whites. Wheat continued his biracial appeals and took 58 percent in the general election.

For the next decade, Alan Wheat maintained a liberal voting record sim-

Table 3.1   Congressional Candidates in Missouri's Fifth District, 1982

Candidate	Party	Political Experience	Vote Percent
Wheat[a]	Democrat	State Legislator	29.0
Carnes	Democrat	City Council	28.0
Campbell	Democrat	State Legislator	22.0
Kenworthy	Democrat	None	9.0
McCanse	Democrat	County Coroner	3.0
Paxton	Democrat	None	3.0
Masterman	Democrat	None	3.0
Price	Democrat	None	3.0
Sharp[a]	Republican	State Legislator	29.0
Lyddon	Republican	City School Board	24.0
Ethington	Republican	State Legislator	16.0
Seward	Republican	City Council	13.0
Collins[b]	Republican	City School Board	9.0
Sollars[b]	Republican	None	4.0
Roach	Republican	None	4.0

Source: Data from *Congressional Quarterly Weekly Report* 40:1911 (August 7, 1982).
[a]Primary winner
[b]Female

ilar to that of most white liberals and blacks in Congress (Swain 1993). He attracted no significant primary or general election opposition, despite representing a heavily white, suburbanizing district. He was renominated with 85 percent of the vote in 1984 and reelected with 66 percent, running twelve points ahead of Walter Mondale. Through 1990, he never garnered less than 70 percent of the primary vote, even when he faced seven challengers in 1986.

In 1994, Wheat sought the open U.S. Senate seat once held by Truman.[3] As table 3.2 reports, another fractious congressional primary ensued in the Democratic camp for the right to represent the Fifth Congressional District. On its face, the scenario for the Fifth District primary seemed familiar: an emergent political minority (a woman) wins over a large field by a plurality to succeed a senior liberal on the Rules Committee. But this case differed substantially. An early frontrunner emerged, nine-term state representative Karen McCarthy. The other two principal contenders were also female legislators, including a black, Jacqueline McGee. However, unlike in 1982 when Wheat sought to build a biracial coalition, McGee more narrowly focused her effort on winning black support. In 1982, Wheat succeeded by being treated gently and "running under radar" to sneak a plurality victory. McCarthy, the apparent nominee, was subjected to constant attacks by her ten primary opponents. Nonetheless, she had obtained a valuable endorsement before the primary and cruised to a comfortable 15,000 vote plurality over the next closest finisher (cf., Smist and Meiers 1995).[4]

Former pro-football player Ron Freeman dominated the Republican pri-

Table 3.2   Congressional Candidates in Missouri's Fifth District, 1994

Candidate	Party	Political Experience	Vote Percent
McCarthy[a,b]	Democrat	State Legislator	41.4
Park[b]	Democrat	State Legislator	17.3
McGee[b]	Democrat	State Legislator	12.6
Moody	Democrat	None	11.9
Smist	Democrat	Legislative Staffer	6.4
Morris	Democrat	None	3.5
Sildon	Democrat	None	3.3
Bassa	Democrat	None	1.9
Three other Democrats with less than 1%			
Freeman[a]	Republican	Congressional Nominee	71.1
Osgood	Republican	Former U.S. Attorney	22.4
Fournier	Republican	None	6.4

[a]Primary winner
[b]Female

mary. Freeman, a black minister, had run previously against Wheat in 1992 and won an impressive primary victory in 1994. He was later a featured presenter—along with another black open seat nominee, Oklahoma's J. C. Watts—at the unveiling of the GOP's Contract with America. However, despite the fanfare surrounding his candidacy, Freeman was easily dispatched by McCarthy.

Both times that the Missouri Fifth came open during the period of our study, it attracted large numbers of candidates of varying backgrounds. Elected officials, activists, and political aspirants of every stripe sought this seat. The Fifth demonstrates how open seats appear to be windows of opportunity for these many and varied candidates. In what is one of the few remaining New Deal Democratic districts in the country (the Fifth voted 60 percent for Michael Dukakis in 1988), the advancement of two legislative minorities has occurred: women and blacks. Democrats and Republicans have both had competitive primaries for the seat and have produced seasoned candidates with the chief prerequisite for electoral success: experience.

WHERE DO THEY COME FROM? PRIMARY CANDIDATES

In open seat contests, Missouri's Fifth generated an extraordinary number of candidates. Opportunity attracts quality candidates, and the 1982 primaries for this seat were decided by relatively small margins. The case study also demonstrates how groups often underrepresented in Congress, such as blacks and women, can make gains in the absence of incumbency.

As illustrated in the Missouri case study, generally the best candidate for a congressional seat—other than an incumbent—is often a state legislator. Three of the four nominees in the Missouri case study, along with four unsuccessful candidates, emerged out of the legislature. Moreover, state legislators are by far the most successful challengers to incumbents (Jacobson 1990). They also have demonstrated strategic thinking in seeking Congress by waiting for open seats (Robeck 1982; Kazee 1994). However, as in Missouri, these open seats that fire the ambitions of state legislators also attract other candidates with varying political backgrounds and experiences.

The data in table 3.3 reveal that from 1982 to 1994, the state legislature was the single largest source of candidates with elective experience competing for open seats (22.2 percent), followed by local elected officials (12.6 percent). Candidates for open seats also came from the ranks of those involved in policymaking activities such as lobbyists, political appointees, and legislative staffers. About 3 percent of open seat candidates held statewide elective office or were former members of Congress. Over half of all candidates, however, had no office-holding or policymaking experience.

Table 3.3   The Professional and Political Experience of Open Seat Congressional Candidates, 1982–1994

Experience	Republicans	Democrats	Total
State Legislator	186 (20.7)	229 (23.6)	415 (22.2)
Former Congressmen	13 (1.4)	13 (1.3)	26 (1.4)
Statewide Elected Official	12 (1.3)	24 (2.5)	36 (1.9)
Local Elected Official	100 (11.1)	136 (14.0)	236 (12.6)
Legislative Staffer	13 (1.4)	30 (3.1)	43 (2.3)
Lobbyist/Political Appointee	65 (7.2)	55 (5.7)	120 (6.4)
All Candidates	898	969	1,867

Note: Numbers in parentheses are percentages.

Table 3.3 shows that more candidates ran as Democrats than as Republicans, with 52 percent of those seeking open seats being Democrats. A major difference is in the prior experience of candidates seeking office. More than 41 percent of candidates seeking the Democratic nomination in open seats had held elective office, compared with about 35 percent of Republican office seekers. Included among the experienced candidates were forty-three more Democratic than Republican state lawmakers.

The emergence of experienced candidates in primaries for open seats is not constant across time. In four of the seven election years examined, at least 10 percent more Democrats than Republicans had previously held office (table 3.4). These differences are most pronounced in 1982, 1984, 1988, and 1992, when the incidence of experienced Democrats was between ten and fifteen points greater than among Republicans. In only two years—1986 and 1990—was experience more common among Republican than Democratic primary candidates. Democrats had their fewest experienced primary candidates in 1994, although these primaries were still highly competitive, as we shall illustrate.

The large number of electorally experienced candidates is a tribute to the depth of Democratic candidate pools in the 1980s, which often touched off primary competition between multiple officeholders. As figure 3.1 indicates, it was only in 1990 that Republicans had more primaries for open seats involving multiple politically experienced candidates than Democrats, and for every year under study except that one, Republicans had more primaries without any experienced candidates than did the Democrats. More than three-quarters of Democratic primaries had at least one electorally experienced candidate in the field, and 47 percent had at least two such candidates.

There is a dramatic shift in primary contestation in 1994. For only the second time in our period of study, more Republican than Democratic open seat primaries had multiple experienced candidates. The bimodal

Table 3.4   Electoral Experience of Congressional Primary Candidates by Party and Year

Year	N	Statewide/ Congress	State Legislator	Local Elected Official	% with Elective Experience
		Republican Candidates			
1982	156	0	29	26	35.3
1984	75	1	23	5	38.6
1986	82	4	22	12	46.3
1988	83	3	9	14	31.3
1990	69	2	30	3	50.7
1992	211	7	37	24	32.2
1994	187	8	36	16	32.0
Total	898	25	186	100	34.6
		Democratic Candidates			
1982	153	4	43	29	49.6
1984	63	5	18	12	55.5
1986	128	4	37	16	44.5
1988	65	3	14	15	49.2
1990	82	6	16	8	36.6
1992	244	7	60	40	43.8
1994	185	8	41	16	35.1
Total	969	37	229	136	41.5

Note: Totals exclude 87 candidates for whom no political or professional experience or occupation could be ascertained.

tendency of electorally experienced GOP candidates in a primary was 0 and 2. By comparison, the modal tendency of Democratic primaries was to attract one experienced candidate. Most experienced GOP candidates emerged in relatively fewer districts. More than 80 percent of GOP officeholders seeking an open seat ran in just 43 percent of the open districts; almost a third of GOP primaries attracted no officeholders.

As the data in figure 3.1 and table 3.4 indicate, differences exist in the emergence and frequency of officeholders as candidates in open seats. The data in table 3.5 further show that disparities in experienced candidate emergence exist across regions and within the parties. For 1982 to 1992, about a quarter of all primaries for open seats had no experienced office-holding candidates. Outside the South, little difference existed between the Democratic and Republican parties in the frequency with which officeholders ran for open seats in Congress. The South was a different story, with the region's long Democratic dominance still visible. In the South, Democrats had far more primaries for open seats with multiple experienced candidates; more than half featured at least two candidates with office-holding experience. By

Figure 3.1 Experienced Candidates in Primary Elections, 1982–1992

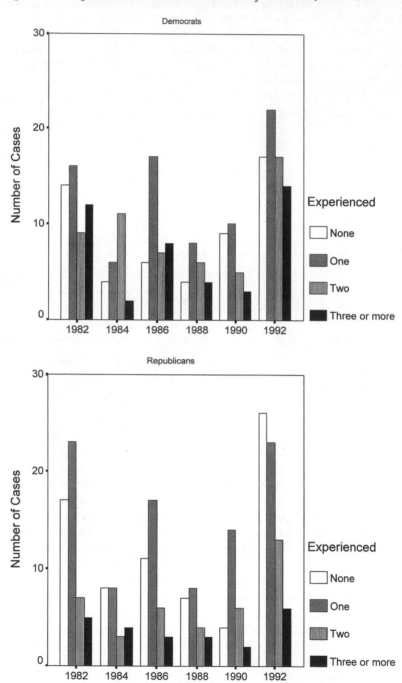

Source: Data from *Congressional Weekly Report.*

contrast, the southern GOP primaries were filled with novices, as only one open seat in five attracted more than one experienced Republican, whereas almost 40 percent had no one who had held office. Given how recently Republicans have become competitive in much of the South, some districts have few if any GOP officeholders, so the Republican contestants will be novices (unless a Democrat switches parties).

In 1994, the patterns of competition for the previous decade were upset, especially in the South. Among Democrats, the share of open seat races attracting no officeholders and those that attracted two remained unchanged from the previous decade. Although the number of campaigns with multiple office-holding candidates held constant, the share of primaries with three or more former officeholders fell by half to 13.3 percent, with the slack taken up by increased numbers of primaries with a single seasoned candidate. Surprisingly, in light of how well Republicans performed in 1994, half of GOP primaries in the South had no officeholders seeking nomination. The proportion of races with two or more experienced candidates increased more than thirteen points over the previous decade, whereas GOP contests with one officeholder plummeted from 41 to 20 percent. The 1994 figures reflect two recent changes. A growing number of southern seats were now so skewed toward the GOP that multiple officeholders emerged in pursuit of the Republican nomination, and an expanding pool of Republicans who have held lower offices was now eager to try for a seat in Congress. Nonsouthern Republican primaries more often had multiple experienced candi-

Table 3.5   Incidence of Experienced Candidates in Primaries, 1982–1994

	None	*One*	*Two*	*Three*	N
	Number of Experienced Candidates				
1982–1992					
North					
Democrats	26.1	36.3	22.9	14.6	157
Republicans	27.7	41.3	19.4	11.6	155
South					
Democrats	17.6	29.7	25.7	27.0	74
Republicans	38.6	41.4	12.9	7.1	70
1994					
North					
Democrats	23.5	47.0	11.8	17.6	34
Republicans	26.5	26.5	38.2	8.8	34
South					
Democrats	20.0	40.0	26.6	13.3	15
Republicans	46.6	20.0	20.0	13.3	15

Note: Cell entries are percentages.

dates, whereas Democratic contests less often had multiple officeholders; the number of contests attracting only novices remained fairly constant.

Increased competition between experienced Republicans is part of a long-term growth in GOP primary competition in general. In the early 1980s, fewer than half of Republican open seat primaries in the South or nonsouth attracted more than two candidates, and one in five contests (one in four in the South) had a single candidate, as reported in table 3.6.

Beginning in 1986, GOP primaries with more than three candidates became more common in the South. From that point until 1992, southern primaries were more likely than nonsouthern ones to attract large fields. The rapid growth in the numbers of southern primaries with at least three candidates may reflect the encouragement afforded contestants in states that have vote-share thresholds for nomination. The regional differences observed in table 3.6 are in line with Bradley Canon's (1978) observation that states that employ runoffs when no candidate achieves a majority of the vote in the initial primary tend to have larger candidate fields than those that nominate with pluralities. The surge in GOP contestants in 1994 also reflects the expectation that the Clinton midterm election would be especially auspicious for Republicans.[5] Only 5.8 percent of nonsouthern nominations and 13.3 percent of southern nominations went to the nominee without opposition.

As a consequence of heightened competition, fewer experienced officeholders obtained a nomination without opposition. As indicated in table 3.7, of the nominations obtained without opposition from 1982 to 1992, more than half in the nonsouth and two-thirds in the South went to experienced candidates. Between 8 and 14 percent of office-holding candidates ran without opposition, and more than one in five officeholders who were nominated won without opposition.

In contrast, in 1994, Republican officeholders received no deference and

Table 3.6   Number of Candidates in Contested Republican Primaries, 1982–1994

Year	% Primaries with One Candidate		% Primaries with Three or More Candidates	
	North	South	North	South
1982	18.8	25.0	43.8	40.0
1984	20.0	25.0	53.3	37.5
1986	33.3	25.0	51.9	62.5
1988	26.7	0	46.7	87.7
1990	27.3	25.0	31.8	75.0
1992	25.0	17.4	56.8	60.9
1994	5.8	13.3	79.4	80.0

Table 3.7 Experience and Unopposed Nominations, 1982–1994

	% of One-Candidate Primaries Involving Office-Holding Candidate	% of Office-Holding Candidates Who Run Unopposed	% of Officeholders Nominated Who Win Unopposed
1982–1992			
North			
Democrats	52.6	9.6	21.1
Republicans	53.8	11.2	23.1
South			
Democrats	71.4	8.1	21.3
Republicans	64.3	14.1	26.5
1994			
North			
Democrats	42.9	3.3	13.6
Republicans	0	0	0
South			
Democrats	50.0	2.7	11.1
Republicans	0	0	0

Democratic officeholders faced more pervasive opposition. No GOP officeholder won nomination without opposition, although four nominations went without opposition to candidates without elective-office experience. Democrats with office-holding experience were only half as likely (proportionally) to win nominations without opposition as in the previous decade, and less than half of unopposed Democratic nominations went to experienced candidates. The drop-off was most pronounced in the South, where the proportion of uncontested nominations claimed by Democratic officeholders fell by more than twenty points.

WHO GETS NOMINATED?

Electorally experienced candidates usually move on to the general elections. Table 3.8 reports the share of the candidates having various types of political experience who actually won nomination. Figures on the incidence of success track with the level of experience. Aspirants with previous success at a high level, those who had served in a statewide post, won two-thirds of the nominations to open seats that they sought. No other group won most of the nominations that it contested. Most Republican legislators (51.6 percent) succeeded, but the figure for Democrats falls to 45 percent. These figures, and those for the other categories as well, are depressed by situations such as those in Missouri's Fifth, in which multiple experienced candidates compete, a point to which we will return shortly. Local elected officials are less successful but win more than a third of the time. Lobbyists and political appointees succeed in almost a third of the contests they enter, whereas legislative staffers secure nominations 30.9 percent of the time. The one group for whom success is not commensurate with experience is former members of Congress, who win nomination less than a third of the time. Although these twenty-six former members join the late author Jacqueline Susann in believing that once is not enough, their constituents usually reaffirm Thomas Wolfe's observation that you can't go home again. Former members of Congress who try to return to their old haunts via an open seat succeed just over 30 percent of the time.

Except for former members of Congress, officeholders competing as Republicans have been nominated at equal or slightly higher rates than Democrats with comparable experience. Somewhat greater deference to experience among congressional competitors on the GOP side is in line with a tendency for Republicans to give their presidential nomination as a reward to the candidate, such as Bob Dole, who has labored long in the party vineyard.

Although officeholders enjoy success at higher rates in the GOP than the Democratic party, the partisan disparity is recent. In the early 1980s, there was virtually no partisan difference in the experience profile of emerging candidates, as Democrats and Republicans nominated similar numbers of officeholders for Congress. More recently, Democrats have been more likely than Republicans to nominate public officials. This persisted in 1994, when the proportion of experienced Republicans nominated was the lowest in seven elections. Republican figures for 1994 are in keeping with Canon's (1990) observation that amateurs are common when what had been the minority party sends a large freshman class to Congress. In contrast, in 1994 as in previous elections, approximately 60 percent of the Democratic nominations went to politically experienced candidates. That greater numbers of Democratic officeholders tried to move up to Congress may reflect the deeper commitment to public service found among those who see the gov-

Table 3.8   The Political Experience and Electoral Success of Primary Winners, 1982–1994

Experience/Occupation	Republicans		Democrats	
	% Nominated	N	% Nominated	N
State Legislator	51.6	186	45.0	229
Former Member of Congress	23.0	13	38.5	13
Statewide Elected Official	66.7	24	66.7	24
Local Elected Official	41.0	100	34.6	136
Legislative Staffer	41.7	12	26.7	30
Lobbyist/Political Appointee	32.3	65	32.7	55

Table 3.9 Success of Candidates with Elective Experience against Other Candidates, 1982–1994

	% Primaries Won by Candidates with Elective Experience	% Primaries Won by Policymakers	% of Elective-Experienced Candidates Losing to Other Experienced Candidates	% Amateurs Who Defeated Elective-Experienced Candidates
1982–1992				
North				
Democrats	60.5	26.5	69.9	33.9
Republicans	58.7	28.0	60.4	32.8
South				
Democrats	63.5	17.8	70.7	51.9
Republicans	48.6	38.5	64.7	25.0
1994				
North				
Democrats	64.7	8.8	72.7	33.3
Republicans	55.9	11.8	64.2	60.0
South				
Democrats	60.0	15.4	50.0	50.0
Republicans	26.7	20.0	50.0	63.6

ernment as a tool for effecting change rather than as an inappropriate intruder in matters better left to the private sector (Ehrenhalt 1991).

Except for Republicans in the South, candidates with elective experience typically win more than 60 percent of all open seat nominations. From 1982 to 1992, success was greater among Democratic than Republican office-holders, especially in the South (see table 3.9).

A consequence of the patterns of competition, however, is that the loss rates of officeholders is skewed by the intensity of competition. We previously noted that the nomination rates of virtually all categories of political experience were below 50 percent, especially in the Democratic party. Of the Democratic officeholders who sought an open seat nomination and lost, more than two-thirds fell to other officeholders. Republicans with office-holding experience were somewhat less likely to lose nomination to another officeholder, although, except for 1994, proportionally fewer experienced Republicans were ousted by "true" amateurs (people with no prior political or elective experience). This higher failure rate among Democrats no doubt reflected the tendency of those primaries to be affairs for career-oriented politicians.

Holding elective office, as noted before, is not the only path to a major party nomination. Before 1994, former lobbyists, political appointees, or congressional staffers, a group we have loosely termed "policymakers," won more than a quarter of the open seat nominations. In the nonsouth, these candidates had virtually identical rates of success across party lines. In the South, where the GOP has traditionally had fewer candidates, policymakers captured a larger share of primary nominations (38.5 percent) than in other parts of the country (28 percent). GOP policymakers won almost twice as many nominations in the South as Democratic policymakers, in part because fewer GOP candidates possessed prior policymaking experience.

Despite the success of policymakers, data through 1992 indicate open seat primaries are much tougher propositions for candidates without office-holding experience to win. When they succeed, nonofficeholders typically win districts that did not attract experienced candidates from either party. In the nonsouth before 1994, GOP and Democratic amateurs prevailed over a field with an officeholder only about a third of the time. Southern Republican amateurs were even less successful, with a quarter of their primary wins coming against office-holding candidates. By contrast, when a southern Democratic primary was won by a nonofficeholder, as often as not, the accomplishment occurred against seasoned opponents. This is more a result of the higher incidence of Democratic primaries that attracted one or more officeholders than of a typical weakness in the ranks of the GOP experienced or a unique prowess among GOP amateurs.

Primary elections of 1994 indicate that a rebellion of sorts occurred against office-holding candidates among GOP primary voters. Before

1994, experienced Republicans lost to amateurs a third of the time in the nonsouth and a quarter of the time in the South. In 1994, table 3.9 shows that the rate at which GOP amateurs bested experienced Republicans hit 60 percent in both regions. Apparently the electorate wanted not simply to replace old faces in Washington; they wanted nominees who had not been tainted by an exposure to politics at any level. In 1994, a result of this attraction to novices was the unwillingness of freshman Republicans to compromise—a skill learned on the job by politicians. Among Democrats, amateurs enjoyed no more success in 1994 than earlier.

The declining enthusiasm for office-holding primary candidates is evident in table 3.10, which reports the mean vote for primary winners of open seats by party, region, and electoral experience. Before 1994 in the nonsouth, primary winners had roughly comparable average support, regardless of office-holding experience. In the South, primary winners with office-holding experience had support that averaged nine points (Democrat) to fifteen points (Republican) higher than that of nonofficeholders. In 1994, winners with office-holding experience saw their average vote fall six (nonsouthern Democrats) to twenty-six points (southern Republicans). Comparing the share of the vote for experienced and nonoffice-holding winners in 1994, the average winning vote for both Republican and southern Democratic officeholders fell to less than a majority,[6] whereas the average for nonofficeholders remained more than 50 percent.

As indicated in table 3.11, the distribution of primary leader ballots reinforces the proposition that candidates had to fight harder to win nominations in 1994. Before 1994, between a third and a half of primary nominees polled less than a majority of the vote, depending on region and party. In 1994, this proportion shifted to between 45 percent and 67 percent. With the exception of southern Republicans, the proportion of candidates nominated with less than majority support increased by at least eleven points for each candidate cohorts.

Table 3.10 Mean Vote of Primary Winners, Controlling for Experience, 1982–1994

	Office-Holding Experience		No Office-Holding Experience	
	1982–1992	*1994*	*1982–1992*	*1994*
North				
Democrats	59.9	53.2	63.9	61.3
Republican	63.2	47.2	61.4	57.1
South[a]				
Democrats	60.5	49.4	51.8	51.7
Republicans	67.7	41.9	52.3	55.1

[a]Percent of first primary vote in runoff states.

Table 3.11   Vote Thresholds of Primary Winners[a]

	<30	<40	<50	<60	<70
1982–1992					
North					
Democrats	9.4	25.6	38.8	57.5	65.6
Republicans	8.3	20.5	33.8	52.6	67.9
South					
Democrats	13.5	28.4	47.3	64.9	77.0
Republicans	2.9	23.2	39.1	63.8	75.4
1994					
North					
Democrats	5.9	29.4	50.0	67.6	73.5
Republicans	11.8	23.5	47.1	76.5	88.2
South					
Democrats	13.3	53.3	66.7	73.3	80.0
Republicans	20.0	40.0	46.7	73.3	86.7

[a]Percent of first primary vote in runoff states.

THE SOUTH IN TRANSITION

The previous section presented differences in primary competition between the South and the rest of the nation. Despite lingering differences, the South has been undergoing transition for decades. V. O. Key (1949) initially noted the dangers to representative democracy of one-party rule and defined for three generations of researchers the problems confronted by the GOP in the South. In districts dominated by one party, most candidacies emerge in the majority party, with minority party nominations going to the candidate brave (or foolhardy) enough to come forward. When the situation is perceived to be hopeless, the minority party may not even be able to find a lamb to sacrifice. In the South, finding candidates has been particularly problematic for the GOP. For example, even though a Republican broke into the ranks of Georgia's all-Democratic delegation in 1964, not until 1990 did the GOP field candidates in each of the state's congressional districts.

Even as the realignment (or de-alignment) of the South opened up unprecedented opportunities for Republicans, the lack of down-ticket development hindered the emergence of GOP candidates, and as the results in chapter 2 indicate, experience is a key factor in open seat races. With ambitious attorneys and entrepreneurs automatically gravitating to the Democratic party—regardless of the candidate's ideology—as the only reasonable avenue for political advancement, the GOP nomination often went to novices. Sometimes the Republican standard-bearer was a successful person of business who decided to run for Congress rather than buy a Jaguar or a new house. At other times, the Republican ballot line was filled by a kook. Either way, the GOP competed poorly against Democratic nominees who far more often entered congressional contests with electoral experience in lower offices already behind them.

The two case studies that follow illustrate changes in the fortunes of the GOP in the South. The first, which examines Arkansas's Second District, shows how, until recently, the Democratic party usually enjoyed a larger pool of experienced candidates, even when the vacated seat had most recently been held by a Republican. By the 1990s, conditions had changed in much of the South so that Republicans now had better and often more numerous candidates vying for open seats. We turn to the transformation of Georgia's congressional delegation to demonstrate how, with a more hospitable environment, Republicans attracted candidates with longer political resumes and achieved new highs of success.

Arkansas Second

The Second Congressional District of Arkansas centers on the state capital of Little Rock and includes seven other counties north and west of the city. Redistricting has done little to alter the shape of this or any other Arkansas constituency since 1962, when Little Rock was shifted into the district of Wilbur D. Mills, noted chair of the Ways and Means Committee. Mills, who retired in 1976 after a series of embarrassing alcohol-related episodes involving a stripper, was succeeded by Democratic State Attorney General Jim Guy Tucker. Tucker might have held the district for years but instead opted to seek election to the U.S. Senate in 1978. His effort failed, and Republican Ed Bethune won the congressional district. Bethune held the seat with an impressive reelection margin in 1980 but failed to make the district safe for other Republicans. When Bethune challenged junior Senator David Pryor in 1984, several serious contenders for the House seat came forward.

Leading the pack eager to succeed Bethune was Arkansas Secretary of State Paul Riviere. A Democrat boasting impressive credentials, Riviere was a member of the thirty-something "Diaper Brigade" led by Bill Clinton that stormed to power in 1976 to 1978. When Bethune announced for the U.S. Senate, Riviere immediately launched a campaign designed to draw on young moderate-to-liberal Democrats who helped return Clinton to the governorship in 1982. Riviere's quiet, moderate image reflected the relatively nonconfrontational nature of his political experience.

Although Riviere was the early front-runner, his principal opposition came from a former Clinton ally, Pulaski County's colorful Sheriff Tommy Robinson. As controversial as Riviere was cautious, Robinson had a strong following in Little Rock and surrounding rural counties, which comprised 40 percent of the district. Robinson had started out as a police officer; became Clinton's director of public safety; and then, with Clinton's support, was elected sheriff of the largest county in the state. While in office, Robinson repeatedly made rash, off-color statements such as his claim of feeding black prisoners at the sheriff's lockup "watermelon and chicken." Robinson, who before focusing on the House, had been mentioned as a potential challenger to his former benefactor in 1984, had access to virtually unlimited funding that ultimately totaled more than $900,000. The sheriff was among the first of the current breed of candidates willing to spend whatever it takes to win. The balance of the Democratic field trailed the front-runners in fund-raising, visibility, and viability.

Only one Republican stepped forward, but she was no novice. Judy Petty was one of a handful of Republicans in the legislature and the only GOP lawmaker from outside the Ozarks of northwest Arkansas. A three-term incumbent, Petty achieved statewide prominence in 1983 by advocating stiffer penalties for drunk driving. Petty's state legislative campaigns had been marked by large numbers of volunteers and a set of conservative policy stands. Before election to the state legislature, Petty had challenged the embarrassed Wilbur Mills in 1974 and had garnered a respectable 41 percent of the vote.

In the initial primary, Robinson led Riviere by 12 percentage points but fell well short of winning a majority of the 134,000 primary votes cast. Robinson then won the free-spending, four-week runoff by a 53 to 47 percent margin and carried every county except his home base of Pulaski County. Robinson was helped by making inflammatory statements, opposing the court-ordered consolidation of the Pulaski and Little Rock School systems,[7] and outspending the secretary of state, who poured more than $500,000 into the losing effort.

Following the hard-fought runoff, Robinson attempted to move closer to the political center by endorsing the Equal Rights Amendment and calling for increased funding for children's and geriatric programs. Petty's efforts to attract moderate Democrats was hindered by her performance at the Republican National Convention where, in a nationally televised speech, she told the delegates that "there are some things worse than war." The exact meaning behind this statement was unclear, but moderates interpreted Petty's statement as discounting the lives of soldiers, and Democrats painted her as an extremist who had neither seen combat nor served in the armed forces. Robinson attracted unflattering publicity about financing his primary campaign with more than $400,000 in unsecured loans. The political drama unfolding between this pair was thrown into further doubt by the emergence of an independent candidate. Jim Taylor, who managed a Little Rock television news monitoring service, ran as an unabashed liberal and pitched his candidacy to nuclear-freeze activists and disaffected Democrats unhappy with their party's choice.

Spending heavily on inexpensive Little Rock media, Robinson took 47 percent of the vote in this high turnout contest. Petty captured the same 41 percent of the vote as in her 1974 challenge to Wilbur Mills, despite a last-minute campaign appearance by incumbent Ronald Reagan.[8]

It is worth noting that Petty was literally the only down-ticket GOP officeholder in the Second District. Arkansas political scientist Robert Savage has referred to GOP growth in the Little Rock suburbs as "sporadic" before 1984. The farm team that was needed to sustain the GOP after Bethune's departure was virtually nonexistent.[9]

The partisan disparity in down-ticket development has often been cited to account for differences in recruiting activity, primary competition, and electoral success. Senator Richard Shelby (R-AL), a former Democrat, characterized the difference between Republican and Democratic prospects in his region. "In the South, Republicans have tried to start at the top, and they have trouble sustaining themselves. The Democrats seem to have a much better farm system to help them develop candidates" (Dewar 1991). Senator Charles Robb (D-VA), the former chair of the Democratic Senate Campaign Committee, concurred, stating, "We [Democrats] have a much more robust farm team, so successful that [the GOP is] always trying to recruit from it" (Dewar 1991). The advantage Democrats had in the South in candidate development and promotion has become less pronounced recently, almost to the point of disappearing.[10]

The Republican March through Georgia

The Arkansas case illustrates the frustrations confronted by Republicans in the 1980s as they failed to hold the seat when the incumbent departed. The GOP held fifty-seven southern House seats between 1964 and 1993 but had only forty as the 1990 elections approached. In the 1990s, however, Republicans realized dramatic gains in candidate recruitment and congressional representation. Nowhere have these efforts produced more dramatic results in a brief period than in Georgia.

Georgia was a tough nut for Republicans to crack. As of the late 1980s, the GOP had less success at all electoral levels in Georgia than in virtually any other state. The Republicans had won in only three of ten congressional districts ever and had not held more than two congressional seats at a time. The GOP had never held the governorship and won only one U.S. Senate election, in 1980. Republican presidential nominees received the electoral votes of Georgia on fewer occasions (four) than in any other southern state. After the 1988 elections, the GOP held exactly one congressional district, Newt Gingrich's Sixth. During the previous two decades, Republican candidates had mounted challenges in only 56.5 percent of the districts held by Democrats.

Not until 1990 did Republicans finally compete in every Georgia congressional district, and their challenge to nine Democratic incumbents netted no electoral changes. However, hints of Republican progress could be gleaned from the election. Johnny Isakson garnered 45 percent of the vote for governor against four-term Democratic Lieutenant Governor Zell Miller. The Republican candidate in the Fourth Congressional District, state representative John Linder, came within 9,000 votes of defeating incumbent Ben Jones.

In the wake of the 1992 redistricting, the GOP exploited the opportunities afforded by the electoral map. Justice Department enforcement of the 1982 Voting Rights Act produced two additional black-majority congressional districts and resulted in more heavily white districts. Whereas five Georgia districts were at least 31 percent black before redistricting, three were more than 55 percent black and eight were less than 23 percent black in 1992. Incumbent retirements and relocations created open seats in the First, Fourth, and Ninth Districts in addition to a new open black-majority district.[11]

The GOP nominees in Districts One and Four were blue-chip candidates, and they succeeded against Democrats who sported impressive credentials. Jack Kingston, the Republican nominee and eventual winner in District One, gave up the safe seat he had held in the state house of representatives for eight years. Kingston became the first Republican elected to Congress from south Georgia by beating a school principal who had led schools in four counties; she won the Democratic nomination by besting a state legislator and a mayor. In the Fourth District, John Linder could draw upon what he had learned in the course of an unsuccessful 1990 congressional bid as well as six terms in the state house. The initial Republican pool in the Fourth included two alumni of the state house, a state senator, and a former county GOP chair, who pushed Linder into a runoff. Linder's Democratic opponent had served in both chambers of the state legislature and had made it into a runoff for a seat on the Public Service Commission, a seat filled through a statewide ballot. A difference in the South between the early 1990s and earlier periods was that Republicans were attracting politically experienced candidates who sometimes had more political seasoning than their opponents, and even when the parties sent forth comparable nominees, Democrats no longer enjoyed an advantage.

Although the GOP registered impressive gains in candidate quality in two of Georgia's districts, the third majority-white district, the Ninth District, produced as its nominee Daniel Becker, who had a background more like those found in previous decades. The nominee's most memorable television ads featured graphic pictures from third trimester abortions. In a pattern reminiscent of the solid South, Democrat Nathan Deal, a twelve-year state senator, scored an easier win in the general election than at the nomination stage. The Democratic primary attracted a set of political pros, as Deal had to overcome efforts by one candidate who had served in both chambers of the state legislature for a total of fourteen years and a second candidate with two terms in the lower chamber.

On November 8, Republican efforts paid off handsomely, as they won two of the three majority-white open seats (in districts One and Four) and defeated one Democratic incumbent to increase their Georgia congressional delegation from one to four. In the four remaining majority-white districts, Republicans polled more than 40 percent of the vote.

Two years later, Republicans completed their conquest of Georgia. There was no GOP primary in the only open seat, the south Georgia Eighth District, where Saxby Chambliss, who had run second in the 1992 GOP primary, continued to campaign throughout the 103d Congress. On the Democratic side, seven aspirants came forward, including a former congressman (Billy Lee Evans, defeated for renomination in 1982) and the son of a former congressman (Craig Mathis, son of the Second District's Dawson Mathis). Significantly, no one in the crowded Democratic field currently held office, and only Evans had ever won an election. Chambliss engaged in extensive fund-raising before the primary and built a sizeable war chest based on the visibility he gained in 1992. In the two other Georgia districts picked up by the GOP, one of the Republican nominees had previous electoral experience (Bob Barr, who nearly won the GOP nomination for the U.S. Senate in 1992). Moreover both Barr, running in the Ninth, and Charlie Norwood, the nominee in the Tenth District, won their nominations by knocking off the 1992 GOP nominees.[12]

The dramatic expansion of the GOP in Georgia is attributable to a favorable redistricting, changes in the relative experience advantages of the two parties' nominees, and partisan realignment among white voters. Efforts to encourage Republicans to seek congressional office were the first step toward viability. Primary competition was followed by electoral success, and nonincumbent Republican nominees in 1994 were either electorally experienced or defeated electorally experienced candidates in the primary.

WHO HAS THE EXPERIENCE ADVANTAGE?

Given the relationship between open seat election outcomes and political experience, it is logical to ask who holds the experience advantage and under what conditions. In this section, we discuss the relative experience of Democratic and Republican nominees. To lend further insight into the analysis of the impact of political experience from chapter 2, we expand our discussion of political experience to encompass the variety of experience discussed by Krasno and Green (1988). Table 3.12 shows the distribution of the experience advantage for open seats in general elections since 1982. During the 1980s, Democrats held the experience advantage more often than the Republicans, although differences were small even in the South. About one-fifth of the cases featured candidates of comparable experience. In 1992, Democrats had an especially experienced team, with their advantage being much more pronounced in the South than the nonsouth.

The impressive Democratic advantage in the South in 1992 is largely attributable to the creation of a dozen new majority-black districts, all but one of which was an open seat. These attracted office-holding black Democrats and for the most part hopeless Republicans. As indicated in chapter 2, the combination of a strong Democratic ticket, the preponderance of black districts, and the presence of quality candidates contributed tremendously to the Democratic performance in open seats.

The regional disparity in candidate experience was even more pronounced in 1994. In the South, Democrats once again held the experience advantage in a majority of open seats, and Republicans held the advantage in proportionally fewer districts than in any year since 1982 (12.5 percent). However, outside the old Confederacy, Republicans actually held the advantage in more open districts than the Democrats (38.9 to 27.8 percent). Democrats and Republicans had similar levels of experience in a third of the contested districts. Data for 1994 in table 3.12 suggest that outside the South, the GOP gained seats through conventional electoral means. In a break with the recent past, Republicans fielded higher quality candidates more often than did Democrats and reaped the expected rewards. In the South, however, Republicans made advances despite having nominees who rarely had more political seasoning than their opponents.

According to Gary Jacobson and Samuel Kernell (1983), partisan success in congressional elections is partly determined by the interpretation of political winds by quality candidates. Put simply, good candidates seek election when the partisan winds are at their backs. Thus, Democrats ran

Table 3.12   Who Had the Experience Advantage in Open Seat Elections? 1982–1994

	1982–1990		1992		1994	
	South	*North*	*South*	*North*	*South*	*North*
Democratic Advantage	44.4	40.7	73.9	46.9	56.3	27.8
No Advantage	17.8	22.1	4.3	22.4	31.3	33.3 ·
Republican Advantage	37.8	37.2	21.7	30.6	12.5	38.9
N	45	113	23	49	16	36

well in 1974 or 1992 because they attracted quality candidates who took advantage of political opportunity. Conversely, negative political tides can be offset by effective recruiting, as Jacobson and Kernell's analysis of GOP prospects in the 1982 elections indicated. Based on those propositions, in 1994, Democrats should have performed worse in the nonsouth, where Republicans fielded strong, experienced candidates but better in the South, where they offered seasoned nominees.

How can the GOP's surprising southern successes be explained? Chapter 2 described how a backlash against experienced Democrats occurred in the South. GOP success in that region was more than a rejection of Democrats, however. Eight of fifteen GOP primary winners in the South were amateurs, and four of the nominees with no office-holding experience overcame primary opponents having greater experience. The potency of knocking off a more experienced opponent in the primary was noted by Canon (1993, 1125), who observed, "amateurs who defeat an experienced candidate in the primary are as likely to beat an incumbent in the general election as an experienced challenger!" If giant killers from the primary are well positioned to defeat incumbents, it is small wonder that they also do well in open seat competition.

Only half of the districts that featured electorally experienced Republicans nominated experienced candidates, suggesting that Republican voters in the South often rejected elected officials in the primary. Because all but one of these states uses a threshold (runoff) rule to nominate candidates, it is reasonable to conclude that a strong distaste for ambitious officeholders permeated the Republican primary electorate. Rejection of seasoned Democrats in the general election and the preference for GOP novices in the primary suggest a component of the electorate eager to sweep clean with a new broom. The political neophytes who won southern Republican primaries seemingly tapped into the deep distrust of government and its programs identified by pollsters involved in refining the Contract with America (Balz and Brownstein 1996). The electorate's choices continued to march to the tune it hummed during the electoral season. Freshman Republicans in the 104th Congress were in the vanguard of those demanding allegiance to the Contract with America and subsequent plans to reshape the budget and health care. The rookies leaned on older members to reject compromise and politics as usual and held out longest during the government shutdown as they demanded a balanced budget.

A Multivariate Test

In chapter 2, we explained our belief that structure and behavior in elections are joined, and we identified several variables that affected open seat election outcomes. In the following section, we describe the direction and size of the experience advantage in open seats while controlling for the impact of multiple independent variables. Our analysis up to now has indicated that regional differences may exist, along with changes over time. In the preceding sections, we uncovered significant differences in the emergence of experienced candidates in 1994.

The only other rigorous examination of the political experience of candidates that deals explicitly with open seats is by Bond, Fleisher, and Talbert (1997), who analyze the quality of nominees. Bond and colleagues define a quality candidate as one who has held elective office. They find that local partisan forces are the key to the emergence of quality candidates for open seats. From 1976 to 1988, they find that these forces exert a stronger effect on Republican candidate emergence, whereas experienced Democrats are more prone to emerge in a variety of districts. Previous research found support for the proposition that quality candidates run in districts that are strong for their party (Bianco 1984; Canon 1990). However, there is disagreement about whether quality candidates are willing to defy negative partisan tides. Canon finds that they will, because an open seat presents a better opportunity than an incumbent-held seat, whereas Bianco does not support this proposition.

Our model of the experience advantage contains seven theoretically important independent variables plus a temporal control for the 1982 to 1992 pool of cases. We tap the partisan history of the district using three variables: the prior GOP presidential vote, the party of the incumbent, and whether the GOP held the seat in the last decade. Other research, including that of Bond and colleagues, indicates that experienced nominees run more often where their party has previously exhibited strength. The past presidential vote closely correlates with normal party measures (Bond, Talbert, and Fleisher 1997) and is therefore a suitable proxy. The incumbent party and prior GOP measure are also introduced in our model because the GOP has often shown presidential strength in districts that elect Democrats to Congress. Similarly, the GOP may be better able to field candidates in districts it does not currently control but has held in the recent past.[13]

Three constituency controls were also introduced in our model based on the relationship exhibited in chapter 2. We expect that GOP candidates will less often have an experience advantage in districts having black or Hispanic concentrations. Districts with concentrations of minorities are likely to have fewer GOP officeholders, and Republicans who have had success in the state legislature or local offices will be less willing to abandon what they have for a long shot at Congress. And although the GOP has realized substantial gains in the South, we include a southern regional control. Racial and regional controls will help to ascertain whether the outcomes observed in the South are the product of racial and partisan factors or some other regional idiosyncrasy.

Finally, in our model, we control for the pool of available "quality candidates" as measured by the number of state legislators in the districts (see also Canon 1990). No direction is specified for this control, but if the availability of potential quality candidates increases the likelihood of such candidates running, we should observe a negative coefficient.

Although guided by the work of Bond and his colleagues, our analysis here differs at several points. We examine the broader measure of candidate quality and experience as tapped by the Krasno-Green index, whereas Bond and colleagues use the dichotomy of office-holding experiences. In addition to the local partisan trends hypotheses advanced by Bond, we include measures of candidate availability and constituency racial characteristics to help understand the relative partisan advantage in open seats.

Models of candidate experience advantage in open seat elections appear in table 3.13. The dependent variable is the experience of the Democratic candidate subtracted from the GOP nominee's experience, so that Republicans who are more experienced than their Democratic opponents have positive scores. When two competitors have equal scores on the Krasno-Green index, the score is 0. For the period 1982 to 1992, five variables are significantly related to net GOP quality advantage. Of particular interest is the relationship between the candidate pool size and Republican political experience advantage. The size of the experience advantage diminishes as the candidate pool grows larger. Partisan influences are also evident. The size of the previous Republican presidential vote in the district is positively and significantly related to the Republican advantage in open seat candidate experience. Likewise, when the retiring incumbent is Republican, the GOP enjoys an experience advantage despite situations such as those in Arkansas's Second District. Democrats tend to have greater political experience than their opponents in districts with Hispanic concentrations, and the Democratic edge grew during the decade. Although black population is not statistically significant at conventional levels, the direction of the coefficient indicates that black populations are associated with a decreased GOP advantage. Republican domination of experience over Democrats is concentrated in constituencies in which the Republican party has enjoyed political success at the district and national election levels.

Holding the political experience advantage in open seat elections is important for sustained Republican electoral success. The regression analysis of open seat elections in chapter 2 indicates a strong significant relationship between relative candidate quality and the Republican share of the vote in open seat contests. According to conventional political sci-

Table 3.13   Regression Estimates of Experience Advantage

| | 1982–1992 | | 1994 | |
Variable	b	t	b	t
Constant	−2.62		−3.85	
Candidate Pool size	−0.02	−3.27**	−0.04	−1.99**
Last GOP Presidential Vote	0.06	3.10**	0.11	2.41**
South	−0.39	−1.04	−1.88	−2.13**
Incumbent Party	0.56	2.21**	0.36	0.59
Prior GOP Seat	0.46	0.95	−0.64	−0.50
Black Population	−0.02	−1.42	−0.03	−0.76
Hispanic Population	−0.03	−2.32**	−0.03	−0.59
Temporal Counter	−0.14	−2.08**	—	
R^2	.33		.37	
Adjusted R^2	.31		.27	
N	230		52	

Note: Experience is measured as the net Republican candidate experience (dis)advantage relative to the Democratic candidate experience (Republican experience minus Democratic experience).
*p < .05, one-tailed test; **p < .01, one-tailed test.

ence findings, to maintain electoral parity with Democratic candidates, the Republican party must recruit even better candidates than the Democrats in a given seat (Bond, Talbert, and Fleisher 1997; Gaddie 1995a). Or given the relative lack of quality GOP candidates, the party has a vested interest in discouraging quality Democratic candidates from running.

The analysis of 1994 reveals few surprises. Republicans held the experience advantage in districts in which the national ticket ran well previously or in which candidate pools were relatively small. However, the relationship between previous incumbency and the quality advantage observed from 1982 to 1992 disappears in 1994, and minority populations are not significantly related to the candidate experience advantage. Republicans were less likely to have the experience advantage in southern seats, all things held equal. The relationship apparent from the descriptive data holds in the multivariate analysis despite the introduction of controls. For Republicans, the availability of quality candidates is not a sufficient explanation; Republican candidates with electoral experience sought nominations in most southern primaries. The southern GOP electorate rejected these candidates as standard-bearers in favor of less-professional candidates. Republican gains came as the party's primary voters' preference for novices was endorsed by a November electorate now weaned from the Democratic party. Fresh GOP faces received an especially warm reception in the South.

WHO WINS?

The ultimate questions regarding candidates and candidate quality are: Who wins, and why? Throughout this chapter, we have noted the success of state legislators in advancing to Congress. The advantages of legislative experience are powerfully demonstrated in open seat elections. As table 3.14 indicates, most experienced nominees are former state legislators, and during the decade 1982 to 1992, they had exceptional political success. More than 60 percent of Republican legislators and nearly three-quarters of Democratic legislators nominated for Congress won. Local officials nominated for Congress also did well, winning most of the time, with Republicans faring better than Democrats. Overall, Democrats with office-holding experience won 63 percent of their contests, whereas experienced Republicans won more than 58 percent of their contests.

Candidates with other political experiences succeeded at lower rates than those who had previously been smiled on by the electorate. Former lobbyists and appointees won about 45 percent of their contests overall, with Democrats being more successful. By contrast, Democratic legislative staffers performed poorly, although the number of cases is very small and therefore limits the generalizability of the results.

In the previous decade, Democratic officeholders generally performed better than their GOP counterparts; in 1994, the figures were dramatically reversed, as 83 percent of Republican candidates with office-holding experience won, compared with fewer than a third of the Democratic office-holders seeking open seats. Fewer than a quarter of the Democratic state legislators, contrasted with almost 90 percent of the Republican solons, realized their dreams and went to Washington. The electoral backlash against officeholders observed in the Republican primaries in 1994 manifested itself against Democrats in the general elections, as more than 60 percent of the GOP novices won.

Table 3.14 Success Rate of Experienced Nominees, 1982–1994

	1982–1992		1994	
Experience	*Republican*	*Democrat*	*Republican*	*Democrat*
State Legislator	79 (60.8)	77 (74.0)	17 (88.2)	21 (23.8)
Former Congressman	3 (33.3)	5 (80.0)	—	—
Statewide Elected Official	5 (40.0)	12 (41.7)	3 (66.7)	4 (50.0)
Local Elected Official	38 (57.8)	41 (46.3)	3 (100.0)	6 (50.0)
Legislative Staffer	3 (66.7)	6 (16.7)	2 (50.0)	2 (50.0)
Lobbyist/Political Appointee	16 (37.5)	11 (54.5)	5 (80.0)	3 (0.0)
N	144	152	30	36

As indicated in table 3.15, politically experienced candidates constituted almost 85 percent of all Democrats elected in open seats and almost two-thirds of Republicans elected to open seats in 1994. These rates were slightly lower for Republicans and slightly higher for Democrats than in the previous decade.

Again, the South appears to be an aberration. Table 3.16 lists the twenty GOP freshmen from the South, thirteen of whom won open seats. Only six of the twenty had previously held office—four elected from open seats and two who beat incumbents. Five (three in open seats) had no office-holding or other political experience, and another seven (five in open seats) had not held political office but had sought legislative office in the past. In one respect, the GOP success in the South did depend on amateurs if that label is applied to anyone who has not held political office. On the other hand, many of the South's new Republicans were not political virgins, for several of them had entered the rough-and-tumble of the campaign, even if unsuccessfully, prior to 1994. Thus, half of the fourteen citizen-candidates had prior campaign experience to guide them.

The relatively high incidence of nonofficeholders on the Republican line in the South is not too surprising. First, there are relatively few GOP office-holders available. For example, in Georgia's Eighth District, won by a Republican in 1994, there were no GOP state legislators representing any part of the district. Second, amateurs are particularly likely to represent the minority party or a party that is emerging to achieve majority status (Canon and Sousa 1992; Canon 1990, 99). The Republican party in the South held most congressional seats and governorships *after* the 1994 election so that our analysis may have caught it in transition.

Table 3.15   Political Experience of General Election Winners, 1982–1994

	1982–1992		1994	
Experience	*Republican*	*Democrat*	*Republican*	*Democrat*
State Legislator	42.2	47.1	38.5	38.4
Former Congressman	0.9	3.3	0.0	0.0
Statewide Elected Official	1.8	4.1	5.1	15.4
Local Elected Official	19.2	15.7	7.7	23.0
Legislative Staffer	1.8	0.8	2.6	7.6
Lobbyist/Political Appointee	5.5	4.9	10.3	0.0
Total Elective Experience	64.1	70.2	51.3	76.8
Total Policy Experience	7.3	5.7	12.8	7.6
Total Political Experience	71.4	75.9	64.1	84.4
N	109	121	39	13

Table 3.16 Republican Freshmen from the South, 1994

State	District	Legislator	Prior Experience
Open Seats			
Florida	1	Joe Scarborough	None
	15	David Weldon	None
	16	Mark Foley	State Legislature
Georgia	8	Saxby Chambliss	Congressional Candidate
Mississippi	1	Roger Wicker	State Senate
N. Carolina	2	David Funderburk	U.S. Senate Candidate
	5	Richard Burr	Congressional Nominee
	9	Sue Myrick	Former Charlotte Mayor, U.S. Senate Candidate
S. Carolina	1	Mark Sanford	None
	3	Lindsey Graham	State Legislature
Tennessee	3	Zack Wamp	Congressional Nominee
	4	Van Hillery	State Senate Candidate
	7	Ed Bryant	U.S. Attorney
Defeated Incumbents			
Georgia	7	Bob Barr	U.S. Senate Candidate
	10	Charlie Norwood	None
N. Carolina	3	Walter Jones, Jr.	State Legislature, Congressional Candidate
	4	Fred Heineman	None
Texas	9	Steve Stockman	Congressional Aide and Nominee
	13	Mac Thornberry	Congressional Aide
Virginia	11	Thomas Davis	County Official

CONCLUSION

The value of political experience in pursuing and attaining congressional nominations and elections cannot be discounted. In our examination of the emergence and success of candidates at the primary and general election levels, the fields of candidates have consistently narrowed to focus on office-holding candidates.

Political experience is more often an attribute of Democratic nominees than Republicans, and among nominees, a political resume is more common for Democrats than Republicans who ultimately win office. These trends support the hypothesis advanced by Ehrenhalt (1991) that Democratic officeholders are more oriented toward political careers, and this careerism results in aggressive advancement through a succession of offices. The difference, however, is just one of degree because well over half the Republicans elected to open seats also boast political pedigrees.

Some trends from the previous decade persisted in 1994. Democratic nomination patterns continued as primary electorates chose officeholders to pursue open seats. When experienced candidates lost, they usually were eliminated by other officeholders. However, the Republican primaries reflected the mood of GOP voters in 1994, especially in the South. In Dixie, the GOP primary electorate summarily rejected office-holding candidates and previous nominees in favor of ambitious amateurs, and in the non-south, the rate of loss by experienced GOP candidates to amateurs almost doubled to about 60 percent.

The magnitude of the switch in primary preferences may have been an aberration. Two hypotheses can be advanced to explain the change in the role of experience in open seats:

1. The rejection of experienced GOP candidates in southern primaries is related to the rejection of experienced Democratic candidates in the South (see chapter 2). White southern voters, who increasingly vote in Republican primaries, rejected incumbents of all stripes in favor of "new faces" and outsiders. Primary elections may return to the "normal" pattern of favoring experience, especially if the electorate joins many political commentators in blaming the inability of the 104th Congress to legislate on the GOP freshmen's unwillingness to compromise.
2. GOP primaries are attracting strong, attractive candidates even though they have not held elective office. Even outside the South, an unusually large number of experienced candidates lost to amateurs. Primary elections will continue to be contested largely by officeholders, as ambitious amateurs move into office at all levels in the GOP majority.

In any case, the evaluation of the role of experience requires further study to understand what happened in 1994.

An immediate explanation for the performance of GOP amateurs in the general elections can be traced back to the GOP primaries. Recall that, of the thirteen open seat winners in the South, nine had no office-holding experience (table 3.16). However, five had sought legislative office, and six defeated officeholders to win nomination. Although these results are speculative, it stands to reason that the amateur who defeats an experienced primary nominee should be a formidable contender in the general election. If we ascribe electoral viability on the basis of the strength of the opposition overcome to gain nomination, then the amateurs carrying the GOP banner in 1994 were an impressive lot.

GOP prospects for sustained electoral success, especially in the South, are unclear. As seats open up, Republicans should be able to recruit quality candidates, especially in light of their new majority status. The behavior of several sitting southern Democrats in 1995 may be indicative of GOP prospects for attracting quality candidates in the future. By December 1995, the last two Louisiana white Democrats followed Georgia's only surviving white Democrat into the GOP. This trio was joined by one convert each in Texas and Mississippi and by Alabama's Senator Richard Shelby. If incumbents—a class reelected more than 90 percent of the time—see an elephant in their futures, it is reasonable to expect aspirants for open seats to move to the GOP with alacrity. If there is a stampede to the GOP, then Republican nominees may include both experienced partisans and some of the South's hordes of state and local Democratic officials who may switch parties if they sense a political riptide running toward the Republican party. In the face of realignment, a novice Republican may have a wider appeal than a Democratic legislator.

NOTES

1. The county judge-executive is a legislative-executive post, not unlike being chairman of a county commission. The post is still used in Kentucky and Missouri.

2. An excellent discussion of Alan Wheat's political rise and subsequent congressional career is in Carol Swain's *Black Faces, Black Interests* (1993, 116–127).

3. Wheat won the statewide primary with a plurality (41 percent), running strongest in St. Louis and Kansas City. The second place finisher was the female county judge-executive of Jackson County (Kansas City), who won 38 percent by carrying eighty-three predominantly rural counties. Wheat lost to former governor John Ashcroft in the general election.

4. McCarthy won with less than a majority, because Missouri has no runoff provision.

5. With rare exceptions such as 1998, midterm House elections are bad news for the president's party. In all but two midterms of the twentieth century, the president's party has lost seats. Research on the phenomenon—also discussed in chapter 2—indicates it is a product of presidential evaluations, changes in voter turnout, and the economy (Tufte 1973; Campbell 1997). Jacobson and Kernell (1982) argue that the early midterm evaluation also affects the decision by potential candidates to run.

6. This is interesting, given the extensive use of the runoff primary in many southern constituencies. Under a plurality rule, the average winning vote dropping below a majority is not a serious threat to leading candidates. However, in 1994, many candidates who in previous years might have commanded majorities and avoided a second primary instead came out of runoffs to win nomination. The precipitous drop among Republicans is another indication of the unprecedented interest in GOP nominations in the region.

7. Desegregation of Little Rock's Central High School in 1957 drew national attention as Governor Orval Faubus's efforts to bar a handful of black students were trumped when President Dwight Eisenhower sent in troops to implement the court order. The political benefits reaped by Faubus encouraged numerous other southern politicians to pledge undeviating support of white superiority. The potency of desegregation as an issue was underscored when the respected local U.S. representative lost to a write-in candidate who claimed the incumbent was "soft" on segregation. (This contest receives coverage in Miller and Stokes 1963). By 1966, Faubus had become a public relations nightmare and the state had become a pariah for industrial recruiters. He was succeeded by racial moderate Winthrop Rockefeller who, along with Florida's Claude Kirk (elected in the same year) became the South's first modern Republican chief executives. By 1984, however, the issue had returned to Little Rock, and to Robinson's advantage.

8. Robinson diffused the Reagan appearance by taking out an advertisement welcoming Reagan to Arkansas. Reagan captured 60 percent of the vote in the Second District but did not have sufficient coattails to pull in Petty.

9. Savage's observations come from personal conversations and interviews.

10. Of course, Arkansas is not the best example of Republican development in the South. Republicanism often had a liberal echo during the tenure of Governor Winthrop Rockefeller, and the GOP did not see the dramatic increase in state legislative representation that it realized in other southern states. As recently as 1997, there were fewer than two dozen Republicans in both Arkansas chambers, or less than 15 percent of the total. Those members were largely from the Ozarks, although a few, such as Petty, came from greater Little Rock.

11. In addition, Fourth District incumbent Ben Jones contested a district (the Tenth) that included only 4 percent of his old constituency. Jones lost in the primary to the general election winner, Don Johnson\ (D).

12. One white Democrat, Nathan Deal, survived the GOP onslaught but changed parties during the spring of 1995.

13. The last Republican presidential vote is coded as the Republican share of the two-party vote. Incumbent party is coded 1 = GOP, 0 = None, −1 = Democrat. Prior GOP seat is coded 1 if a Republican held the seat at some point during the prior ten years and 0 otherwise.

Chapter 4

Investing in the Future

The way to change the Congress usually isn't by beating incumbents—you do that through open seats.
—Corporate Political Action Committee Director, 1998

This chapter examines fund-raising by candidates for open seats. Campaign finance studies that concentrate on incumbents indicate that the political attributes of the incumbents' challengers and the competitiveness of their districts explain variations in challenger funding. As a general rule, incumbents dramatically outspend their challengers, and this spending is often preemptive, intended to scare off prospective candidates from even entering the race. Incumbent and challenger spending is often intertwined; increases in challenger spending are matched by increases in incumbent spending. The sources of support are often determined by the incumbent's committee or leadership positions or specialization. As discussed in chapter 1, challengers face daunting obstacles as they try to offset the name recognition, campaign visibility, and fund-raising advantages enjoyed by incumbents. Open seats presumably eliminate these obstacles.

Candidates need to create linkages with centers of political power and with voters; if they cannot do this, they will certainly fail. Money is a vehicle for creating, expressing, and maintaining these relationships, and an open seat candidate's fund-raising capability is the best sign of his or her ability to create and maintain these important links. Candidates who can generate campaign dollars prove their viability to the power brokers behind the purse strings.

To better explain the role of money in open seat elections, we overview the regulatory environment of campaign finance and the scholarship applicable to the study of fund-raising in open seat contests. We then develop and test models of fund-raising by open seat candidates and discuss the behavior of political action committees toward open seat candidates. In the end, we find that the factors affecting the overall funding of open seat competitors are unlike those in incumbent-challenger contests.

THE CAMPAIGN FINANCE REGIME AND
POLITICAL ACTION COMMITTEES

The financing of congressional elections is governed by the Federal Elections Campaign Act of 1971 (FECA) and the 1974 and 1976 amendments to the act that regulate individual, party, and registered political organization contributions to candidates for federal office. Since 1972, campaign costs have increased substantially; spending, especially by incumbents, has spiraled upwards and the number of organizations making contributions to candidates has grown dramatically. According to Federal Election Commission (FEC) figures, the total number of PACs increased from fewer than 700 in 1974 to more than 4,000 in 1988 (Stanley and Niemi 1993). Growth in the number of PACs has tapered off, although the amount of money they provide to congressional candidates remains substantial. PACs contributed a majority of all money given to incumbent congressional candidates in the 1980s and 1990s and also gave large amounts to open seat candidates (Jacobson 1989).

Under the 1925 Federal Corrupt Practices Act, political candidates were allowed to accept political donations through committees that they organized in their home states. Corporations were forbidden from making direct campaign contributions to these candidates or to their committees, but corporations nonetheless remained politically active by giving through their employees and corporate officers. Subsequent to the passage of the Hatch Act (1940) and Taft-Hartley Act (1947), labor unions were not able to make financial contributions to political candidates, although a 1952 Supreme Court decision, *Pipefitters' Local 52 v. United States*, allowed labor unions to create committees to engage in political action.

The labor PACs, most notably one organized by the Congress of Industrial Organizations (CIO), worked to promote liberal Democratic candidates nationwide. The CIO-PAC was especially notorious in the South, where CIO-supported candidates often found themselves at odds with the business-oriented, segregationist establishment. CIO-PAC did serve a critical role, however, by financing and supporting candidates for office who might not otherwise have taken the field.

The campaign finance reforms of the 1970s dramatically altered the ability of corporate and other interest groups to channel money into election campaigns. Demands for campaign finance reform had started in the 1960s, when President Lyndon Johnson called for legislation to close the "more loophole than law" 1925 statute. It was not until 1971 that FECA created the FEC to oversee the conduct of candidates for federal office. The subsequent 1974 Federal Election Campaign Act made it possible for corporations, trade associations, issue groups, and parties to create campaign committees for the purpose of donating or spending money in congressional and presidential elections. The major impetus for the 1974 reform was the revelation of campaign improprieties by President Nixon's 1972 reelection campaign. However, abuse of money on Capitol Hill was also of concern. Democratic Senator Edward M. Kennedy, in voicing his support for the 1974 FECA, argued that "abuses of money did not end at the other end of Pennsylvania Avenue" (Regens and Gaddie 1995, 99); they were also present in congressional campaigns.

The 1974 FECA included provisions for the public financing of congressional campaigns and imposed spending limits on candidates for congressional office. These provisions were thrown out by the Supreme Court in *Buckley v. Valeo*. According to the *Buckley* decision, spending money in political campaigns is an act of free speech, and thus cannot be constrained by law. Limitations on individual and PAC contributions were allowed to stand and are in place today. A person cannot give more than $1,000 to a single candidate or campaign, and a PAC cannot give more than $5,000 per election. As a result of inflation, the purchasing power of a maximum contribution has fallen by two-thirds since 1974.

The modern Washington establishment, with its professional interest groups and hired-gun lobbying operations, only emerged with the Great Society in the late 1960s (Sinclair 1989). Until the 1970s, political action committees were not widely used by interest groups, being largely restricted to labor unions. PACs were regulated by the laws governing corporate political activity and the circumstances under which candidates might take money, so this limited the growth of PACs. Trade associations and firms began to develop closer ties to government and organized PACs to help them gain access to members of Congress by paving the way with generous campaign contributions. Between 1972 and 1980, the number of corporate PACs grew from less than fifty to well over one thousand.

This revised FECA, designed to limit the flow of money in political campaigns and to bring campaign finance out into the open, has met with mixed success. Certainly the flow of money has been brought into the sunshine; however, sunshine has not dried up the flow. The demand for money in congressional campaigns has reached record levels as a result of incumbents' increased expenditures. It is this flood of money into incumbent campaigns that is often cited to explain the incumbency advantage. Incumbents, by virtue of their political positions and the high probability of reelection (House member reelection rates regularly exceed 90 percent), are able to attract more money to their campaigns than are challengers (Jacobson 1990). Because they perceive the need for ample money to secure reelection, incumbents who face competitive races will act to attract special interest support and thereby secure campaign financing. There is ample empirical evidence to support this proposition, including sophisticated multivariate studies of corporate, labor, and trade PACs (Grier and Munger 1993; Grier, Munger, and Torrent 1990). The challengers who emerge to contest incumbents are often underfunded, either as a result of their own poor connections or because of the unwillingness of political contributors to finance their campaigns (Kazee 1994).

Jacobson (1990) observed that the spending habits of incumbents have become less reactive and more preemptive. His bivariate regression analyses of the relationship between challenger and incumbent spending show that the change in incumbent spending as it relates to changes in challenger spending has been relatively stable since the 1970s. The slope of the increase in incumbent spending, as it relates to challenger spending, varied between forty-nine cents and eighty-two cents spent by an incumbent for every additional dollar spent by challengers (constant 1994 dollars). However, in general, incumbents have dramatically increased spending. Figure 4.1 shows the intercepts from each election year from 1972 to 1996 of these regressions (cf., Jacobson 1997). The intercept, which reflects the amount of money spent by an incumbent assuming no challenger spending, increased from $116,000 in 1972 to more than $450,000 in 1996 (constant 1994 dollars). Incumbents are investing more money in campaigns, even without a serious financial challenge.

The goal of the congressional incumbent is not just to spend more money than the challenger but to prevent the challenger from having money to spend. In this respect, incumbents often succeed. Thomas Kazee (1994) notes that the resource context of congressional elections—having money—often affects the decision of potential candidates to run. In 1992, the advantages of incumbency in fund-raising were laid bare: the average expenditure by an incumbent was $425,000, whereas the average challenger raised and spent only about $80,000. Many challengers, especially the hopeless amateurs (Canon 1990), did even worse.

Even when challengers have money, they are at a disadvantage. Incumbents have outspent their general election challengers by a ratio of approximately 3:1 since 1982. In 1996, the ratio of incumbent to challenger spending was down slightly, to 2.5:1. The average amount of money spent by an incumbent in 1996 was more than $660,000, compared with the average challenger expenditure of $255,000. Only twenty-five challengers—eighteen Republicans and seven Democrats—outspent their opponents, and an additional thirteen spent about as much as the incumbent. Another eighty-seven challengers were outspent by 2:1. However, the majority of challengers found themselves completely financially outclassed, outspent by the incumbent by more than 5:1; a plurality (159 or 43.6 percent of chal-

Figure 4.1   Estimated Incumbent Spending, Assuming No Challenger Expenditures, 1972–1996

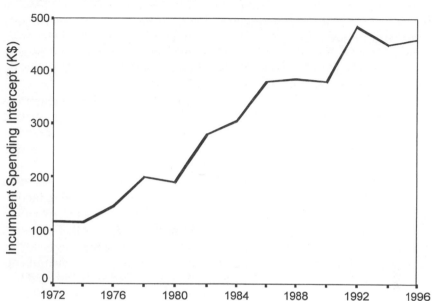

Year

lengers) were outspent by more than 10:1. Most incumbents figuratively buried their opponents in an avalanche of dollars.

Differences in fund-raising amounts primarily derive from the connections incumbents make with PACs. Congressional challengers rely heavily on individual contributions; in the 1980s, they typically raised less than 20 percent of their money from political action committees. By comparison, incumbents garnered almost half of their campaign cash from PACs; and PACs gave more than 75 percent of their money to incumbents.

How do incumbents get this money? Why do they need it? Why do they have such tremendous fund-raising advantages? In no small part, it is a product of their presence in Congress. Richard Fenno (1973) observed that members of Congress pursue three possible goals: gaining reelection, crafting policy, and wielding institutional power. The second and third goals—policy and power—are necessarily predicated by the first—reelection. If you are not in Congress, you will have greater difficulty affecting policy or exerting political power in the chamber. Legislators will use their institutional positions to attain reelection, with reelection their top priority.

According to all of the major research on political action committees,

PACs prefer incumbent legislators because they are better positioned to affect legislation, influence bureaucracies, and generally help interest groups obtain their political and policy goals. The division of the House of Representatives into highly specialized committees corresponds roughly to the structure of the regulatory bureaucracy and to the organization of interest groups. For example, the Environmental Protection Agency is under the principal oversight of four House committees; contributions by PACs affiliated with polluting industries that bear the weight of air pollution control costs tend to track to those principal oversight committees (Regens, Elliott, and Gaddie 1991). PACs give money in a manner that reflects the concerns of George Stigler's (1971) economic theory of regulation: they give to legislators who can affect the bureaucracy that oversees industry regulation.

PACs, especially those affiliated with economic interests, tend to be pragmatic in their campaign contributions. They donate money to incumbents of both political parties. A recent study of the changes in allocation strategies by corporate political action committees in the 1990s uncovered evidence that, despite the changes in the majority party in Congress, corporations continue to pursue a bipartisan strategy to protect incumbents in both parties while largely ignoring challengers (Gaddie, Mott, and Satterthwaite 1999). Interviews with corporate PAC directors echoed what previous research had indicated before the change in party control: PACs have friends in both parties who can affect policy, and although they have partisan preferences that make Republicans more attractive, the reality of a helpful incumbent is of greater value than the possibility of an even more-helpful challenger (see also Su, Neustadl, and Clawson 1995).

Fund-raising helps to support the activities in which legislators engage to maintain their electoral security. Political scientist Richard Fenno (1978) has traveled for years with congressional incumbents, observing how they relate to their constituents. Their activities and statements encompass what Fenno calls a "home style," a set of behaviors designed to connect the legislator to his constituency. Mayhew (1974b) argued that part of relating to the constituency was a matter of advertising accomplishments and taking credit for improvements in the district. The growth of media and direct mail means that, in the election campaign, more information needs to be channeled into the political environment, which in turn drives up the cost of advertising and credit-claiming during the campaign season. To harken back to the work of Gary Jacobson and the observations of Rep. Frank Lucas reported in chapter 2, part of the increase in campaign spending is driven by fear: politicians run scared, with the fear that they might lose. Or as Jacobson wrote, "because of uncertainty, members tend to exaggerate electoral threats and overreact to them. They are inspired by worst-case scenarios—what would they have to do if everything went wrong?—

rather than objective probabilities. Hence, we find members who conduct full-scale campaigns even though the opposition is nowhere to be seen" (1997, 77).

Since the late 1980s, when incumbent retention rates peaked at 99 percent, calls for reform of election financing have intensified, and some experimentation has occurred with notions such as public financing (see Wetherell 1991; Alston 1992a, 1992b).[1] Most calls for reform include proposals to cap candidate expenditures or limit the total amount of political action committee money a candidate can receive. The 1992 campaign reform bill vetoed by President Bush included public matching funds provisions as well as incentives to observe voluntary spending limits. If as suggested in chapter 1, incumbency is an amulet, then the money given to incumbents is the gilder from which the amulet was cast.

Recent efforts at reform have not met with success. In 1993, the U.S. Senate passed legislation (the Ford-Boren-Byrd Bill) similar to the legislation vetoed by President Bush. The House, however, passed legislation that did not address the campaign spending or PAC concerns expressed by critics or the previous legislation, but instead maintained the current system of political action committees and unlimited spending. A pledge by President Clinton and Speaker Newt Gingrich in 1995 to work together to reform campaign finance remained a hollow promise, as the Speaker never named appointees to the proposed bipartisan commission. The controversy over the contribution of funds by the Indonesian-owned Lippo Group to Bill Clinton's reelection campaign returned campaign finance reform to the center of the political debate in the closing days of the 1996 election and may have cost Democrats control of the House. Efforts to pass reform legislation sponsored by senators John McCain (R-AZ) and Russell Feingold (D-WI) encountered substantial resistance in both chambers of Congress but became an important feature in McCain's presidential bid.

The effort to address campaign finance reform is closely tied to concerns about incumbency advantages and influence-buying in Congress. Many of the supposed unsavory "by-products" of the current campaign finance regime—especially the cozy relationships between PACs and legislators—also concern term-limit advocates. Incumbents are the target of critics of the current system, and the arguments made for reforming the system are based on incumbent-election data. Term limits would presumably disrupt the interest group-to-legislator connection that is so troubling to reform groups such as U.S. Term Limits and Common Cause.

The assumption that disrupting incumbency affects the role of money in politics is based on a conventional wisdom that expects to see something fundamentally different in open seat campaigns. Gary Jacobson articulates this belief: "Candidates for open seats face somewhat different electoral situations, because none of the contestants is an incumbent or challenger with the accompanying advantages or disadvantages." There is no incumbent with overwhelming interest group and constituency connections from which to obtain campaign support. Challengers are more likely to come to the contest with similar levels of interest group connections or ties to "electorally important segments of [the constituency]" (Jacobson 1997, 77). Therefore, the overwhelming dominance in campaign financing enjoyed by incumbents when challenged will not be as common for candidates when challenging one another in open seat contests. And as Jacobson observed, spending should matter more in open seats because these candidates have yet to convey their message to a large part of the electorate. An examination of the distribution of money in open seat elections will help inform the discussion of how campaign finance and election reforms might affect congressional elections.

PATTERNS OF FUND-RAISING IN OPEN SEATS

Richard Fenno observed that "campaigning is getting more expensive for everyone" (1982). Despite the widespread perception that campaign costs have become uncontrollable, candidates' receipts, adjusted for inflation, indicate a restrained growth in fund-raising in open seat contests (figure 4.2). The average funds raised by Democrats and Republicans seeking open seats increased by 35 percent and 20 percent, respectively, from 1982 to 1994, but the growth has not been constant. After a more than 20 percent jump between 1982 and 1984 and additional increases in the fund-raising average in 1986, spending stabilized in 1988.

Democrats' fund-raising spiked in 1990 but then fell off by an average of almost $100,000 per candidate in 1992. Republican fund-raising fell off even further in 1992, by almost $200,000 per candidate. Much of this drop-off can be attributed to the large number of minority–majority open seats created in 1992 in which the GOP saw little hope of success. By 1994, the average raised by an open seat Democratic candidate stood at the 1986 level when adjusted for inflation, whereas Republican fund-raising had receded to the 1984 level.

The falloff in average Republican fund-raising after 1986 is indicative of a general decline in Republican financial competitiveness in open seats. As indicated in figure 4.3, the percentage of open seats in which the GOP candidate enjoyed a monetary advantage over the Democrat decreased steadily after 1986 until 1992. In 1986, almost 60 percent of Republicans enjoyed a financing advantage in open seats; by 1992, only about a third of the Republicans were better financed than their opponents. In 1994, however, Republican financial competitiveness recovered dramatically, as just

Figure 4.2   Spending in Open Seats, 1982–1994

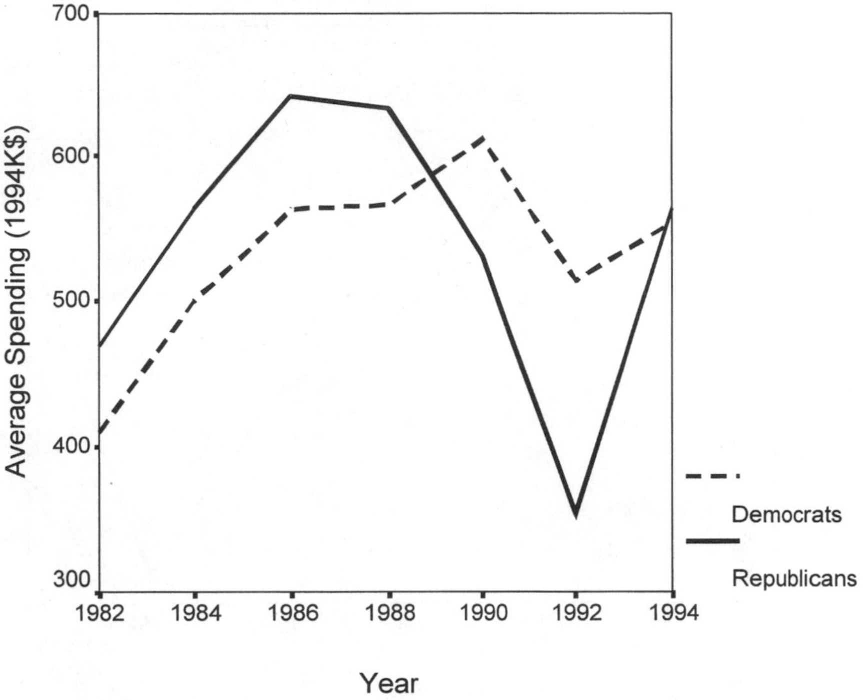

under half the open seat Republicans had a fund-raising advantage. Over-all for 1982 to 1994, Republicans had the financing advantage in almost half of the cases; however, they only held that edge in 38 percent of cases from 1988 to 1992. As indicated by the analysis in chapter 2, the ability to out-spend an opponent is crucial to success in open seats.

Republican efforts in the South have had an impact on the structure of the financial advantage in House races. In 1980, the Republican party committed itself to funding challengers and open seat candidates in the South. However, GOP efforts to capitalize on its initial gains under Rea-gan flagged after 1984. The emphasis on challenger funding shifted to picking up open seats, but overall Republican success in southern open seats was not realized. From 1982 to 1992, Republicans won thirty of sixty-eight (44.1 percent) of the South's open seats; eighteen of these thirty wins were retentions by the GOP, whereas nine had been held by a Democrat and three were newly created. During the decade, Republicans failed to retain four seats when their incumbent retired.

Southern open seat races are far more expensive, on average, than open

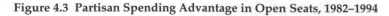

Figure 4.3 Partisan Spending Advantage in Open Seats, 1982–1994

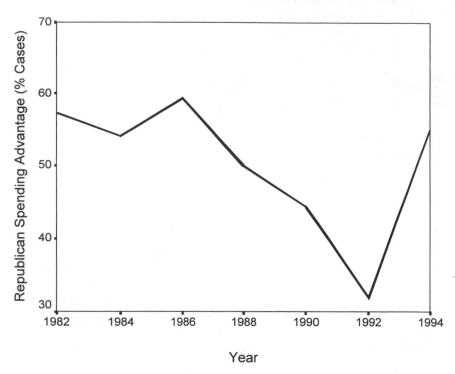

Year

seat races outside the region. As indicated in figure 4.4, GOP candidates averaged more funding than their Democratic opponents in both 1984 and 1986 and again in 1994. Republicans raised nearly as much money as Democrats in 1982, when GOP resources were dedicated to protecting incumbents (Jacobson and Kernell 1983).

In line with national patterns, after 1986, Democrats had a financial advantage in southern seats. Democrats increased their average funds raised in constant dollars from about $585,000 in 1982 to 1986 to almost $740,000 in 1988 to 1990, or an increase of more than 26 percent. At the same time, average Republican fund-raising held constant ($595,000 in 1982 to 1986, $586,000 on average in 1988 to 1990). The average amount raised by southern Democrats far exceeded the amounts available to Republicans in 1990 and 1992. The Democratic advantage in those years is also captured in figure 4.5, which shows southern Republicans outspent about 75 percent of the time. Only in 1986 did most Republicans have more money than their opponents, although in 1982, 1984, and 1994, the two parties were evenly balanced in spending advantage.

Figure 4.4 Average Spending in Southern Districts, 1982–1994

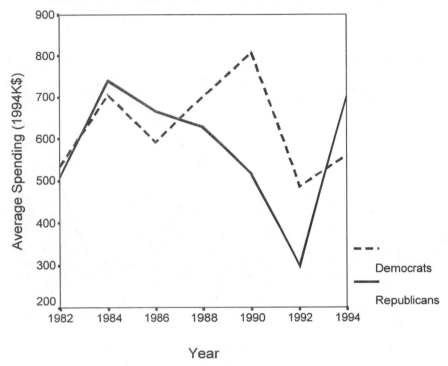

MODELING CAMPAIGN FINANCE

The literature on campaign finance, like most legislative research, has been dominated by incumbency questions. Gary Jacobson (1978) observed that incumbent spending in congressional elections was not significantly related to election outcomes but that increased challenger spending diminished incumbent performance. Subsequent research revealed a relationship between incumbent spending and incumbent reelection percentages, but the slope of that relationship is consistently less than the slope for spending (Jacobson 1985; 1990). In the two decades since Jacobson popularized the study of this phenomenon, tremendous effort has gone into exploring the role of money in congressional elections, but little attention has been given to the financing of open seats.

In specifying an open seats model of funding, we begin with the findings and assumptions of the incumbency-based campaign finance literature. The core assumption of money in politics has been: If you can win, you get money; but you need money to win. Chapter 2 demonstrated the powerful relationship between money and victory in open seats. Incumbency–chal-

Figure 4.5 Spending Advantage in Southern Open Seats, 1982–1994

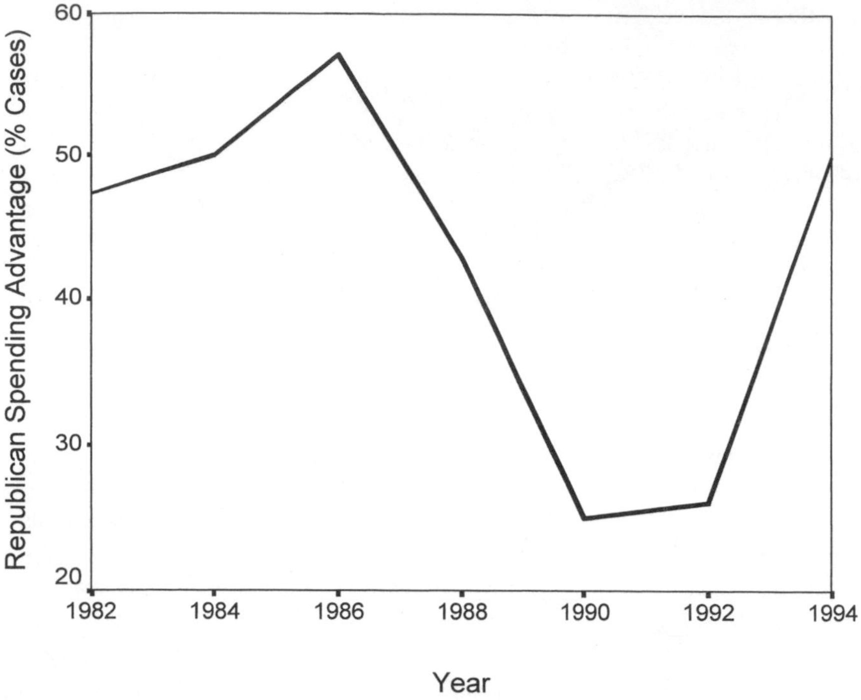

lenger models focus on measures of incumbent vulnerability and challenger strength as indicators of the electoral vulnerability of the former and the viability of the latter. The research emphasizes the institutional, partisan, and personal attributes of legislators and challengers that reflect electoral competitiveness and financial attractiveness. Findings from that research can help in the analysis of the financial quality of open seat candidates.

Experience

The first finding from the campaign finance literature is that experience matters. According to Jacobson (1978, 1990), state legislative experience is significantly and positively related to the ability of a congressional challenger to raise money. State legislators are advantaged for a variety of reasons. In the course of becoming officeholders, they have raised money, created organizations, and honed campaigning skills. As policymakers, they should be able to leverage their positions to obtain additional support from relevant special interests (Denzau and Munger 1986). Their state legislative constituency may provide a base of support that indicates to monied interests a greater likelihood of victory.

Service in the state legislature is not the only type of experience that may enhance prospects for winning a congressional seat and thus cue contributors. Bond, Covington, and Fleisher (1985) and Krasno and Green (1988) provide expanded definitions of experience, and Krasno and Green found that a variety of other political experiences were related to fund-raising. In specifying their index of political experience (see chapter 2), Bond and colleagues accounted for a variety of office-holding and campaign activities. Abramowitz (1989) and Squire (1991) found similar challenger experience and celebrity effects in U.S. Senate elections. Political experience makes a candidate into a known commodity, and investors in political campaigns are presumably more comfortable with candidates they know or of whom they know. Experienced candidates of both parties are expected to be similarly prolific fund-raisers.

Party Support

Political scientists have made much of the decline of party influence in the latter half of the twentieth century. The study of campaign finance has similarly scoffed at parties, in part because for years, parties were constrained by campaign finance laws from channeling large amounts of money directly to candidates. Party organizations also have little control over legislative initiatives or party agendas. Groups interested in obtaining preferred policy can go straight to legislators. This leaves American political parties with less control of campaign finance than their counterparts in most parliamentary democracies. The limited financial resources available to the parties means they often have had to prioritize giving to party nominees. When parties make their campaign finance allocation, they tend to emphasize incumbents over challengers and open seat candidates. Incumbents are better bets to be reelected; they possess expertise and are known commodities to state and congressional party organizations. Parties acknowledge the role of party loyalty when allocating funds to incumbents (Leyden and Borelli 1994). After incumbent needs are satisfied, the parties contribute to open seat candidates and challengers.

Open seat candidates generally obtain more party support than do challengers to incumbents. After 1982, the Republican party abandoned challengers and instead emphasized protecting incumbents and financing open seat candidates. Sorauf and Wilson (1992) observed the shift in party emphasis toward using coordinated funds (which the party controls) instead of direct contributions. Coordinated funding also allows the party to direct more money into a campaign than it might otherwise be able to through direct contributions. In regard to open seats, we follow the lead of Fowler and McClure (1989), who found that the parties serve as gatekeepers to other forms of finance, such as party fund-raising lists and PACs. By extension, if the financial effort of the party reflects its endorsement or intensity of support for a candidate, then money from PACs and individual contributors will flow to candidates the party is betting on (Fowler and McClure 1989). Party funding is likely to be significantly and positively related to overall candidate fund-raising. Given the ability of the GOP to raise money and coordinate funding to their candidates (Jacobson 1989), Republican fund-raising should show greater sensitivity to party investment than should Democratic fund-raising to the investments by the more-atomized Democratic party.[2]

Demographics and Funding

Because the decision to invest in a candidacy is in part related to the perception of a candidate's likelihood of success, the partisan history and racial profile of a district should be related to fund-raising. Bond, Covington, and Fleisher (1985) found that challengers raised and spent more money in districts that were more competitive. Bullock and Shafer (1994), in their study of Georgia state legislative campaigns, found that the Republican party targeted money to nonincumbent GOP candidates running in areas where Republican statewide and national campaigns had performed well in the past.

Racial characteristics also can play a role in funding. Wilhite and Theilmann (1986) found that black incumbents raised less money from PACs than did other incumbents. However, they attributed that discrepancy to the safety of black constituencies and the subsequent low cost of campaigns in those districts rather than to racism. The descriptive analysis in Wilhite and Theilmann indicated that there are differences in GOP and Democratic candidate funding related to the racial makeup of congressional districts, suggesting that Democratic and Republican candidate funding was lower in majority-black districts than elsewhere. Democratic funding should initially increase as black populations grow in a district. As black population approaches 40 percent, the likelihood of a Democratic victory becomes nearly certain so that Democratic fund-raising should taper off as black populations grow very large. Republican fund-raising should also decrease as the black population in a district increases but level off before black population reaches a majority. We have specified a similar control for Hispanic populations.[3]

Descriptive analysis indicated that differences existed when southern fund-raising is compared with that in the rest of the nation. Southern races were more expensive on average except in 1992. The designation of the South as a "battleground" by the GOP in the early 1980s contributed to increased GOP efforts. Another possible explanation is that southern Democrats who encounter unprecedented GOP challenges have access to broader sources of funds than their nonsouthern colleagues.

Alternative Cues

In the absence of incumbency cues, assessing a candidate's electoral prospects becomes more difficult. As noted above, political experience may influence the level of support candidates obtain from political action committees. Krasno and Green (1988) and Jacobson (1990) find politically experienced challengers are more adept at raising money for congressional campaigns. More experienced candidates already have relationships with monied interests; they also possess greater fund-raising experience than amateur candidates. The higher profile and greater experience of candidates who have held electoral office make them more promising prospects in the upcoming election, and that attracts more money.[4] Dealing with how the financial quality of competing candidates affects each of them is necessarily more difficult.

A common assumption in politics is that expensive contests should feed themselves and become even more expensive. Box-Steffensmeier (1996) finds a temporal dimension to congressional candidate fund-raising and that fund-raising is candidate-responsive; campaigns tend to increase fund-raising simultaneously. Our data indicate that the same may not be true for open seats. Table 4.1 reports the funds raised by Democrats as a percentage of funds raised by Republicans. In only 16 percent of the contests did the amounts raised by the two parties' candidates come within 20 percent of each. In 58.2 percent of the pairings, one candidate had at least 150 percent as much money as the opponent, with Democrats more likely than Republicans to hold a substantial advantage. Focusing on actual dollars rather than funding ratios shows only a few districts with candidates who raise funds in roughly equal amounts. Only 8.7 percent of open seat campaigns had candidates who raised within $50,000 of each other, whereas in another 8.9 percent of races, candidates raised within $100,000 of each other. Of course, when spending is great, as it is in open seats, candidates from both parties may appear to be highly competitive even though one candidate may enjoy a six-figure fund-raising advantage.

Table 4.1 Proportional Fund-Raising by Democratic and Republican Candidates

Democratic Dollars as % of Republican Dollars	N	Percent
< 50	55	23.9
50.1–80	38	16.5
80.1–120	37	16.0
120.1–150	21	9.1
>150	79	34.3
N	230	99.8[a]

[a]Does not total 100, due to rounding.

Analysis

The results of the multivariate regression model of candidate receipts appear in table 4.2. Although the model fits the data on Republican fund-raising better (adjusted-R^2 = .45 versus adjusted-R^2 = .27 for Democratic fund-raising), the results of both regression analyses confirm hypotheses about the structure of fund-raising by open seat candidates. However, some of the relationships observed when predicting challenger financial quality were not related to the overall financial quality of open seat candidates.

The most prominent difference observed for open seat candidates involved the role of candidate political experience. The slope for the opponent's experience was positive in both the Democratic and Republican analyses, but in neither instance was experience significantly related to candidate receipts. Democratic funding did not decline in the face of a more experienced Republican opponent, although Republicans had greater difficulty raising money when facing experienced Democrats. Analyses of the financial quality of challengers to incumbents revealed that experienced challengers raised more money than amateurs (Krasno and Green 1988).

The financial quality of Republican and Democratic candidates is inherently entangled. As the financial quality of an opponent increases, fund-raising by both Republicans and Democrats goes up. Republican candidates raised significantly more money in districts in which their party had demonstrated strength in the past. The prior partisan strength of the district, as measured by the last two-party presidential vote, was positively related to GOP fund-raising and negatively related to Democratic fund-raising. Republicans also fared significantly better—and Democrats significantly worse—when the GOP had held the district some or all of the last decade.

The value of the candidate to the party plays a role in candidate fund-raising. Although the Federal Election Campaign Act limits the size of party contributions in congressional elections, PACs and other contributors look to the parties to identify the more viable nonincumbents. The results of the regression analyses indicate that candidates who attract party funds also raise more money than other candidates. Whether this relationship is necessarily causal cannot be determined. The anecdotal evidence presented by Fowler and McClure and the discussion of PAC funding patterns later in this chapter indicate that party investment decisions do lead other sources to invest in candidates.

The partisan electoral history of a district foreordains the outcome of many elections. Jacobson (1990, 1997a) presents evidence that districts are less prone to switch hands when experienced, well-financed candidates emerge to carry the incumbent party banner. The results of our analysis

Table 4.2   Open Seat Candidate Receipts, 1982–1992

	Republicans	
Variable	*b*	*t*
Candidate's Experience	11,162.41	1.12
Opponent's Experience	−30,687.27	−3.01**
Opponent's Financial Quality	0.27	5.46**
Last GOP Presidential Vote	9,416.17	4.18**
Prior GOP Seat	77,016.36	1.95**
Spending by Party	2.16	3.37**
Black Population	−6,608.50	1.79*
Black Population^2	92.27	1.71*
Hispanic Population	−1,955.90	−.56
Hispanic Population^2	22.11	.38
South	8,415.91	.18
Temporal Counter	−11,947.91	−1.54+
Constant	−139,541.46	
R^2	.48	
Adjusted-R^2	.45	

	Democrats	
Variable	*b*	*t*
Candidate's Experience	7,412.88	.54
Opponent's Experience	−3,320.03	−.26
Opponent's Financial Quality	.49	6.29**
Last GOP Presidential Vote	15,979.50	5.63**
Prior GOP Seat	−95,352.95	−1.86*
Spending by Party	3.21	2.37**
Black Population	7,826.38	1.63+
Black Population^2	−202.26	−2.95**
Hispanic Population	5,785.81	1.29
Hispanic Population^2	−143.04	−1.89*
South	10,5651.54	1.79*
Temporal Counter	2,0057.86	2.03**
Constant	922,028.65	
R^2	.31	
Adjusted-R^2	.27	
N	230	

+$p < .10$, one-tailed test; *$p < .05$, one-tailed test; **$p < .01$, one-tailed test.

indicate that much of a candidate's financial quality is dependent on the district's partisan history, although the national party can influence candidate receipts from other sources by anointing them with the most crucial form of political endorsement—cash. Stable seats therefore become self-fulfilling political prophesies by providing a quality candidate pool, ensuring quality candidate emergence, and supporting quality candidate fund-raising ability.

As indicated in figure 4.6, Republicans have been advantaged in party funding. In 1982, the ratio of average party money given to the GOP candidate for an open seat compared with Democratic party money given to the Democratic opponent was more than 8:1, and the typical Democrat received less than 10 percent of the allowed party maximum contributions. Democrats subsequently placed greater emphasis on supporting candidates; by 1992, the average Democratic party support to open seat candidates was approximately 60 percent of that accorded on average to Republicans, constituting a three-fold increase over 1982. In the critical 1994 elections, Democrats made a valiant, although ultimately unsuccessful, push and narrowed the gap in party aid to an average of $6,500. In contrast, Republican party funding to open seat candidates has remained relatively constant since 1982, save for a dip in 1992. Despite heavy GOP funding in 1984 and the lower contribution levels in 1992, average Republican support to open seat candidates increased less than 10 percent in the 1980s. Until 1992, the ratio of Republican party funding to Democratic party funding was approximately 2:1.

Republicans faced greater difficulty, or had less interest in, raising money

Figure 4.6   Party Spending in Open Seats, 1982–1994

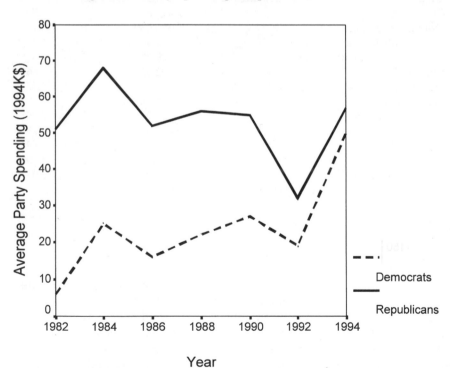

as the black population in a district increased. This effect is most pronounced as the black population approaches 40 percent. In fact, Republicans have not been successful in a majority-black congressional district
since two-term incumbent Webb Franklin held Mississippi's 53 percent
black Second District from 1983 to 1987, and the GOP rarely wins in districts more than 40 percent black. Democrats fared much better in raising
funds for election as the proportion of the black population increased; additional funds raised by Democratic candidates for open seats increased dramatically until the black population reached 25 percent. In districts with
larger black constituencies, the additional funds raised, all things held
equal, tapered off until no positive benefit to fund-raising was observed in
districts with more than 50 percent black population (see figure 4.7).

What are the reasons for this upward spike and subsequent decline in
fund-raising that is related to black population? To recap minority voting
behavior: black voters cast ballots overwhelmingly for Democratic party
candidates. As the proportion of blacks in a district increases, the core vote
for the Democrat increases. The existence of a significant core constituency
promotes the electability of a candidate and facilitates collecting funding:

**Figure 4.7   The Relationship between District Racial Composition and Candi-
date Funds Raised**

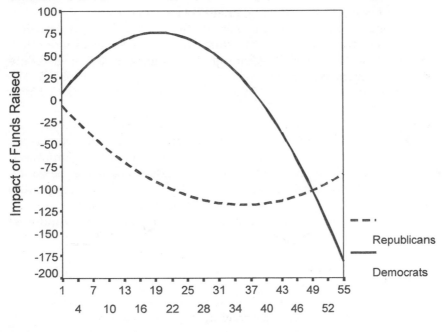

Percent Black Population

money follows success. However, the need for substantial money decreases as the core constituency becomes so large that the partisan outcome is preordained. The likelihood of Democratic success is sufficiently high in districts that are more than 30 percent black, so quality GOP candidates often do not emerge, meaning less money is needed to campaign against them. In neither 1992 nor 1994 did Republicans win a single southern congressional district that was at least 30 percent black. In the 102d Congress, however, Republicans did hold eight southern districts with black percentages between 30 and 38.[5]

Although the uniformity with which African Americans vote Democratic reduces that party's campaign costs, there are other factors that help Democrats cheaply win districts that have concentrations of blacks. Most of these districts are urban, which lowers costs in part because television is not sufficiently cost-effective to be an option. The political strength of institutions such as black churches—and in some areas, political organizations such as the SOUL, BOLD, and LIFE organizations in New Orleans—allows Democratic nominees access to low-cost vehicles for mobilizing voters. Conversely, the lack of Republican sympathies in the black community means that the costs of campaigning in the district are high for a GOP candidate; this is why Republicans have difficulty fielding attractive candidates or raising money in those districts. If a nominee emerges, it may be a throw-away, long-shot candidacy.

The average Republican in a majority-black district raised less than $80,000, compared with the Democratic candidate average of more than $350,000 in the same districts. Although the Democratic advantage is substantial, the average funds raised by a Democrat in a majority-black district is only about 60 percent of the average Democratic funds raised in whiter districts. Attributing the Democratic advantage in fund-raising in the South to the perception of victory as a result of black populations is not sufficient to explain the phenomenon. Even after party and the racial make-up of the district are controlled for, Democrats in the South raised more than $100,000 more than their fellow candidates outside the South, indicating that the perceived Democratic advantages in southern politics ran deeper than the effects of incumbency when raising money.

The absence of a relationship between candidate quality and fund-raising is surprising. Although Republicans who faced experienced Democrats raised less money than Republicans who did not face these seasoned candidates, the lack of any effect for a politician's own experience defies assumptions about fund-raising. The literature on challenger competitiveness suggests that candidates with electoral experience constitute better investments and will therefore attract more money. In open seats, experience is not a crucial variable in determining a candidate's total budget once other factors are held constant. This may in part be a function of the hurdles overcome by open seat nominees. Chapter 3 noted that the amateurs who were nominated often overcame experienced candidates in the primary. As shown in the next section, experience does matter when open seat candidates raise money from organized economic interests.

When turning from the question of how much money individual candidates raise to consider who has the financial advantage, a very different picture emerges. As indicated earlier in this chapter, in more than 80 percent of districts, one candidate raised at least 20 percent more money than the opponent, and in more than half of all districts, one candidate enjoyed a 50 percent advantage in funds raised. To find the conditions under which the parties hold the funding advantage in open seats, a logistic regression of partisan advantage in fund-raising was estimated. The model, which appears in table 4.3, is based on the Ordinary Least Squares regression (OLS) analysis, with the exception that the opponent financial quality variable is removed. The dependent variable is coded 1 for a Republican funding advantage, 0 otherwise; the candidate who had more money is assumed to hold the financial advantage.

The bottom of the table reports the null prediction, which is the proportion of cases correctly predicted if we guessed the most frequent outcome for each case and relied on no other information. The "percent correct prediction" tells how many cases would be correctly predicted based on knowledge of the other values in the model. The proportional reduction in error (PRE) reports what share of the errors made using the null prediction are eliminated by having the knowledge from the other variables in the model. Thus

$$PRE = \frac{\text{Percent correct predicted by the model} - \text{null prediction}}{100 - \text{null prediction}}$$

If all cases are correctly predicted by the model, then PRE = 100. If the model makes no improvement over the null, that is, the information in the model adds nothing to our knowledge, then PRE = 0. The model in table 4.3 improves over the null prediction by 28.9 percent and correctly predicts 80.4 percent of cases. The model was consistent in correctly predicting both GOP and Democratic funding advantages; no categoric bias was evident.

The logistic regression results indicate that, although the funds raised by candidates are related to partisan and constituency factors, it is candidate–political quality and partisan indicators of success that predict who will have the funding advantage. The coefficients of Democratic and Republican political quality are both statistically significant and perform in the hypothesized manner. More experienced candidates tend to have

Table 4.3   Who Has the Spending Advantage in Open Seat Races?

Variable	b	t
Democratic Experience	−.251	−2.43**
Republican Experience	.234	2.26**
Last GOP Presidential Vote	.122	4.63**
Prior GOP Seat	.469	1.28
Black Population	−.046	1.05
Black Population^2	.001	0.75
Hispanic Population	−.057	−1.38
Hispanic Population^2	.001	0.88
South	.541	1.11
Temporal Counter	−.252	−3.15**
Constant	−5.62	
Null Prediction	72.5	
Percent Correct Prediction	80.4	
PRE	28.8	
N	230	

**p < .01, one-tailed test.

an advantage in fund-raising. Partisanship as measured by prior GOP presidential vote was positively related to the GOP funding advantage. The temporal decline from 1982 to 1992 in GOP candidates holding the financial high ground is part of a larger decline in Republican congressional fortunes during that period. No regional or racial/ethnic effects were directly observed in the analysis.

Fund-Raising in 1994

The model of open seat fund-raising in table 4.2 does not adequately explain candidate fund-raising patterns in 1994. As indicated by the descriptive data in the initial section of this chapter, the GOP fielded better-funded open seat candidates in 1994 than in the previous decade and, for the first time since 1988, GOP candidates enjoyed higher average funding than their Democratic opponents. For the first time since 1986, Republicans had the funding advantage in a majority of open seats, and their spending was significantly higher in the South.

Table 4.4 contains regression estimates for open seat funding based on the initial model presented in table 4.2. Only 7 percent of the variance in GOP fund-raising is accounted for and virtually none of the predictors are in the expected direction. The application of the model to Democratic candidate fund-raising was also unsuccessful, with none of the predictors achieving statistical significance.

In part, the failure of the model to explain variations in funding is first a

Table 4.4 Candidate Fund-Raising in 1994

	Republicans		Democrats	
Variable	b	t	b	t
Candidate's Experience	−21,933.04	−.586	27,788.44	.785
Opponent's Experience	−24,713.74	−.680	−13,695.12	−.364
Opponent's Financial Quality	0.27	1.204	.14	.968
Spending by Party	−2.88	−.681	.61	.186
Last GOP Presidential Vote	3,990.19	.404	−10,116.83	−1.025
Prior GOP Seat	−192,234.94	−1.373	18,074.23	.130
South	−59,102.81	−.310	83,398.72	.458
Black Population	24,762.86	1.494	−6,386.36	−.387
Black Population^2	−570.30	−1.803*	−11.94	−0.38
Hispanic Population	54,336.51	2.179**	15,447.36	.585
Hispanic Population^2	−1,883.06	−2.162**	−484.53	−.553
Constant	432,695.82		859,743.17	
R^2	.27		.11	
Adjusted-R^2	.07		−.15	
N	52		52	

*p < .05; **p < .01.

product of the relative lack of variation in the values of the independent variables in 1994. The cases from 1982 to 1992 demonstrated considerable variation along partisan and racial/ethnic demographic lines. Districts ranged from those having virtually no Hispanic or black population to clear majorities, and many cases were one-quarter to one-third minority by population. Districts varied in terms of the partisan normal vote for president. In 1994, most of the open seats, including virtually all of the seats in the South, were predominantly Caucasian districts with a substantial core of presidential Republicans. Second, Republican and Democratic challengers in 1994 were generally well financed; the investment in open seats was generally higher and may have reached the point of defying the usual cues that structured giving by financial interests. Third, there was a dramatic increase in the average party contribution to the open seat candidates. Average party support to open seat candidates nearly doubled for both Democrats and Republicans, and for both parties, this was the highest average contribution to open seat candidates in a midterm election for the period we study. The coefficient of variation (standard deviation/mean) was the smallest for the Democrats ever and the smallest for Republicans since 1984. Contributions by the parties were generally up, but an increase in funds raised by the receiving candidates did not follow.

An analysis of who holds the spending advantage fares far better. The model of the funding advantage, as indicated in table 4.5, correctly predicted three-quarters of cases and improved on the null prediction by 23 percent. The distribution of correct predictions is the same across the null cases and the cases of interest. Unlike the model estimates for 1982 to 1992 in table 4.3, the measures of candidate quality are not significantly related to who holds the funding advantage, although the coefficients are in the correct direction. As in the examination of the previous decade, the presidential vote is significantly and positively related to determining who will have the funding advantage.

The only other significant difference in the results of the funding advantage model is the emergence of the South as a significant predictor. When the South is controlled for in the analysis of all open seats, however, it is negatively and significantly related to the GOP holding the financial advantage. As indicated in the discussion of the 1994 election in chapter 2, the Democrats and Republicans each held the spending advantage in eight southern open seats. The GOP held the fund-raising advantage in twenty of thirty-six nonsouthern open seats (55.6 percent).

A final possible explanation for the failure of the fund-raising model in 1994 relies less on statistical evidence than on a contextual explanation of the 1994 election. The election of 1994, it has been argued, constituted a fundamental shift in the electoral balance of the nation. For a variety of reasons related to their evaluations of President Clinton or dissatisfaction with the Democratic Congress or particular issues of concern, a share of the public turned against congressional Democrats of all stripes and types. The analysis in tables 4.2 through 4.4 indicates that partisan factors, such as latent Republican strength as indicated by presidential voting, were more

Table 4.5   Logistic Estimate of the Funding Advantage in 1994

Variable	b	t
Democratic Experience	−.327	−1.21
Republican Experience	.157	0.63
Last GOP Presidential Vote	.279	3.07**
Seat Previously Republican	−1.725	−1.65*
Black Population	.172	0.89
Black Population^2	−.004	−0.50
Hispanic Population	.178	0.96
Hispanic Population^2	−.003	−0.47
South	−2.695	−2.05**
Constant	−12.724	
Null Prediction	67.5	
Percent Correct Prediction	75.0	
PRE	23.0	
N	52	

*p < .05; **p < .01.

important to determining who had the fund-raising advantage than candidate characteristics. If, as Gary Jacobson (1997) argues, open seats are more vulnerable to national partisan tides, this should impact fund-raising, especially when the national political climate enhances those tides and indicates a clear division between the two parties.

PACS AND OPEN SEAT CANDIDATES

Earlier in this chapter, we noted the emergence of political action committees as major players in congressional politics. Conventional research on PAC allocations emphasizes an access/influence paradigm to explain PAC behavior toward incumbents (Grier and Munger 1993, 1991; Wright 1989; Denzau and Munger 1986). The rich campaign finance literature discusses the origins and variety of political action committees as well as their contribution strategies in incumbent elections (see Sorauf 1992; Grier and Munger 1991; Sabato 1985). The appropriateness of the access/influence paradigm is drawn into question, however, when examining open seats because of the underlying assumptions that explain the behavior of economic interest groups.

PACs have been the largest source of money for House candidates since 1978. Research indicates that interest groups seek access to the legislative process to obtain tangible economic gains, either through the receipt of a subsidy or contract or though the creation of beneficial regulation (Stigler 1968; Posner 1986). Among legislators, the ability to obtain benefits from economic actors is related to their institutional position and the issue areas in which they have influence (cf., Grier and Munger 1991). Legislators are spurred to seek additional support when they fear electoral defeat. Are access/influence strategies evident when the benefits to be obtained from recipients of support are entirely prospective, as in an open seat election? In open seat contests, do PACs pursue strategies that emphasize bet-covering (supporting both parties' candidates), which is an extension of the bipartisan relationship between private sector interests and incumbents? Or in the absence of incumbents, do PACs revert to partisan behavior emphasizing the classic business–labor allegiances of the respective parties?

The Federal Election Commission divides nonparty, noncandidate PACs into six distinct categories: nonconnected (ideological), cooperative organization, labor union, corporate, corporate (nonstock), and trade association.[6] The first category of PAC is the largest, encompassing a variety of ideological and social issue-oriented committees affiliated with special interest groups as diverse as National Right-to-Work, National Rifle Association, Realtors PAC, and EMILY's List. Cooperative organization PACs include about sixty PACs affiliated with agricultural cooperatives. They contribute heavily and almost exclusively to members of the

House and Senate agriculture committees and demonstrate no discernable pattern of investment in challengers or open seats (Grier and Munger 1991; Gaddie 1995c). Labor union PACs are overwhelmingly partisan in their giving, preferring Democrats in both open seat and incumbent races. They demonstrate some regional prejudices, investing less often in southern Democrats. The last three categories of PACs are what are often referred to as "investor" PACs—committees affiliated with corporations or professional trade associations. Their behavior is the most intriguing because these PACs most often engage in bipartisan behavior. They usually support Republicans but may also back Democrats, especially incumbent Democrats who are either ideologically moderate or on committees important to business, such as the Ways and Means Committee or the Commerce Committee. Collectively, the investor PACs—corporations and trade associations—along with labor PACs constitute the economic PACs, committees affiliated with institutions that have a primary interest in economic, rather than social, policy. The overarching political goals of economic PACs are more clearly defined than are the goals of ideological PACs, and their policy priorities also tend to fall along partisan lines. Therefore, these PACs better lend themselves to an empirical analysis of PAC strategy in open seats (Gaddie 1995c; Gaddie and Regens 1997).

This section examines economic PACs' contributions in open seat House elections. The extant literature on PAC allocations indicates that economic PACs pursue highly specialized contribution strategies that are clearly related to their economic needs and that also reflect the political needs of incumbents. Do the same considerations guide contributions when neither candidate has the inside track of incumbency?

The importance of such an analysis is underscored by the observations of PAC directors in Washington. These interviews, conducted by Gaddie, Mott, and Satterthwaite (1999) revealed a keen interest in open seat contests.[7] They touched on corporate PACs' funding priorities and political goals, indicating a unanimous belief that open seat contests reveal an interest group's "true" priorities, as open seats are perceived to be the principal vehicle for changing the composition of Congress. One PAC director observed the following:

> Incidentally, one of the real indicators of a PAC's ideological or partisan leanings is their giving behavior in open seat and competitive races. You can tell a lot about a PAC by looking at their giving in those kind of races. I like to go into both open races and races where there's a strong challenger. Those are chances for us to move the Congress in our direction.

The importance of open seats was also noted by two other PAC directors. According to one, "A key focus in getting [a Republican majority was] open seats. We absolutely look at those seats because there are big opportunities there. It's almost impossible to defeat an incumbent, but you can pick up an open seat much more easily." The second director, who represents a major transportation corporation, observed: "The numbers speak for themselves. In 1994, we gave 45 percent of our money to nonincumbents. There were a lot of opportunities with all of the retirements and open seats and vulnerable incumbents to elect some people that would be more friendly to us." Giving in open seats offers PACs a greater opportunity to affect political change because challengers require a greater investment to overcome the advantages of incumbency.

Any examination of corporate PACs that compares the partisanship of their giving in incumbent races with open seats shows the influence of incumbency, especially Democratic majority incumbency in the late 1980s. After the 1984 elections, a systematic growth in corporate contributions to Democrats occurred, although the balance of corporate money typically favored Republicans. During this same period, corporate contributions skewed heavily toward Democratic incumbents, primarily as a result of the efforts of the Democratic leadership in the House of Representatives (a matter discussed at length below). The change in political control affected the funding priorities of corporations. Gaddie (1995c) concluded that the shift of open seat money toward Democrats was the result of Democrats exploiting political experience and fielding candidates under conditions that heightened their prospects for electoral success. Favorable local conditions and political experience increased the value of many Democratic candidates to private sector interests that first seek to back winners in the open seats. The proportion of open seat receipts to Democrats is not as great as the proportion garnered by Democratic incumbents.

The existence of a bipartisan corporate strategy is important in explaining the electoral advantage enjoyed by Democrats in open seat elections during the 1980s. Open seats figure prominently in the Republican electoral frustration of the 1980s and are also important to the Republican breakthrough in 1994. Gilmour and Rothstein (1993), Abramowitz (1991), and Gaddie (1997) observed that the disproportionate retirement of Republican incumbents in the 1970s and 1980s left more GOP seats exposed;. Gilmour and Rothstein estimated that this retirement cost the GOP between ten and fifteen seats. The Democrats countered GOP efforts to keep these seats, gaining six seats from 1982 to 1990 (Gaddie 1995a). Corporate PACs' bipartisan support for open seat candidates defies the expected ideological and partisan loyalty toward GOP candidates. As one corporate PAC director put it,

Generally speaking, business PACs don't care which party members [of Congress] belong to as long as they help them. Again generally speaking, though,

Republicans are more likely to support what business PACs want than Democrats. This was the difficulty we faced when Democrats were in the majority. Some business PACs didn't and don't care about upsetting Democrats and they give their money to Republicans regardless of who is in control of the Congress. We have probably been more pragmatic than some.

To explain the pattern of corporate giving in open seat contests, we specified a regression model, drawn from Gaddie (1995c). Six theoretically important variables are included in the analysis. Three of these variables control for candidate-specific attributes that previous research has found to be important in explaining financial quality or political action committee allocations. The other three variables control for constituency attributes that affect the movement of PAC money. The candidate-specific variables are candidate experience, the investment decision of the PAC cohort in the candidate's opponent, and the investment by the candidate's party in her/his candidacy. Previous research on open seats found that corporate PACs responded to the experience of Democratic candidates but not of Republicans (Gaddie 1995c). The Krasno-Green index of candidate quality is used to measure candidate political experience.

Although some scholars denigrate the role of parties in modern politics, the parties are still relevant to the campaign finance process. They are limited in the amount of direct resources that they can provide candidates, but they continue to have a prominent role in open seat campaigns. One PAC director we spoke to noted: "Obtaining non-PAC money establishes their credibility as a candidate. If you could just come to Washington and pick money off of trees, it'd be too easy for anyone to run for Congress. The ability to raise money is an excellent barometer of a candidate's political strength." Gaddie (1995c) found that party financing of open seat campaigns was a reasonable surrogate for party endorsement, representing an expression of a candidate's value that is meaningful to economic interests.[8]

Previous research also noted an exchange in economic PAC behavior. Gaddie's analysis (1995) of corporate and trade PACs found that they reduced contributions to candidates as they increased support to the opposition. When candidate divestiture occurred, it usually meant less money for Republicans and resulted in a bipartisan bet-covering strategy in which private interests supported both Democrats and Republicans.[9] Despite evidence of bet-covering in the aggregate, corporate PAC directors discount this behavior. One director was most explicit, stating flatly: "Another ground rule we operate under is that we never give to both sides in an election. You hear about that, and I guess people think they're covering their bets or something, but we don't do that. You're just canceling out your own money. It's just awful. I don't think that's the way to wield political influence." Nonetheless, when aggregated, there are races in which both candidates draw substantial support from the same corporations and trade associations.

We do not examine cooperative agriculture and nonassociated PAC giving behavior. The former are almost entirely wedded to supporting incumbents on the Agriculture Committee, and previous research has uncovered no meaningful pattern in their contributions to open seat candidates. Nonassociated PACs encompass a vast variety of issue groups so that it is unreasonable to expect that, in the aggregate, these groups would follow a single strategy. In contrast, economic PACs have clear-cut preferences regarding the market and the type of government they desire. An examination of their contributions in the absence of incumbents reveals what candidates they prefer when the cues and biases of incumbency are absent.

The distribution of economic political action committee money to open seat congressional candidates is illustrated in table 4.6. The average corporate receipt for a Republican was about $35,000 more than for the average Democrat, whereas, on average, labor PAC support for Democrats was $80,000 more than for Republicans. Republicans averaged $12,000 more than Democrats when passing the hat among trade associations. Comparable numbers of Democrats and Republicans received corporate and trade PAC support. Although virtually all Democrats received labor PAC contributions, only four in ten Republicans got money from labor, and the Republicans who did attract funding got relatively little. Nonlabor sources give broadly but generously to Republicans, whereas labor gives more heavily and exclusively supports Democrats.

The more open seat campaigns there are, the more they increase in importance to economic PACs. In table 4.7, a set of bivariate regressions

Table 4.6   Open Seat Candidate Receipts from PACs, 1982–1994

PAC Source		Republicans	Democrats
Corporate	Mean	56,178.40	20,508.90
	SD	43,521.37	23,091.22
	Maximum Receipt	180,025.40	120,290.40
	Received Contribution	92.6%	92.3%
Labor	Mean	2,440.93	84,123.70
	SD	5,751.47	58,979.60
	Maximum Receipt	40,195.31	298,227.70
	Received Contribution	40.4%	97.2%
Trade Association	Mean	46,736.50	34,726.00
	SD	33,736.60	29,080.15
	Maximum Receipt	126,355.80	141,077.20
	Received Contribution	89.7%	93.7%

Note: All financial data are expressed in constant 1994 dollars.

are presented to illustrate the relationship between the number of open seats in an election year and the percent of money given by economic PACs to open seat candidates. As indicated in table 4.7, the pattern of giving to open seat candidates since 1982 is directly related to the number of open seats. The PAC cohorts gave a greater share of their funding to open seat candidates as the number of open seats increased. The table shows the coefficients and R^2s between the number of open seats and the percent of total PAC money of each cohort directed to open seats. Giving by labor, trade, and corporate PACs moved in concert with the number of open seats. The fact that economic PACs shift their resources so dramatically with the incidence of open seats underscores the importance of how they allocate their funds in the absence of incumbency.

Analysis

To test these assumptions about PAC allocations in open seat elections, ordinary least squares regression (OLS) is used to estimate the receipts from corporate PACs, labor PACs, and trade PACs. The equation specified to explain PAC contributions to open seat candidates is

$$Y_i = a + b_1X_1 + b_2X_2 + b_3X_3 + b_4X_4 + b_5X_5 + b_6X_6 + b_7X_7 + b_8X_8 + b_9X_9 + b_{10}X_{10} + b_{11}X_{11} + b_{12}X_{12} + e$$

where: Y_i = dollars to the candidate from economic PAC cohort I; X_1 = candidate experience; X_2 = opponent dollars from economic PAC cohort i; X_3 = South; X_4 = party contributions and coordinated spending; X_5 = seat formerly republican in last decade; X_6 = Republican presidential vote in the most recent election; $X_7 - X_{12}$ = year controls for 1982–1990 inclusive; e = error term. Separate analyses are performed for Republican and Democratic candidates

The same set of variables is used in the analysis of labor PAC giving to Republicans, but a different statistical technique is used. Because so many

Table 4.7 Open Seats and Aggregate PAC Allocations, 1982–1994

PAC Cohort	b	Beta	t	Adjusted-R^2
Corporate	.088	.663	1.98*	.44
Labor	.147	.844	3.53**	.71
Trade	.153	.966	8.40**	.93

Note: Dependent variable is percent of each PAC cohort's total contributions directed to open seat candidates; independent variable is the number of House seats open in a given election year ($N = 7$).

*p < .05, one-tailed test; **p < .01, one-tailed test.

Republicans got no money from labor PACs, the analysis could be distorted if OLS regression were used. To avoid that difficulty, the data on labor contributions to Republicans are analyzed with logit in which the dependent variable is a dichotomy where a value of 1 is assigned if the Republican received any labor PAC money and 0 if he or she received none. Thus in the analysis of the relationship between Republicans and labor PACs, the model focuses on whether any contribution was received and not the amount given.

PAC Allocations, 1982 to 1992

As reported in tables 4.8 to 4.10, all three types of PACs give more generously to candidates with greater political experience. This pattern holds for both Democrats and Republicans. The private-sector PACs gave more to Republicans than Democrats based on political experience; the slope for political experience was twice as large for Republican as for Democratic candidates. Labor PACs, although less responsive to Republicans (only 40 percent of Republicans received any labor PAC contribution), were most generous to Democrats with experience. The slope for experience in table 4.10 showed labor to be more responsive to Democrats for each increment in experience ($6,385.49) than were corporations ($4,638.14) or trade associations ($4,906.19) when giving to Republicans. Labor seemingly weighed experience more heavily in its decisions on giving than did the other economic interests.

Corporations and trade associations demonstrated a trade-off that weighed disproportionately on Republican candidates. As corporate or trade support for Democrats grew, support for the competing Republican decreased by roughly thirty cents for each dollar given a Democrat. Trade PAC contributions to Democrats decreased by about seventeen cents for every dollar given to the GOP opponent. The net effect of trade-off behavior by trade PACs favored Democrats, who saw their funds diminish at half the rate of that of the Republican opponent. Corporate PAC giving to Democrats was unaffected by amounts given to opposing Republicans.

As noted above, campaign finance laws constrain the ability of the parties to make substantial contributions to individual candidates; however, the gatekeeper role ascribed to parties by Fowler and McClure (1987) is evident. All three major economic PAC cohorts responded positively to party cues. Corporate giving was strongly related to Republican party giving and increased funding to GOP candidates by more than 40 percent of the party's contribution. Democrats' receipts from corporations increased by 18 percent of the sum that the party provided (see table 4.8). Trade PACs were more responsive to cues from the Democratic party. According to table 4.9, trade PACs matched 60 percent of the Democratic party contribution to

Table 4.8 Corporate PAC Support to Open Seat Candidates, 1982–1990

	Democrats		Republicans	
Variable	b	t	b	t
Candidate Experience	2,055.12	2.57**	4,638.14	3.14***
Opponent PAC $	−0.05	−1.56	−0.28	−2.14**
Prior GOP Seat	−7,447.86	−2.59**	7,052.52	1.24
Last GOP Presidential Vote	−278.24	−2.02**	661.58	2.50**
Spending by Party	0.18	2.40**	0.41	5.31**
South	19,280.13	6.84***	2,020.22	0.34
Year 1982	−2,588.49	−0.72	−5,695.82	−0.79
Year 1984	−6,773.44	−1.42	20,767.01	2.17**
Year 1986	2,364.46	0.59	8,452.06	1.09
Year 1988	3,632.53	0.78	−5,180.91	−0.56
Year 1990	11,516.02	2.65**	14,337.40	1.71*
Constant	23,299.25		−20,313.30	
R^2	.38		.43	
Adjusted-R^2	.35		.40	
N	230		230	

Note: Dependant variable is the amount of money given to a candidate by corporate PACs, expressed in 1994 dollars.

*p < .05, one-tailed test; **p < .01, one-tailed test; ***p < .001, one-tailed test.

their candidates, all other things held equal. Republican candidates received a 32 percent match to party contributions.

Labor PACs, as noted above, are far more partisan in their giving, and this is reflected in table 4.10. The receipt of labor money by Republicans is in no way related to contributions received from their party. However, labor funnels overwhelming amounts of money to Democrats who are generously supported by the party. Although PACs are generally more partisan when giving in open seat contests, it is labor that is the most partisan, giving overwhelmingly and almost exclusively to Democrats. Party support also pays its most handsome reward to Democrats seeking labor dollars.

All the major economic PAC cohorts followed the partisan behavior of the constituency. Labor unions and corporations gave more heavily to Democrats in heavily Democratic districts, and corporations and trade associations gave more heavily to Republicans in districts where the GOP nominee ran well in the previous presidential election. Trade PACs also tended to give more to Republicans and less money to Democrats when the seat had been held by the GOP some time during the previous decade.

These patterns, when considered together, indicate that the major economic PACs pursued a sophisticated pattern of contributing in open seats based on factors that reflected the prospects of success for the individual

Table 4.9   Trade Association PAC Support to Open Seat Candidates,
1982–1990

Variable	Democrats		Republicans	
	b	*t*	*b*	*t*
Candidate Experience	1,488.22	1.68*	4,906.19	5.23***
Opponent PAC $	−0.17	−3.25***	−0.34	−4.87***
Prior GOP Seat	−11,791.60	−3.65***	10,512.81	2.83**
Last GOP Presidential Vote	−119.43	−0.79	459.94	2.74**
Spending by Party	0.60	7.28***	0.32	6.30***
South	10,626.39	3.34***	−5,738.27	−1.59
Year 1982	−17,758.00	−4.53***	−16,435.90	−3.22***
Year 1984	−23,089.00	−4.57***	−106.82	−0.02
Year 1986	−9,863.48	−2.30**	−3,600.43	−0.70
Year 1988	−444.72	−0.09	5,886.27	0.98
Year 1990	11,457.65	2.42**	8,972.66	1.67*
Constant	39,588.28		−2,973.66	
R^2	.55		.60	
Adjusted-R^2	.53		.57	
N	230		230	

Note: Dependant variable is the amount of money given to a candidate by trade association PACs, expressed in 1994 dollars.

*p < .05, one-tailed test; **p < .01, one-tailed test; ***p < .001, one-tailed test.

candidates. These patterns were partisan, reflecting the status quo and rewarding candidates who had political experience and/or had the financial support of their party. The bipartisan tendencies of trade and corporate PACs were skewed to the Republican party; however, the overwhelming partisanship of labor meant that open seat Democrats had the privilege of fishing off both sides of the political bridge by taking a substantial, though not majority, share of private sector money while receiving the almost exclusive support of labor.

The Turning Tide of 1994

The 1994 election represented a departure from the pattern of PAC giving witnessed in the previous decade. In the aggregate, the patterns of PAC giving appeared to be unchanged: Democrats and Republicans both benefited from corporate and trade contributions, whereas labor gave overwhelmingly to Democrats. Within each cohort of candidates, however, there was a change in the significant predictors of receiving money from economic political action committees.

Tables 4.11 to 4.13 present regression models used in the preceding analysis to examine receipt patterns for open seat candidates in 1994. The

Table 4.10   Labor PAC Support to Open Seat Candidates, 1982–1990

	Democrats		Republicans (logit)	
Variable	b	t	b	t
Candidate Experience	6,385.49	3.21***	0.31	3.21***
Opponent PAC $	−0.21	−0.38	−0.00001	−3.27***
Prior GOP Seat	−7,582.97	−1.05	0.23	0.63
Last GOP Presidential Vote	−656.69	−1.96**	0.01	0.52
Spending by Party	1.76	9.34***	0.00006	1.22
South	−22,282.80	−3.15***	−0.21	−0.62
Year 1982	13,149.34	1.44	−0.31	−0.64
Year 1984	−12,847.70	−1.11	−0.30	−0.49
Year 1986	36,553.42	3.68***	0.93	1.84*
Year 1988	35,501.64	2.99***	0.98	1.64
Year 1990	21,252.59	1.94*	−0.37	−0.65
Constant	57,922.75		−1.60	
R^2	.45			
Adjusted-R^2	.42			
Null Prediction			57.4	
Percent Correct Prediction			70.9	
PRE			31.7	
N	230		230	

Note: Dependent variable is the amount given to a candidate by labor PACs, expressed in 1994 dollars.

*$p < .05$, one-tailed test; **$p < .01$, one-tailed test; ***$p < .001$, one-tailed test.

results for 1994 are similar to those observed in the analysis from 1982 to 1992, with two exceptions: first, the relationship between candidate experience and PAC receipts changed; second, party and partisanship was less of a cue for PAC contributions. With regard to experience, two changes occurred. Corporate PAC giving to Democrats was not significantly related to candidate experience. The slope of experience in table 4.11 was only 60 percent of that observed in table 4.8. Experience continued to be a significant predictor of Democratic candidate receipts from trade associations and labor unions. Seasoned Republicans continued to receive significantly more trade and corporate money as these PACs placed a higher premium on candidate experience than in the preceding decade. The slopes of both corporate and trade receipts related to experience increased from less than $5,000 to approximately $8,000.

The importance of party giving declined as a cue for PACs. In the 1980s, the evidence confirmed the conventional wisdom espoused by Fowler and McClure (1987) that in open seats, PACs followed the cues of parties, thereby allowing parties to control access to the riches of PAC coffers. In 1994, party contributions were not a significant predictor of candidate

Table 4.11   Corporate PAC Support to Open Seat Candidates, 1994

Variable	Democrats		Republicans	
	b	*t*	*b*	*t*
Candidate Experience	1,205.38	0.65	8,039.22	3.12***
Opponent PAC $	−0.01	−0.08	0.16	0.72
Prior GOP Seat	−7,229.20	−1.09	339.21	0.04
Last GOP Presidential Vote	−1,457.94	−2.74**	2,121.40	2.98***
Spending by Party	0.12	0.72	−0.14	−0.71
South	28,270.64	3.46**	2,020.22	0.34
Constant	79,553.90		−62,953.96	
R²	.43		.41	
Adjusted-R²	.34		.32	
N	52		52	

Note: Dependent variable is the amount of money given to a candidate by corporate PACs, expressed in 1994 dollars.

**p < .01, one-tailed test; ***p < .001, one-tailed test.

receipts from corporate or trade PACs. Only when it came to labor's support for Democrats did party giving play a role, but even here the relationship was weaker with the slope for 1994 (b = .57), only a third as large as reported for the previous decade in table 4.10. Party receipts became less important as a discriminating cue for PACs in 1994 because they made more generous contributions to a variety of open seat candidates.

Table 4.12   Trade Association PAC Support to Open Seat Candidates, 1994

Variable	Democrats		Republicans	
	b	*t*	*b*	*t*
Candidate Experience	4,874.57	2.06*	7,964.58	3.25***
Opponent Experience	−0.17	−1.26	−0.12	−0.80
Prior GOP Seat	−6,035.64	−0.72	−340.82	−0.04
Last GOP Presidential Vote	−857.19	−1.38	808.09	1.24
Spending by Party	0.28	1.36	−0.25	−1.35
South	9,443.44	0.92	−12,632.67	−1.12
Constant	57,080.35		11,058.04	
R²	.31		.37	
Adjusted-R²	.21		.28	
N	52		52	

Note: Dependent variable is the amount of money given to a candidate by trade association PACs, expressed in 1994 dollars.

*p < .05, one-tailed test; ***p < .001, one-tailed test.

Table 4.13   Labor PAC Support to Open Seat Candidates, 1994

	Democrats		Republicans (logit)	
Variable	b	t	b	t
Candidate Experience	7,677.19	1.99**	0.44	1.97*
Opponent PAC $	−0.63	−0.26	−0.00002	−0.25
Prior GOP Seat	−17,113.90	−1.24	0.72	0.87
Last GOP Presidential Vote	−1,344.59	−1.40	0.14	2.06*
Spending by Party	0.57	1.66*	0.00002	1.22
South	−12,191.00	−0.75	−2.27	−1.99*
Constant	110,950.60		−6.24	
R^2	.45			
Adjusted-R^2	.42			
Null Prediction			54.1	
% Correct Prediction			80.9	
PRE			58.4	
N	52		52	

Note: Dependent variable is the amount of money given to a candidate by labor PACs, expressed in 1994 dollars.

*$p < .05$, one-tailed test; **$p < .01$, one-tailed test

Observations on Economic PAC Contributions

In 1984 and 1994, labor found its proven friends in the Democratic House under siege from a strong national Republican campaign against the Democratic party. Labor gave top priority to incumbent Democrats, thereby reducing funds available for open seats. In 1984, labor PACs were pressed by incumbent Democrats for additional support to offset the potential drain of a weak Democratic presidential candidate, and in 1994, the onslaught of media and strong campaigns against incumbent Democrats in several states again knocked the Democrats back on their heels and taxed the financial capacity of labor. Gaddie (1995c) found that labor PACs directed significantly more money to Democratic open seat candidates in 1982, further supporting the hypothesis that labor emphasized supporting expansionist Democratic efforts in "good" Democratic years and then shifted its focus away from open seats when the national Republican party launched an offensive they sought to repulse.

As candidates seek to have interest groups and others pay large shares of the campaign costs (Paul and Wilhite 1990), nonideological contributors will assume those costs with one eye toward maximizing the likelihood of a return on their investment. Before winning election, open seat candidates cannot produce goods or policy outputs, but as legislators, they will have that ability. By selectively investing in experienced candidates who run in favorable constituencies, monied interests maximize the likelihood of obtaining a return on their investment.

The ability of Democratic incumbents to obtain corporate and trade support has been ascribed to the legislator's institutional power (committee assignments, leadership) and ideological orientation (voting record) (Grier and Munger 1991). Without the benefit of these established institutional and behavior cues, open seat Democrats obtained less support from corporate and trade interests. Democrats received approximately 30 percent of corporate and trade contributions to open seat candidates from 1982 to 1988, though the amount increased to more than 40 percent by 1988. In the absence of incumbency, such contributions to Democrats seem unnecessary. For business PACs to extend a modified version of the bipartisan contribution strategy to open seats was not unreasonable prior to 1995, especially if doing so would be viewed favorably by the long-standing House Democratic majority.

Former congressman Tony Coelho (D-CA) inspired bipartisan giving by business and trade PACs. As chair of the Democratic House Campaign Committee in 1981, Coelho took over a virtually bankrupt organization that possessed no realistic fund-raising or campaign strategy. Confronted with the prospect of Republican-leaning PACs supporting exclusively the bids of GOP candidates seeking to take control of the House in 1982, Coelho began courting business and trade officials. According to Brooks Jackson (1990), Coelho's most important—and in terms of impact—longest-lasting activity was his "door-to-door" visits to virtually every major PAC in Washington. In these visits, the chair emphasized to industry, trade, and other capital PACs, that "we control every committee and subcommittee in the House, and we keep score." This none-too-subtle threat alerted private sector PACs that they should become bipartisan in their giving. The financial support of private sector PACs to Democratic incumbents and open seat candidates throughout the 1980s indicates that Coelho's message lasted longer than his own tenure in the House (Gaddie 1996; Jackson 1990).[10] Political analyst Michael Barone attributes the Democratic party's retention of the House in the mid-1980s directly to the efforts of Tony Coelho.

Unlike corporate and trade PACs, labor had the advantage in the 1980s of trying to extract policy from a receptive legislative majority. Labor PAC investments sought to reinforce the partisan majority, although the allocations they made among Democrats were sensitive to the candidate's attributes. The more numerous liberal and moderate Democrats should be more willing and able to provide benefits for labor, whereas Republicans are presumed to have much higher marginal costs for providing similar benefits (see Parker 1992a; 1992b; 1994). For labor, shopping for policy outputs does not presume an increase in allocations across party lines.

Instead, labor maximizes support to the most viable likely supporters. Toward this end, labor money went to experienced nonsouthern Democrats. The benefits reaped by labor's single-minded support of nonsouthern Democrats provided access to key legislators during decades of Democratic dominance, but this strategy serves them poorly in the dawn of Republican resurgence. Even in the salad days of the Democratic dynasty, labor, because of its inability to fashion a majority exclusively from the nonsouthern wing of the party, faced frequent disappointments, such as the inability to repeal Section 14B of the Taft-Hartley Act, failure to establish a right of common sites picketing, and culminating in enactment of the North American Free Trade Agreement approval (on labor's relative weakness even in the Democratic party, see Mayhew 1966).

Explaining 1994

An examination of PAC open seat giving broken down by time period indicates that major PAC cohorts did not depart from patterns established in the last decade until midway through the summer of 1994. As table 4.14 indicates, PAC contributions through March 1994 favored Democratic candidates. Trends in giving by trade association and labor PACs mirrored giving since 1990, whereas corporate PACs gave more heavily to Democrats early in the 1994 campaign than in the preceding decade. Between April and July 1994, corporate contributions started to shift away from Democratic candidates. Corporate giving flipped from a 53 to 47 Democratic advantage in the first quarter to a 53.5 to 46.5 Republican advantage in the second quarter of 1994.

Table 4.14   The Movement of PAC Money in the 1994 Elections

	Contributions Between		
PAC Cohort	Jan. 1, 1993– Mar. 31, 1994	Apr. 1, 1994– June 30, 1994	Jul. 1, 1994– Nov. 8, 1994
Corporate			
Democrats	53.2	46.5	23.9
Republicans	46.8	53.5	76.1
Trade Association			
Democrats	53.9	51.7	39.7
Republicans	46.1	48.3	60.3
Labor			
Democrats	98.9	99.6	97.3
Republicans	1.1	0.4	2.7

Note: Cell entries are the percentage of a PAC cohort's dollars given to the respective party's open seat candidates between the dates above.

The dramatic shift in PAC allocations came in the last four months of the campaign. From the beginning of July until election day, Republicans dominated the receipts from trade and corporate PACs. In the immediate run-up to the election, corporate PACs largely abandoned the bipartisan strategies of the previous decade to support GOP candidates.

Did PAC managers sense that 1994 would break four decades of Democratic dominance long before anyone other than Newt Gingrich believed his rhetoric of change? Or did groups intimidated by Tony Coehlo become emboldened to return to their ideological roots, thereby forsaking a bipartisan strategy and in so doing produce the GOP win? We do not know which came first—belief that Gingrich could lead Republicans to a political promised land in a Moses-like fashion or such alienation of the American public from Bill Clinton and his party so as to propel the GOP to victory. Gaddie, Mott, and Satterthwaite's interviews (1999) of political action committee directors shed light on the change in funding priorities. In this section, we draw heavily on their original interviews with PAC directors to craft a discussion of the role congressional leaders played in affecting PAC priorities. We were curious how the efforts of Republican leaders compared with the actions, a decade prior, of former Democratic campaign committee leader Tony Coehlo.

PAC directors were most forthcoming in discussing the role of Republican leadership in engineering a shift in economic PAC funding; indeed, it is apparent that efforts to engineer a business-interest-backed Republican majority predated 1994. When asked, "What has been the general reaction to the Republicans' efforts to 'encourage' PACs to give more money to Republican candidates?" the responses varied. One respondent said: "I haven't seen any overt efforts by the Republicans to move money their way, but I've heard rumblings about that. I'm not sure if that would have much effect on us one way or the other, though." (Gaddie, Mott, and Satterthwaite 1999, 20.) The other directors acknowledged Republican efforts to encourage corporate partisanship in the following statement:

> There were some efforts on the part of the Republicans before 1994 . . . [Former Republican National committee chairman] Haley Barbour pushed PACs hard to give more money to Republicans, but he wasn't successful because people don't like to be told what to do. It's too simplistic to tell us to up the percentage of money we give to them. Some jawboning is okay. [Representative Bill] Paxon did it the right way, I think. He said, "we don't mind if you give 20 percent of your money to [Democratic] incumbents, but we want you to work for our side or stay out of open races or where we have winnable challenger races in play." (Gaddie, Mott, and Satterthwaite 1999, 20)

One interviewee, citing the role of both the Republican National Committee (RNC) and the GOP leadership in the U.S. House of Representatives, confirmed the role of Republicans changing corporate priorities. In the wake of the 1991 to 1992 reapportionment, the vulnerability of the Democratic majority was apparent to Republican leaders. When GOP campaign officials met with political action committee representatives, they emphasized the potential for a Republican majority.

> We all went to RNC meetings in 1992 and 1993 and listened to [Republican Congressional Campaign Committee chairman Guy] Vander Jagt tell us we only needed to elect twenty-five more Republicans to take control of the House. We knew that was doable, something within striking distance, but nobody really believed it would [be] imminent. Many of us took note though and did what we could to bring that about. If you look at the records you'll see that some business PACs gave 70 percent of their money to non-incumbent challengers in 1993, 1994 and even earlier. (Gaddie, Mott, and Satterthwaite 1999, 21)

Another PAC director identified a specific source of efforts to alter corporate PAC thinking away from the emphasis on incumbent partisanship and challenger neutrality.

> As a PAC, we were not actively engaged in trying to change the majority party of the Congress. We were not involved in any party PACs in 1994. But I think they made a difference. I think Bill Paxon, as the NRCC Chairman, is more responsible for the 1994 takeover than Newt Gingrich. Republicans really sat on their haunches for awhile in the late 1980s and early 1990s and lost some opportunities. (Gaddie, Mott, and Satterthwaite 1999, 21)

Since the Republican takeover of Congress, the balance of corporate political action has favored the GOP. The distribution of this money has been the most favorable to the GOP since 1978. The effort to redirect corporate PAC money indicates an undoing of the Coelho strategy. In particular, many Republican leaders find it unthinkable that corporate PACs continue to contribute to Democrats, especially when the Republican party is the "pro-business" party. The activities of GOP Whip Tom DeLay (R-TX) stand out in both press accounts and in the minds of PAC directors:

> Tom DeLay . . . played a big role in the effort to remind PACs that the Republicans are the majority party now. DeLay called people in on the carpet. He wasn't extorting people, he was calling it like it is. Business PACs should be with the Republican party. Coehlo was more vindictive and shrewd, more intimidating. Business should be happy to respond to the Republican challenge. (Gaddie, Mott, and Satterthwaite 1999, 21)

Two other directors fell back on an institutional power argument to explain the post-1994 increase in corporate support to Republican incumbents. The first had this comment:

The Republicans are in the majority now so they should get more PAC money. It's totally inaccurate to suggest, as some people have, that Paxon wasn't as good at shaking down the PACs as Coehlo. And it's also a bit sour grapes for the PACs to complain about it. It's reality. Paxon was really just asking them to come back home. (Gaddie, Mott, and Satterthwaite 1999, 22)

Another PAC director had this to say:

You have to remember that politics is about power and it's about people. Everyone around here wants to succeed, to be good at what they do. They're successful, competitive people. They like to deliver when asked to perform. Coehlo may have set the standard for asking PACs to deliver; maybe not. He more probably just exemplified a long line of people in this town who are driven to succeed and try to motivate others to help them succeed. There are lots of people in this town who did that before he did it and a lot of people still do that. (Gaddie, Mott, and Satterthwaite 1999, 22)

That effort has come with some costs:

There has been a big Republican effort, headed up by Tom DeLay, to be as aggressive as Coehlo in demanding business PAC money. But I think it has backfired. It pissed people off. Maybe it's easier to say no to your friends and because they were friends they didn't feel like they had to go along. DeLay didn't do as good a job as the Democrats at convincing PACs to change their giving patterns. The Republicans, I think, just weren't as good at selling it as the Democrats. (Gaddie, Mott, and Satterthwaite 1999, 22)

The effort of Republican leaders had an impact. A quantitative analysis of incumbent receipts from corporate PACs by Gaddie, Mott, and Satterthwaite (1999) indicates that the balance of corporate giving shifted toward the GOP but that the shift was not a product of moving money away from Democrats; it was instead a way of putting more money into the system. The distribution of funds described by one of their interviewees illustrates this point while also indicating the limits of partisan control to leverage money: "I'd say about 80 percent of our money goes to Republicans. When the Democrats were in power, we gave more of our money to them—maybe about 50 percent. We gave to them because we worked with them—we had to because they were in the majority. But even then, the ones we gave money to were the people who agreed with us on our issues." (Gaddie, Mott, and Satterthwaite 1999, 22) Corporations did not abandon Democrats altogether but placed a greater emphasis on their market-oriented, Republican friends, especially after the Republicans won their majority. Interviews with PAC directors indicate that this emphasis extended into the open seats.

CONCLUSION

Chapter 2 demonstrated the critical influence of money in open seat House elections. The dynamic of who receives money in open seats reflects the previous advantages of candidates in congressional elections. Open seats are among the most expensive, but in relatively few contests do both major candidates have equal access to substantial funding. Open seats tend to be won by the candidates who raised the most money, and determining which candidate will raise more money is multifaceted. Our analysis indicates the following about financing open seat contests:

In neither party were open seat candidates' financial resources related to their political experience, although from 1982 to 1992, Republicans who faced experienced Democrats raised less money than other Republicans. Fund-raising skills of the opposition are, however, related to campaign funding. Although we cannot ascribe causal order, it is apparent that until 1994, expensive races fed on each other in the open seats, much as Box-Steffensmeier's (1996) research on incumbent congressional elections found.

Although candidate experience was not related to total funds raised, it was linked to the successful soliciting from PACs. Among the cohorts of economic PACs examined, all demonstrated some responsiveness to candidate quality.

The analysis supports the proposition that parties are important in cueing PAC contributions as well as money from other givers. Candidates who received more party money enjoyed greater total receipts and more generous PAC contributions until 1994.

Constituency characteristics affect financial quality. Some of the most powerful drivers of overall fund-raising are the ethnic composition and partisan history of a constituency. In all of the analyses for 1982 to 1992, the partisan and ethnic makeup of the district affected the fund-raising of candidates. Southern Democrats also demonstrated greater success in drawing support from private-sector PACs prior to 1994.

PACs are strategic when supporting open seat candidates. The partisan behavior exhibited by corporate PACs during the late 1970s disappeared in the 1980s, giving way to bipartisan contributions that ultimately helped Democrats. The intervention with corporate and other business-related PACs by DCCC chair Tony Coelho carried over to giving to open seat candidates. The bipartisan strategy of economic PACs continued into the 1994 congressional election cycle. The last-quarter shift of support to Republicans indicates that corporate and trade PACs anticipated (or facilitated) the November 8 outcome by a late shift in the bulk of their largesse.

As long as Republicans hold a majority in the House, we expect PAC giving to open seats to be more partisan. Corporate and trade interests no longer confront the explicit threat initially offered by Coelho; market-oriented Republicans are in control of the House, and the recent progress on issues such as development, environmental regulation, and changing the capital gains tax structure indicates that the majority is responding to its constituency.

Why did the models of candidate financial quality and spending advantage not perform the same in 1994 as in the prior decade? Several factors explain the differences:

1. Democratic and Republican party funding was up in 1994, and with more candidates receiving large amounts of party money, the distribution of these funds was flattened. Party giving, especially among Democrats, had been more discriminating in the 1980s. The reduced variation in party financing in 1994 weakened this cue to other interests that give to open seat candidates.
2. PAC funding turned away from Democrats at the end of the 1994 campaign cycle. The initial trend in 1994 showed Democrats continuing to benefit from bipartisan giving by business-oriented interests. In the last reporting cycle, business PACs abandoned Democrats and fueled Republican campaigns in the stretch run to the election.
3. Experience failed as a predictor of who would hold the spending advantage in 1994 despite its utility for explaining individual candidate fund-raising from 1982 to 1992. More experienced Republicans often lost primaries to relatively inexperienced opponents, especially in the South. By winning a contested primary, the amateur usurpers demonstrated political viability that went beyond the measures used in political science research.

The failure of the model in 1994 was not related to a decline in the money-to-votes relationship. Chapter 2 indicated that candidate spending was significantly and positively related to candidate performance in 1994.

Financing of open seat contests is unique in many ways. The absence of incumbents removes cues that PACs and individual contributors rely on to target their giving. The absence of institutional structures seemingly divorces fund-raising from the expectation of buying policy. However, the amount of money required to win an open seat is greater than that spent by most incumbents seeking reelection, and the advantages of name-recognition and office assets that come with incumbency are absent (or diminished, in the case of an ambitious officeholder). To presume that open seat candidates are freed from the influence of monied interests or particularized constituencies when seeking office is naive. To assume that incumbency-interest linkages are broken in open seats is to ignore the reality of how these seats are funded. Experienced lesser-office candidates may be more likely to raise large sums of money from PACs than other nominees. Similarly, the parties, by serving as gatekeepers, exercise some influence with candidates, forging linkages to incumbent government.

NOTES

1. These reforms are being tried at the state level and therefore have little impact on federal elections.

2. Party funding is coded as the direct contributions plus coordinated party contributions expressed in constant 1994 dollars.

3. Minority population effects are controlled using, respectively, the percentage of black and percentage of Hispanic population in the district, and the quadratic of the two population terms.

4. Candidate experience is measured with the Krasno-Green candidate quality index described in chapter 3.

5. In the 105th Congress, Republicans again held some districts that were more than 30 percent black. For the most part, these districts had Republican incumbents but were made blacker in the course of court-ordered redistricting in Georgia and Louisiana.

6. Party committees are governed by different rules than those for other political action committees. Nonconnected PACs encompass a variety of issue groups, good-government or advocacy groups, and political leadership PACs (e.g., Henry Waxman's Twenty-fourth Congressional District PAC).

7. Subsequent quotations from PAC directors come from unpublished interviews conducted by Keith Gaddie, Jonathan Mott, or Shad Satterthwaite during 1999.

8. Party support is measured as the amount of party contributions plus the level of party coordinated expenditures on behalf of the candidate, all expressed in constant 1994 dollars. Party financial data came from the Federal Election Commission.

9. The opponent's support from a PAC cohort is measured in constant 1994 dollars.

10. Coelho was forced to resign in disgrace from both his post as majority whip and his seat in June 1989 amid allegations of unethical conduct related to the collapse of the savings and loan industry.

Chapter 5

Women and Open Seat Congressional Elections

For most of the three generations since Jeanette Rankin became the first female member of Congress in 1916, the number of congresswomen has grown slowly. The "Year of the Woman" in 1992 produced an unprecedented increase in females in the U.S. House. In this chapter, we examine whether gender makes a distinct contribution to the explanation of candidate performance in open seat contests.

The combined effects of redistricting and incumbent retirement created the largest number of open seats in the post-World War II era in 1992. The elimination of entrenched male incumbents may have significantly enhanced opportunities for female advancement (Burrell 1994; Pritchard 1992 a,b). Do women utilize the same stepping stones as used by males—political experience and plentiful campaign funds? Are candidate quality, campaign finance, and presidential coattails as useful in explaining congressional election outcomes for women as they are for all candidates?

WOMEN AND LEGISLATIVE ELECTIONS

Before the 1970s, women in Congress often followed a funeral procession into the chamber. Bullock and Heys (1972) examined the careers of sixty-six women elected to the House of Representatives between 1917 and 1970. They found that almost half of those women (47 percent) succeeded to their late husbands' seats, exploitation of a specific type of open seat. Widows, however, tended to play only bit parts, being more than twice as likely as nonwidows to serve one term and then quickly opt out of electoral politics (Bullock and Heys 1972). Women subsequently entered Congress largely in their own right (Gertzog 1979), although their numbers remained small. Before 1980, most research examining this phenomenon ascribed the paucity of women at all levels of public office to a lack of motivation or ambition or to family-related or traditional cultural factors (Carroll 1983; Darcy and Hadley 1988). Recent research has turned away from cultural and motivational influences on female representation. Carroll (1985; also see Thomas 1994) made the following observation:

> [w]hile lower levels of political ambition may be one reason why fewer women than men seek political office in the first place, women's aspirations relative to men's are not a factor holding them back once they have achieved the basic threshold of election to a public office. (Carroll 1985, 1242)

If women who hold elective office are no less ambitious than men who hold comparable positions, then a lack of motivation cannot explain low female representation (but see Bledsoe and Herring 1990). Instead, factors such as candidate availability, elite support of candidates, and campaign financing may affect female electability.

Anderson and Thorson (1984) claimed female representation was inhibited by the presence of incumbents who hold institutional advantages in seeking reelection and by the scarcity of female nominees. This argument was supported by Volgy, Schwartz, and Gottleib (1986), who argued that women are outsiders in American politics. Darcy and Choike's (1986) examination of the impact of legislative turnover on female representation found that the rate of incumbent turnover and the presence of female candidates were the two driving forces behind female representation. Assuming constant rates of incumbent success and of female candidate emergence, they predicted that beginning in 1986, the numbers of women in Congress would increase slowly before stabilizing at forty-three (10 percent), sometime around 2010. The results of the 1992 elections, when forty-seven women were elected to Congress, disproved that prediction. Most of these women were either reelected incumbents or open seat winners. Only two of forty-one female challengers defeated incumbents in 1992, a rate comparable with the general rate of incumbent defeats in the 1980s and 1990s (Fowler 1993).

Dramatic changes in representation as a result of episodic events are not unusual in American politics. Historic shifts in voter preferences or strong presidential coattails have altered the composition of legislatures. When the status quo is upset by events such as redistricting, cues used by voters and politically powerful elites can be muted, and the natural advantages that incumbents enjoy may be attenuated. "Outsider" candidates may perceive the openings created as a result of the displacement of incumbents as opportunities to advance politically. Redistricting and incumbent turnover have been tied to the influx of women into Congress (Burrell 1994) as well as the Florida legislature (Pritchard 1992b), but not into the North Carolina or South Carolina legislatures (Bullock and Gaddie 1993).

This chapter examines four aspects of female representation: (1) candidacies and candidate political experience, (2) nominations (winning primaries), (3) financial support, and (4) general election success. The preponderance of evidence regarding female advancement in politics emphasizes the importance of women running for open seats. EMILY's List president Ellen Malcolm argued a month before the November 1992 elections that the biggest problem facing women in recent elections was the lack of "realistic opportunities"—the opportunity to compete against a candidate without the incumbent's advantage. If this is correct, a better understanding of the role of gender in the nominating, fund-raising, and elections of new representatives through open seats is warranted.

RECENT FEMALE SUCCESS: FLORIDA, 1992

The success story of the Year of the Woman was the performance of female candidates for election in Florida. Before 1992, Florida had one female U.S. Representative: Ileana Ros-Lehtinen, elected in 1989.[1] Female congressional representation in the Sunshine State increased substantially after the 1992 elections, rising from one to five[2] (from 5.3 percent representation to 21.7 percent, the highest level of any state with more than five congressional seats). Women continue to represent all major racial/ethnic groups in the state as well as both parties.

The story of the emergence and advancement of women in Florida is fascinating and offers insights into the variety of conditions under which women advanced to Congress. As indicated in table 5.1, women ran successfully and in force in 1992. Ten women sought nine major party nominations in eight of ten open congressional districts.

Female success is readily apparent in 1992, especially when compared with the success of men. Six of ten women (60 percent) seeking nominations finished first in the initial primary, compared with fourteen of thirty-eight men (36.8 percent); of those women, three were involved in runoff elections, and two were victorious. Of the five women nominated in open seats, all but Republican Tillie Fowler faced primary opposition. Four of five women nominated in open seats were victorious, compared with just six of fifteen men holding major party nominations.

Female representation in Florida increased entirely as a result of the performance by women in open seat elections, although the creation of open seats alone was not sufficient to guarantee increased female representation. Without exception, the women elected to Congress from open seats in Florida possessed exceptional political and fund-raising experience.

Table 5.1   Women in Florida Open Seat Elections, 1992

	Men	*Women*
1st Place Finishes	14	6
Nominations	15	5
General Election Wins	6	4
Legislative/Council Experience	15	6
N	38	10

Women seeking open seat nominations more often had prior elective experience than men. Of the ten women candidates, six (60 percent) had held either local or state legislative office before seeking congressional office. Only fifteen of thirty-eight men (39.5 percent) running in those districts had comparable experience. Of the six women with office-holding experience in open seat races, five led the initial primary, and the four who won nominations were elected to Congress; only six of fifteen men with comparable experience led their initial primary, and four of those were subsequently elected to Congress.

Typical of the elections of new women in 1992 was the story of Karen Thurman, elected from Florida's Fifth Congressional District. Thurman's election to the House followed a political career that began as a middle school math teacher in Dunnellon, Florida, where she urged students to get involved in a political issue of importance to them. She was subsequently elected to the Dunnellon Council and then mayor. After holding local office for eight years, Thurman moved on to the state senate. Elected in 1982 with 54 percent of the vote, Thurman quickly established herself as a strong "hyperactive" legislator (Barone and Ujifusa 1993), offering an average of sixty bills per session covering topics from education to the environment to agriculture.

No doubt Thurman's advancement was expedited by the scrambling of the Florida maps in 1992. As chair of the state senate subcommittee on congressional reapportionment, she was positioned to affect the political map. However, the final disposition of the Florida map was decided by a federal court and drawn by a Tulane University law professor. This map had to meet minority-access requirements under the Voting Rights Act of 1965. Thurman's decade-long political history and her familiarity with the constituency strengthened her candidacy for U.S. Congress in 1992. Although Barone and Ujifusa (1993) characterized the seat as marginal, Thurman capitalized on her experience to raise two and half times as much money as the former prosecutor nominated by the GOP and won a 6 percentage point victory.

The creation of minority–majority districts in the Jacksonville and Miami areas contributed to the success of three women in 1992, Democrats Corrine Brown and Carrie Meek and Republican Tillie Fowler. Brown advanced to Congress after a decade in the state house from a district that wended its way from Orlando north to Jacksonville then back south to the college town of Gainesville. This district was carefully crafted to achieve a 55 percent black majority by uniting heavily black neighborhoods while avoiding concentrations of whites, with about half the population being from Jacksonville, Brown's home. Another new majority-black district, but this one in Miami, promoted Meek from the state senate. Like Brown, Meek bested a black male state legislator on the way to winning the Democratic nomination. Fowler, the other woman assisted by the racial gerrymanders found in several southern states, won a Jacksonville-based northeast Florida district rendered only 6 percent black as a result of the creation of Brown's neighboring district. Fowler's predecessor, Charles Bennett (D), had represented a united Jacksonville in a district more than one-fourth black at the time of the 1990 census. Fowler would have been hard pressed to assemble 57 percent of the vote had she run in the old Bennett district, which the concentration of blacks made much more hospitable to a Democrat.

The female-friendly conditions evidenced in 1992 in Florida were not unprecedented or unique. Instead, they represent the broad emergence of conditions that preceded female congressional advancement throughout the 1980s and into the 1990s. In Georgia and Texas, woman state legislators in were active in drawing congressional districts and as a result, won open U.S. House seats in 1992, much like Florida's Meek, Brown, and Thurman did. At the state legislative level, Anita Pritchard (1992b) argued that the disruption of elite and structural barriers through redistricting prompted the growth of female representation there. Although evidence from North and South Carolina did not support this contention (see Bullock and Gaddie 1993), the disruption resulting from redistricting advanced a generation of political women in Florida.

Broadening the examination of Florida's 1992 female congressional nominees to include challengers and incumbents shows that the re-mapping in 1982 and 1992 coincided with the attempted and actualized political advancement of several female politicians. Of the ten women holding major-party nominations in 1992, one was an in-cumbent U.S. representative, four were state legislators, and another female state legislator lost a runoff to a black man. If the six women candidates with state legislative experience are considered, including the female legislator who led her initial primary and Congresswoman Ros-Lehtinen, the influence of the previous redistricting is apparent. As indicated in table

5.2, four of these six women initiated their legislative careers in 1982 or advanced to the state senate from the state house in 1982, and Lois Frankel succeeded to the Florida house seat of a woman who advanced to the state senate in 1986. The creation of open seats from events that suddenly disrupted the political balance in the constituencies (U.S. Representative Claude Pepper's death and the 1992 redistricting) subsequently created opportunities for four of these women to advance to the U.S. House.

EARLY FEMALE SUCCESS: CONNECTICUT, 1982

The conditions of female advancement in 1992 were not new to congressional elections or confined to that year. A review of data on open seats from the 1980s shows that female success often occurred under conditions similar to those in Florida in 1992. An excellent example of the success of women in open seats comes from Connecticut in 1982. That year's race for the open Sixth District illustrates how the Republicans' ability to recruit and fund a candidate paid off in the capture of a previously safe Democratic seat; however, it also represents the success of a progressively ambitious woman who saw her opportunity and took it. The nomination and election of Republican Nancy L. Johnson from a Democratic district in a Democratic year is evidence that women need not rely on broad national tides for their electoral success.

The 1982 election was not supposed to be a banner year for Republican congressional prospects because the president's party usually loses seats at the midterm election. The elections of 1982 turned out better than anticipated for the GOP, and one reason was the combination of strong recruiting and adequate financing of challengers and open seat candidates. The Sixth District is one of the more politically and geographically diverse congressional

Table 5.2   Women Congressional Nominees in Florida with State Legislative Experience

| | | State Legislative Experience | |
District/Candidate	Status	House	Senate
3rd Corrine Brown (D)	Open	1982–1992	N/A
5th Karen Thurman (D)	Open	N/A	1982–1992
17th Carrie Meek (D)	Open	1978–1982	1982–1992
18th Ileana Ros-Lehtinen (R)	Incumbent	1982–1986	1986–1989
22nd Gwen Margolis (D)	Challenger[a]	1974–1980	1980–1992
23rd Lois Frankel (D)	Open[b]	1986–1992	N/A

[a]Lost general election challenge.
[b]Lost primary runoff after leading primary field.

districts in the Northeast. Alan Ehrenhalt (1983) observed that the ideo-logically distant William F. Buckley and Ralph Nader both hail from there, and it was carried in 1980 by Democrat Chris Dodd for the U.S. Senate and Republican Ronald Reagan for president. The principal city, New Britain (population 73,000 in 1980), is the home of the famous Stanley Tool Works.

The incumbent in the Sixth District, Democrat Toby Moffett, was tremendously popular in his constituency. Rather than seek reelection, Moffett opted to challenge incumbent Republican Senator Lowell Weicker (R) in 1982, and two attractive, experienced challengers emerged to vie for Moffett's seat. The campaign conducted by these formidable candidates indicates the importance of money in determining electoral outcomes.

The Republican nomination was contested by three candidates. The front-runner, state senator Nancy L. Johnson, had won three consecutive elections in the largest metropolitan area in the district. Johnson's attrac-tiveness as a candidate came from her appeal to blue-collar Democrats. In 1977, she became the first Republican elected to the state senate from New Britain since World War II. Her combative spirit is evident to even casual observers. When asked about her eager entry into the race for the Sixth, she responded, "When women have the opportunity to move up, they must" (Ehrenhalt 1983, 269). Her record on anticrime and education issues helped attract Reagan Democrats and her impressive record in con-stituency service bolstered her appeal. The GOP primary was of little con-cern, as Johnson won more than 70 percent of the vote against conserva-tive businessman Nicholas Schaus, who had opposed Moffett in 1980.

Democrats nominated William E. Curry, Jr., a young state senator who represented Farmington, a traditionally Republican area. Curry's cam-paign sought to maintain the liberal coalition that had propelled Moffett to four victories, and toward that end he built a campaign organization around youthful volunteers and young, liberal professionals. Curry pitched himself as a consumer advocate and sought to reinforce this image at a fund-raiser at which Winsted, Connecticut, resident Ralph Nader appeared and extended an endorsement.

In the general election campaign, Curry attempted to turn the strengths of Johnson's primary campaign against her. Despite expecting an easy nomination, Johnson had positioned herself to the right of Schaus and went to great lengths to remind primary voters that she directed Reagan's 1980 presidential primary campaign in Connecticut. In the general elec-tion, Curry attempted to turn those words on Johnson by tying her to the 1982 recession. Debates between the candidates, however, showed John-son to be the more effective speaker, whereas Curry "showed the not-very-helpful habit of drifting into political theory" (CQ 1982, 2503).

The effectiveness of the campaigns hinged on the ability of the candidates to communicate their messages to voters. Johnson raised almost twice as much money as Curry; this proved essential in purchasing media in expensive western Connecticut, which is effectively part of the New York media market. To offset his financial disadvantage, Curry concentrated on developing a grassroots organization to contact Moffett voters in metropolitan New Britain. His efforts paid off with a three-thousand-vote plurality in the city. Johnson countered by carrying the rest of the district by more than ten thousand votes.

Chapter 2 shows that open seat outcomes are tied to the prior political experience and financial support of the candidates. In this case from Connecticut, the success of a woman nominated by the "out" party was seemingly predicated on these factors. (Recall that candidates who hold both the spending and experience advantages win 80 to 90 percent of the time.) Is Nancy Johnson's case unique or does the outcome of female candidacies fit the conventional findings about open seats?

BACKGROUND ON WOMEN IN OPEN SEATS

The critical factor in electing women to Congress is getting them to run. Although open seats represent the best opportunity for the electoral advance of women, winning nominations to the seats is, of course, a prerequisite. The problems faced by the parties in fielding experienced candidates are reflected in the literature on candidate recruitment (Fowler and McClure 1989). The dominant position held by incumbents, even when confronted by experienced challengers, prompts most risk-averse politicians to wait for open seats (Jacobson and Kernell 1983). As chapters 3 and 4 demonstrated, experience is important to candidate electoral success. For the period under study, Democrats have been advantaged in recruiting experienced candidates for open seats, in part as a result of the activist government role articulated by the party.

The 230 open seats drew 1,502 candidates, of whom 191 (12.7 percent) were women. The evidence of female candidacies is skewed, with 40 percent of the 191 women running in 1992. Over the course of the six elections (1982, 1984, 1986, 1988, 1990, and 1992), women won sixty-one nominations, including four districts in which they carried both parties' banners.

Although relatively few women have sought congressional nominations, those who did were remarkably successful. Women won only 13 percent of the open seat primaries, but they did not contest 68.5 percent of all such primaries, so they won 42.7 percent of the nominations they sought. Female success is greatest in the redistricting years (1982 and 1992) as illustrated in table 5.3, with women winning 45.8 percent of their bids in 1982 and 56.9 percent in 1992. In non-redistricting years, women only won 27.9 percent of nominations contested. Women sought more Democratic than Republican nominations (eighty-nine versus fifty-four) but demonstrated comparable success across parties, winning 43.8 percent of Democratic nominations they contested and 40.7 percent of Republican nominations contested. Although men won more nominations than women, the rate of nomination among all candidates was slightly higher among women than men: 31.9 percent of female primary candidates were nominated, compared with 30.4 percent of male primary candidates. Most female electoral successes are recent, with thirty-three of the sixty-one major party nominations coming in 1992. In 1992, 44 percent of all women candidates secured nominations, compared with just 27.3 percent of men who sought open seats.

Women who won nominations usually won the elections, prevailing in thirty-two of the fifty-seven open districts (56.1 percent) in which a man held the opposing party nomination; in another four districts, women took both nominations. Female candidates prevailed in twenty-one of thirty-one female–male contests (67.7 percent in 1992), which constituted 65.6 percent of all female open seat victories since 1982. The high incidence of female candidates, nominations, and elections in 1992 underscores the appropriateness of dubbing 1992 "Year of the Woman."

Table 5.3   **The Emergence and Success of Women Seeking Open Seat Congressional Nominations**

Year	Party	Primaries[a]	Female Candidates	% Females Running	Female Nominees	% Females Nominated[b]
1982	Democrat	51	11	11.5	5	45.5
	Republican	52	13	25.0	6	46.2
1984	Democrat	23	4	17.4	1	25.0
	Republican	23	8	34.8	1	12.5
1986	Democrat	35	13	37.1	1	7.7
	Republican	34	8	23.5	4	50.0
1988	Democrat	22	10	45.5	3	30.0
	Republican	22	3	13.6	0	—
1990	Democrat	27	10	37.0	6	60.0
	Republican	27	5	18.5	1	20.0
1992	Democrat	70	41	58.6	23	56.1
	Republican	68	17	25.0	10	58.8

[a]Primaries are not held in all states; therefore, district column totals are not equal for the parties and do not equal the total number of open seat general elections.

[b]Number of females nominated as a percent of districts contested by female candidates.

EXPERIENCE

Among female open seat candidates, 45.4 percent had prior electoral office experience, compared with just 38.2 percent of male candidates, with women more likely to have held local office. Experience as a lobbyist, political appointee, or legislative staffer was equally prevalent among the men and women vying for open seats. The Krasno-Green index of politically relevant experience reveals minimal gender differences.

Although most congressional candidates lacked office-holding experience, the one in three who secured nominations typically had prior electoral success, a background feature shared by almost 60 percent of men and 54 percent of women in our study. These modest gender differences are largely a product of men dominating the ranks of statewide officials—the group most advantaged in the primaries and the only group to win more nominations than it loses.

Table 5.4 indicates that winners in congressional elections tend to be more experienced regardless of gender. Successful female candidates had greater political experience, on average, than their opponents, and there was less variation in the levels of experience. The average winning Democratic woman's experience (4.58 on the Krasno-Green index) was twice the average of her opponents (2.29), whereas losing Democratic women had experience levels (3.38) a full point lower, on average, than their successful sisters. The mean experience of opponents who defeated Democratic women was almost identical to the 4.58 mean for successful Democratic women. Results are similar for successful Republican women who had greater average experience than their opponents, whereas experience levels for losing Republican women were 60 percent of their opponents. Successful Democratic women averaged more experience than successful Republican women and generally faced less-experienced opponents.

Table 5.4   Mean Political Experience Index of Candidates by Gender and Electoral Success

	Candidate	Opponent	N
Contests with Women			
Winning Democrat	4.58 (1.10)[a]	2.29 (2.10)	24
Losing Democrat	3.38 (1.71)	4.56 (1.31)	16
Winning Republican	4.25 (1.83)	3.25 (1.83)	8
Losing Republican	2.54 (1.61)	4.31 (.95)	13
Contests with Men Only			
Winning Democrat	4.39 (1.55)	2.68 (2.00)	87
Winning Republican	3.78 (1.58)	2.94 (1.76)	86

Note: Candidate experience is measured on the Krasno-Green (1988) index.
[a]Standard deviations in parentheses.

Experience patterns in all-male contests are similar to those in female–male elections. Successful Republican men possessed greater political experience than their Democratic opponents but less than successful women. The magnitude of winning GOP men's experience advantage over opponents is slightly less than the 1.0 experience advantage enjoyed by winning Republican women, although the average experience of Republican males' opponents is less than that faced by Republican women. In contrast, Democratic men who won election had mean levels of experience just slightly below the 4.58 of their winning female colleagues and faced slightly more experienced foes than did female Democratic winners. The magnitude of the Democratic male experience advantage over opponents is only three-quarters that enjoyed by successful Democratic women, but it is still the third-largest average advantage enjoyed by any cohort of candidates. The consistency in experience across gender of successful candidates indicates that it does not take "super-woman" to win a seat in Congress.

GENDER AND MONEY

In contrast with the argument that women must rely on exogenous, non-traditional sources of funding when seeking political office (Volgy et al. 1986), research finds women no less able to attract money than men. To a degree, fund-raising for women has been facilitated by the efforts of EMILY's List (Democratic) and WISH (Republican), which have directed money to viable female contenders in recent elections. Wilhite and Theilmann (1986), who analyze all congressional elections in 1980 and 1982, find no evidence of a female disadvantage in attracting votes or PAC support. Uhlaner and Schlozman (1986) note smaller female war chests in the 1980 elections but attribute these discrepancies not to gender but to other political characteristics, such as incumbency. They conclude that "any reluctance to encourage women to run for Congress on the grounds of inability to raise funds has no basis in fact" (46). Open seats were not explicitly analyzed in either study because of insufficient cases.

As the figures in table 5.5 indicate, in 1992 and in the preceding decade, prevailing female candidates generally outspent their opponents. The seven Democratic women who won in the 1980s outspent their opponents by almost 1.7 to 1; in 1992, the seventeen successful Democratic women outspent their opponents by almost 1.9 to 1—an advantage of more than $300,000 per campaign on average. Successful Republican women generally outspent opponents in 1992, although the magnitude of spending advantage is less than among successful Democrats.

In the 1980s, unsuccessful women of both parties were usually outspent

Table 5.5 Mean Expenditures of Open Seat Candidates by Gender and Electoral Success

	1992[a]				1982–1990			
	N	Candidate	Opponent	Ratio of Winner to Loser	N	Candidate	Opponent	Ratio of Winner to Loser
Contests with Women								
Winning Democrat	17	678,360 (502,385)[b]	360,527 (321,385)	1.9	7	747,602 (257,234)	452,491 (379,314)	1.7
Losing Democrat	6	485,737 (402,509)	495,788 (176,617)	1.0	10	326,109 (253,425)	665,902 (297,457)	2.0
Winning Republican	4	598,712 (91,458)	523,843 (255,619)	1.1	4	955,447 (314,049)	1,184,745 (919,687)	.8
Losing Republican	7	417,937 (353,025)	857,980 (721,369)	2.1	6	593,344 (679,877)	946,325 (375,909)	1.6
Contests with Men								
Winning Democrat	22	456,589 (259,023)	206,607 (192,725)	2.2	65	579,250 (364,470)	393,439 (283,937)	1.5
Winning Republican	20	444,182 (239,663)	477,669 (286,370)	.9	66	686,369 (286,985)	378,637 (317,426)	1.8

[a]1994 dollars.
[b]Numbers in parentheses are standard deviations.

by their opponents; Republican women who lost were outspent by their opponents by 1.6:1, and Democratic women averaged spending only half as much as their opponents. In 1992, unsuccessful female candidates of both parties had lower spending averages than their opponents, although the differences were only $10,000 in races lost by Democratic women. In the 1980s, four Republicans won despite spending only 80 percent as much as their opponent.

In all-male contests, spending patterns were similar to those observed in contests involving women. In the 1980s, successful Democrats averaged spending 150 percent as much as their opponents, a margin that swells to 220 percent for 1992. During the 1980s, successful Republicans spent 1.8 times as much as the Democrats they beat. As with successful GOP women in 1992, spending by winning Republican men approximated the expenditures of their opponents. Successful Republican women narrowly outspent their opponents, whereas GOP men won despite being slightly outspent.

GENDER AND OPEN SEATS ELECTIONS

The preceding analyses examined variations in financial quality and political experience among candidates by gender and party. Tables 5.4 and 5.5 suggest that experience and campaign funding are related to candidate success regardless of gender. We now examine whether these relationships persist when combined with other variables in multivariate formulations. Of particular interest is whether gender exhibits an explicit impact on open seat election outcomes after controlling for other influences that have proven to be important in open seat elections.

The multivariate analysis is similar to that presented in chapter 2. To assess the independent variable of interest, candidate gender, dichotomous variables are included in the equation to indicate whether the Democratic or Republican candidate is female. The dependent variable is the percent of the two-party vote for the Republican candidate with uncontested seats excluded from the analysis. Ordinary least squares regression is used to estimate the relationship between the dependent and independent variables.

The results of the multivariate analysis appears in table 5.6. As the adjusted-R^2 indicates, the equation explains two-thirds of the variance in the Republican vote share.[3] Individual candidate attributes exhibited strong, statistically significant influences on open seat congressional elections and are virtually unchanged from the results presented in chapter 2. The gender coefficients are negative for GOP women but positive for Democratic women, although neither is statistically significant, which means that being a woman confers neither a benefit nor a cost.[4]

Table 5.6   OLS Estimates of Gender Impact on Open Seat Elections

Variable	b	t
Constant	43.09	
Female Democratic Candidate	.79	.59
Female Republican Candidate	−.55	−.31
Democratic Candidate Experience	−1.76	−5.87*
Republican Candidate Experience	1.92	6.96*
Democratic Spending (in $100K)	−.84	−5.89*
Republican Spending (in $100K)	1.42	7.81*
Year 1984	−27.88	−5.09*
Year 1988	−27.71	−5.60*
Year 1992	−19.73	−5.10*
Presidential Coattails	.53	6.32*
Temporal Counter	.23	.52
R^2	.69	
Adjusted-R^2	.67	
N	230	

Note: Dependent variable is the Republican candidate's percentage of the two-party vote.
*$p < .05$, one-tailed test.

The analysis in table 5.6 indicates no relationship between gender and open seat election results. To ascertain more explicitly whether the conditions that lead to female and male electoral success are the same, we specified an equation to examine the performance of female candidates against male opponents. Slightly less than a quarter of the cases examined (57 of 230) involved female candidates. Four cases were female-versus-female contests, leaving fifty-three instances of intergender competition. The equation specified to explain female candidate performance included seven variables: female candidate experience, male candidate experience, female candidate spending, male candidate spending, female candidate party, the Year of the Woman (1992), and a temporal counter.[5] Specifying this equation allowed us to test explicitly and simultaneously the effects of experience, spending, and episodic effects on gender electoral success.[6] The results of the regression analysis appear in table 5.7. The model explains 62 percent of the variance in the female candidate's vote share. The results of this analysis confirm our initial observations based on table 5.6: political experience and adequate funding are the twin engines that drive female electoral success. In similar fashion, experienced, better-funded men have stronger showing against women. Neither partisan nor episodic Year of the Woman effects were observed, although a significant temporal growth in female vote share is apparent.

Table 5.7   OLS Estimates of "Year of the Woman" Impact on Female
Performance in Open Seat Elections

Variable	b	t
Constant	43.20	
Female Candidate Experience	3.04	3.83*
Male Candidate Experience	−2.46	−3.54*
Female Spending (in $100K)	.66	1.75*
Male Spending (in $100K)	−.88	−2.47*
Female's Party	2.17	.75
Year of the Woman	−5.22	−1.04
Temporal Counter	1.83	1.79*
R^2	.67	
Adjusted-R^2	.62	
N	53	

Note: Dependent variable is the female candidate's percentage of the two-party vote. Four districts where women opposed each other are excluded.
*p < .05, one-tailed test.

CONCLUSION

The presence of large numbers of open seats coincides with greater numbers of female candidates and nominees in 1992. Redistricting in 1982 had some, albeit a less dramatic, impact on female candidacies and nominations. Thus the unsettling effects of decennial redistricting operating alone did not promote the political prospects of women.

Women in 1992, particularly those running as Democrats, could exploit the opportunities offered by large numbers of open seats because they were politically and financially competitive. During the previous decade, successful women generally had experience and funding profiles similar to their successful male counterparts and were just as skillful in obtaining nominations. The ranks of congresswomen swelled because women ran for an unprecedented number of open seats (fifty-eight in primaries and thirty-two in general elections) in 1992 (cf., Bledsoe and Herring 1990).

The case of expanded female representation in Florida indicates that down-ticket development of experienced candidates promotes up-ticket success. Florida also illustrates the importance of institutional changes and the disruption of incumbency to female advancement. Florida's three new congresswomen previously ascended the office-holding ladder as a direct result of redistricting in 1982 and 1992. All of the women who were major party nominees and had legislative experience initially entered the state house or state senate through open seats. The creation of open congressional seats a decade later allowed four to win nominations and three to advance to the next level.

Results from 1994 suggest that several factors must coincide for women to enjoy the kinds of gains registered two years earlier. In 1994, women had net gains of one in each chamber as the House welcomed thirteen new women, but nine female incumbents lost and three others left voluntarily. Seventeen women won nominations for the fifty-two contested open seats (32.7 percent), a rate less than that at which women had won open seat nominations in 1992. The pattern for most of the previous decade recurred in 1994 as women disproportionately ran as Democrats. This gender gap in contestation for Congress parallels gender differences in voting in recent presidential elections. Burrell (1994) speculates that the tendency for women to run as Democrats may reflect several factors: the greater likelihood of winning as the nominee of the majority party, more Democratic than Republican female state legislators, more open seats in Democratic districts, or a culture less receptive to female candidates in the GOP. Whatever the reason in 1992, holding the Democratic nomination often helped; in 1994, women were disproportionately candidates for the disadvantaged party. Four of the six women seeking open seats as Republicans in 1994 won. In comparison, five of eleven female Democratic open seat candidates succeeded. Democratic women seeking open seats in 1994 nonetheless fared better than comparable males.

When the great success of women in 1992 is compared with the modest gains of 1982 and 1994, open seats appear to be necessary but by no means sufficient for increasing the ranks of congresswomen. With GOP women winning two-thirds of their contests in 1994—a rate less than that of Republican men competing for open seats—it seems likely that had more women run as Republicans in 1994, that year might have been a reprise of the Year of the Woman.

NOTES

1. Ros-Lehtinen was a trailblazer among Cuban American politicians. She was the first Cuban American female elected to the Florida house of representatives, the first Cuban American elected to the Florida senate, and the first Cuban American elected to the U.S. Congress. Ros-Lehtinen came to the House in an August 1989 special election following the death of Claude Pepper (D).

2. A Caucasian woman, Lois Frankel, ran a strong primary campaign in the majority-black Twenty-third Congressional District. She led the initial primary but lost a runoff to impeached federal district court judge Alcee Hastings, who is African American.

3. Examination of variance inflation factors revealed no problem with multi-collinearity.

4. A model that included terms that interacted gender and party with spending and experience was estimated but provided no additional insights beyond the more parsimonious model presented in table 5.6.

5. Experience variables, funding variables, and the temporal counter are coded in the same fashion as in the partisan model with female party = 1 if Democrat, and Year of the Woman = 1 if 1992.

6. Tests for multicollinearity were performed by examining the variance inflation factors of the independent variables; no problem is evident. A model also was specified that included presidential coattail effects; however, the results of that analysis were no better than those presented in table 5.7.

Chapter 6

Special Elections:
The Other Open Seats

A manifestation of open seats that is often forgotten is the special election, or by-election.[1] Although these elections rarely attract attention, even from the constituents of the vacated district, these seats represent a substantial source of new members of Congress. Occasionally, one of these unique elections will receive intense scrutiny by the media, political observers, or scholars as a source of national political trends. Results in those cases are treated as referenda on national issues or indications of future partisan tides. It is these treatments of special election results that often lead to comparisons with British by-elections.

This chapter examines the political dynamics of special elections in the United States. First, we review the admittedly sparse literature on American special elections and discuss the theoretic issues emphasized in both that research and research performed on British by-elections. Then, we present examples of U.S. special elections that illustrate the referendum and partisan trend interpretations that are often ascribed to these races. The chapter next turns to an examination of special elections since 1982 to draw conclusions about candidate emergence, financing, and outcomes based on a comparison with regularly scheduled open seat elections. We conclude by discussing our findings in light of existing research on by-elections and special elections.

THEORIES OF SPECIAL ELECTIONS

The little that has been written on American special elections is heavily flavored by studies of British by-elections. In Great Britain, by-elections are seen as bellwethers of the popularity of the incumbent government, and a literature has grown up around their interpretation (Mughan 1986). With a new parliament elected only every four or five years, British by-elections occur in far greater frequency than they do in the United States. As Butler and Kavanaugh (1981) point out, in closely divided parliaments, by-elections have cost governments their majorities, as happened to Britain's last Labour government. A poor electoral performance can erode public credibility and undermine party morale. Mughan (1986) says that in 300 by-elections from 1950 to 1983, the incumbent government's vote share in the district dropped in 86 percent of cases, with an average vote loss of almost 10 percentage points.

Mughan (1986) presented three models of incumbent government vote loss. The first theory focuses on voter turnout as the source of declining governmental support. The subjective interpretation of the turnout model by the media ascribes losses to disillusionment among the government's supporters who fail to turn out.

The second theory, tested elsewhere (see Norris 1990; Feigert and Norris 1990; Norris and Feigert 1989), sees by-elections as referenda. According to the referendum theory, the voters of the district are representative of the entire national electorate. Outcomes in a by-election are considered to reflect the general taste or distaste of the nation for the incumbent majority. Because the British electorate is relatively unmoved by local forces, the referendum hypothesis is a reasonable one (Stokes 1967; Mughan 1986; Feigert and Norris 1990), although others (Pollock 1941) reject this interpretation.

The third theory emphasizes the personal vote. According to this perspective, the vote for the incumbent party depends in part on the strength of the personal following and prestige of the member vacating the seat. Members of Parliament are able to build up a personal vote using constituency service and the visibility of incumbency, much like American legislators (Cain, Ferejohn, and Fiorina 1984). Accordingly, the departure of the incumbent should increase the likelihood of a change in party control of the seat. Mughan (1986) found no support for the personal vote theory in Great Britain.

Although Frank Feigert and Pippa Norris do not directly test the personal vote hypothesis, their conclusions regarding the role of party system and electoral structures rely on this argument. The differences between U.S. special elections and the by-elections of Great Britain, Australia, and Canada are reflected in the movement of support for the incumbent governing party in by-elections and the approval of the incumbent government in national polls. In Canada, Australia, and Great Britain, the patterns of by-election support and national government approval generally track together. In the United States, these two factors have been largely separated since 1948. Feigert and Norris (1990) conclude that this disjunction reflects the weak nature of the U.S. party system and the institutional independence of Congress from the president when ascribing electoral responsibility. Because the outcomes of special elections are likely to reflect local concerns, understanding them requires a localized perspective.

Sigelman (1981) and Studlar and Sigelman (1987) produced the only other research on special elections in the United States. In his initial study, Sigelman examined special elections from 1954 to 1978 to develop what he termed "descriptive generalizations" about these elections. Sigelman found ninety-seven "true" special elections—elections not held concurrent with general elections in November in even-numbered years. This examination produced six generalizations:

1. Turnout tends to be lower consistently in special elections than in general elections in the same districts, even in off-year general elections. Turnout is also more variable across districts than in general elections.
2. Special election victors tend to win by comfortable margins, but special elections are more closely contested than the preceding general election.
3. House seats remain in control of the party that already holds them. When party change does occur, it is usually at the cost of the incumbent president's party.
4. The party that wins a special election almost always retains the seat in the next general election.
5. Seat changes occur much more rapidly in special elections.
6. Party control changes more rapidly in open seat general elections than in special elections. Midterm open seat elections and special elections change at similar rates.

In concluding his generalizations, Sigelman noted that although special elections did not produce dramatic partisan change, they did result in greater change than general elections, primarily because they were open seats. The partisan shifts away from the incumbent presidential party indicate a referendum-like effect. Studler and Sigelman (1987) extended this work by comparing U.S. and British special elections. They found that special elections were manifestations of the normal partisan forces found at work in general elections. A greater impact by third-party intervention occurred in British than U.S. cases, although such interventions were significant in the United States. Support for the incumbent government candidate decreased when the special election was further removed from the last general election, in keeping with the referendum theory noted earlier.

PERSPECTIVES ON U.S. SPECIAL ELECTIONS

Special congressional elections receive relatively little attention from the media or the voters in most districts unless there are unique conditions or outcomes; for example, a partisan change in a supposedly safe district, as happened when two border-South Democratic districts went Republican in early 1994, or the emergence of a celebrity candidate, such as Jesse Jackson, Jr.'s, candidacy for the Illinois seat vacated by Mel Reynolds in 1995. The election may receive attention when interesting hot-button issues take center stage, as when Harris Wofford (D) rode the health care issue to victory in the 1991 election in Pennsylvania to fill the Senate vacancy caused by the death of John Heinz (R). A year later, presidential candidate Bill Clinton followed Wofford's lead of promising affordable medical care. Pundits, like Clinton's handlers, sometimes see in special elections the foreshadowing of the electorate's emerging policy concerns.

We offer two cases to illustrate interpretations of special elections. The first, more historical case illustrates how the injection of national political issues into a special election creates the conditions of a referendum. The other case shows how an unexpected outcome is interpreted as a bellwether in congressional and presidential politics.

Referendum in Texas

A fine example of how a by-election was perceived as a barometer of national politics occurred in 1937 in Texas's Twelfth Congressional District. The incumbent, James P. Buchanan (D), died suddenly in the summer of 1937. Unlike the president bearing the same name, Buchanan left a widow, and one of the great traditions of special elections, especially in this era, was to allow a widow to succeed (preferably without opposition) to her husband's seat. Bullock and Heys (1972) observed that this form of succession was the traditional route for women to enter Congress, in part because they would serve as caretakers of the seat and because they usually retired when the term ended. Before Buchanan's widow could announce her candidacy for the hill-country seat, an upstart Texas politician had already thrown his hat into the ring, and seven other candidates quickly followed suit. Mrs. Buchanan decided to forego the special election, clearing the way for the inauguration of one of the great American electoral careers: Lyndon B. Johnson, the upstart politician and former congressional staffer, was headed back to Washington (Caro 1982; Kearns 1976).

At the time of Buchanan's death, Johnson was the director of the state's National Youth Administration. In that capacity, he expanded the connections he created in college at San Marcos and during his years as the top staffer to south Texas Congressman Richard Kleberg. In many respects, Johnson represented the prototype of the modern career politician described by Alan Ehrenhalt in *The United States of Ambition:* young; ambitious; and dedicated to creating public policy, wielding policy levers, and accumulating political influence. Johnson worked systematically to develop his constituency service techniques and also to develop his institutional skills in the Little Congress.[2] All these efforts were made with an eye toward the opportunity to move onto the political stage as a legislator.

In his conversations with Doris Kearns, LBJ related his decision to jump into the race for the Twelfth. The decision was made immediately after he saw the news of Buchanan's death in a newspaper left on a park bench in Houston:

> I kept thinking that this was my district and my chance. The day seemed endless. [Johnson's visitor][3] never stopped talking. And I had to pretend total interest in everything we were seeing and doing. There were times when I thought I'd explode from all the excitement bottled up inside. . . . As soon as I got home, I talked with Bird [Lady Bird Johnson] and then I called Senator Wirtz. (Kearns 1976, 86)

After conversing with Mrs. Johnson and his mentor, LBJ secured a $10,000 loan from his father-in-law to support the campaign and announced his candidacy the week after the incumbent's funeral.

As the race in Texas's Twelfth District was heating up, the Roosevelt scheme to pack the Supreme Court became a significant issue. The continuation of Roosevelt's initiatives under the second New Deal hinged in part on a friendly Court, which in turn required an endorsement from the electorate. Johnson's closest advisors encouraged him to seize on the court-packing scheme and endorse it in an effort to co-opt Roosevelt's popularity. In taking the court-packing scheme as an issue, Johnson separated himself from his seven opponents (who universally supported Roosevelt) and characterized his opponents as enemies of the president for not endorsing the plan. Four of LBJ's opponents tried belatedly to endorse the plan, but their me-tooism was too late to prevent a Johnson victory.

FDR in turn seized on the results from Texas as an affirmation of his policies by the electorate. The press touted the victory as an endorsement of the second New Deal and the Roosevelt presidency. Although the court-packing scheme never came to fruition, Johnson forged a link with Roosevelt that would influence the rest of his career and underscored the president's continuing popularity. Still it is not the success or failure of the policy itself that is important; it is the fact that local politicians and national political leaders both interpreted the results of the Texas election as a referendum in support of the relevant policy.[4]

Bellwether in Kentucky

Occasionally, special congressional elections are interpreted by the press and politicians as indicators of coming broad national electoral trends. Commentators interpreted special election results for the House and Senate during the first two years of the Clinton administration as indicative of the continued erosion of support for the often-embattled incumbent and, subsequently, as harbingers of the November 1994 Republican revolution. The best known of these cases is the special Texas U.S. Senate election in early 1993, where appointed Senator Bob Krueger was beaten handily in a special runoff by a GOP challenger, State Treasurer Kay Bailey Hutchison. In May 1994, the Republican party continued its run when it scored an upset in Kentucky's Second District, left vacant by the death of twenty-one-term incumbent and Appropriations Committee Chair, William Natcher (D).

Natcher was initially elected in a special election in 1953 and never missed a roll-call vote until he was hospitalized in the month preceding his death. Even at age eighty-three, Natcher continued to perform his own research and to document all of his activities in a journal. His low-cost campaigns were paid for out of pocket and usually conducted on weekends by visiting the courthouse towns. Despite challenges both within the party and from the GOP, Natcher continued to roll up impressive victory margins.

After his death, a special election was called to coincide with the May 17th congressional primaries. Kentucky parties choose nominees in caucuses. Democrats selected one of the best-known and influential members of the state legislature, Senator Joe Prather. The GOP choice of fundamentalist minister Tom Lewis was viewed by many as conceding the seat to the Democrats.

Although largely unnoticed, the Second District was changing. For most of Natcher's tenure, the district centered on the traditionally Democratic towns of Owensboro and Bowling Green. With the post-1990 census reapportionment, Kentucky lost a district, and the Second was reshaped to include the Republican-leaning suburbs in southern Jefferson County (Louisville) that were previously in Jim Bunning's (R) Fourth District. Natcher held the district with strong pluralities outside of Louisville and through the application of his well-worn homestyle but was pressed in Jefferson County. The changed district boundaries meant that the Second District encroached into three television markets. For a candidate who lacked the name recognition enjoyed by the twenty-one-term incumbent, a change in campaign style would be necessary.

This lesson apparently was lost on the Democratic nominee. Prather campaigned for Congress much as he had for the state legislature, using an approach similar to that of the late incumbent, visiting the courthouse towns and not spending money on consultants or media. Although charm and sentiment make for good literature, they do not necessarily make for good politics. Tom Lewis, the Republican nominee, advertised heavily on Louisville television (which was disseminated into much of the district, courtesy of cable television) and tested the first application of the now-famous "morphing" technology.[5] This technique linked Democrat Prather to President Clinton and the policies of the national Democratic party, even as Prather was running away from both the party and the president. Lewis won decisively with 55 percent of the vote.

Democratic party professionals pinned the blame for the loss of the Second on the candidate, citing his refusal to conduct a modern campaign. Republicans, however, characterized this victory in a district never represented by the GOP as an indication of good things to come. The national media bought the Republican interpretation and characterized the victory in Natcher's district as an indication of trouble on the horizon for the Democrats and Bill Clinton.

Given the results of the 1994 election, the outcome in Kentucky's Second does seem prophetic. Political scientist and Kentucky politics expert Penny Miller told us that the role of the emerging GOP in organizing support for Lewis may have helped create the bellwether result. Miller noted that Republican U.S. Senator Mitch McConnell had worked feverishly throughout his first two terms to build an organization in rural western Kentucky. McConnell apparently activated his organization in support of Lewis's candidacy so that the GOP victory was facilitated by long-term political engineering. Whatever the explanation, in a year in which Democratic incumbents and professional politicians were often punished at the polls, an amateur minister defeated a major state legislative power broker. The modern campaign technology applied in the contest was used with great effect in several subsequent campaigns. Moreover, the spin placed on the outcome of the Second District campaign by Republicans was validated by exit-polling on election day, which indicated extensive anger and frustration with professional politicians in general and President Clinton in particular.[6]

The Lewis victory in Kentucky was not the only by-election that pointed to problems for the Democrats. Some see the first hint of difficulty coming just three weeks after the Clinton election, when Georgia voters narrowly ousted one-term Democratic Senator Wyche Fowler in a runoff election necessitated by the state's requirement that general election winners poll a majority. The victory of Senator Kay Bailey Hutchison in the Texas special election in the spring of 1993 was followed up by a razor-thin margin in Wisconsin for Peter Barca, the Democrat seeking to hold the seat vacated by Les Aspin when he was named secretary of defense in the new administration. In 1994, Republicans took the special election to fill the Sixth District of Oklahoma in a situation much like the Kentucky case chronicled above. The nineteen-year Democratic incumbent vacated a personally safe seat, which was won by Frank Lucas, the Republican favorite of the Christian Coalition (Bednar and Hertzke 1995).

In the next section, we examine all special elections for indications of partisan switches or other indicators of referenda in the outcomes; alternatively, we expect that these races are driven by the localized dynamics and partisan tendencies that Sigelman (1981) observed in special open seat races from 1956 to 1980.

SPECIAL ELECTIONS SINCE 1982

Of particular interest when examining U.S. special elections is what is missing. The bulk of research on incumbent and open seat elections has emphasized a variety of variables to explain election outcomes. These variables—candidate experience, campaign finance, district demographics—remain untested in special elections. In the remainder of this chapter, we examine whether these factors—previously shown to be so important in open seat elections—also influenced the results of special elections. This is critical for an understanding of the role of a personal vote in special elections. Because these elections occur in effective isolation, the results should depend more heavily on the political dynamic of the constituency and on the political assets that the respective candidates bring to bear, that is, political experience or fund-raising ability.

In the following section, we examine special elections since 1982, a period coterminous with the data used throughout this volume. Based on an examination of these data, we can discuss special elections as a special type of open seat election. In particular, we are concerned with six questions about special elections: (1) why they occur, (2) what rules are used to fill vacancies and how these varying systems affect the candidate emergence and partisan change, (3) what sort of candidates emerge in special elections, (4) who wins, (5) why these candidates prevail, and (6) how these results differ from or parallel the results of normal open seat elections.

The Data

From 1982 to 1994, fifty-eight House vacancies occurred between elections. Of those, forty-eight were resolved in special elections; ten others were filled concurrent with the general election and were included in the open seats data base analyzed in chapters 2 to 5.

We collected data on special elections from a variety of sources. Vacancies were initially identified in *Congressional Quarterly Weekly Report*. Special elections that coincided with general elections for the same seat were discarded; in all but one case, the same candidate won both elections.[7] Primary and general election data and candidate backgrounds were gathered from various issues of *Congressional Quarterly Weekly Report* and the *Almanac of American Politics.* Campaign finance data were obtained from the Federal Election Commission and the *Almanac of American Politics.*

When Vacancies Occur

Table 6.1 reports the reasons for open seat vacancies in special elections. The most common cause of vacancy was the death of an incumbent, with 45.8 percent of the forty-eight special elections following the demise of an incumbent. Another 43.8 percent occurred because the incumbent resigned for noncontroversial personal or political reasons, usually related to health, or to assume other political or private duties, such as the decisions by Norman Mineta (D-CA) to leave Congress to rejoin the private sector and Kweisi Mfume (D-MD) to take over the leadership of the NAACP. A few incumbents vacated their seats because of scandalous or unbecoming behavior, such as the 1995 vacancy caused by the resignation of Mel Reynolds (D-IL) because of a felony sexual assault conviction. Among the most prominent cases of incumbent vacancy in recent years are the almost simultaneous resignations of House Speaker Jim Wright (D-TX) and Majority Leader Tony Coelho (D-CA) in the spring of 1989 because of unrelated scandals.[8]

Ten of the forty-eight open seats examined switched party control in the special elections. Of the four seats opened up by resignations of scandalized incumbents, one changed parties. Only three of twenty-one seats created by other resignations led to partisan switches, whereas six of twenty-two cases in which incumbents died set up party switches. These differences were not statistically significant.

The Conduct of Special Elections

The literature on U.S. special elections assumes that they are conducted under the same rules and in the same manner as British elections. However, this is most definitely not the case. The timing and format of special elections vary with state election laws. In some states, the special election rules vary substantially from the rules in normal elections. Other states

Table 6.1 Reasons for Departures, 1982–1994

N	Death	Resigned	Resigned in Disgrace	Declared Vacant
48	22 (45.8)	21 (43.8)	4 (8.3)	1 (2.1)

Note: Figures in parentheses are percentages.

have altered their election rules in the wake of partisan change. In Georgia, for example, the governor can actually exercise discretion in deciding whether to hold partisan or nonpartisan special elections. In the 1980s and 1990s, California used a plurality rule for nomination and election in regular elections but used an open primary with runoff for special elections. In response to a Republican ascendancy in the late 1970s, Mississippi changed its special election law from an open primary with plurality winner to an open primary with runoff. Texas made a similar change in its special election law in the 1960s after the special election victory of John Tower to succeed Lyndon Johnson in March 1961.

Our research identified four principal formats for conducting special elections. The first in table 6.2 is the conventional format, in which parties hold primaries (and runoffs, if required by state law) to pick nominees and then hold a general election. Under this format, the voters will cast ballots in at least two elections and possibly three in runoff-primary states.[9] The campaign period is often compressed, with primaries and elections occurring within six weeks of each other. The second format is the party caucus format, in which district party organizations, either in executive session or through caucuses, choose party nominees. The nominees then immediately proceed to a general election. This format is often used in convention states in which party nominees are chosen through a convention rather than a primary, such as Colorado and Connecticut and in the mid-Atlantic states with strong party organizations (New York, Pennsylvania, New Jersey). The third format is the open primary, which provides for all candidates, regardless of party, to run in one heat. The candidate with the most votes wins election. Most recently this format has been used only in Hawaii, although Texas and Mississippi have used it in the past. The fourth format is more common than we expected: the open primary with runoff format. If no candidate wins a majority in the open primary, the top two finishers proceed to a runoff election two to four weeks later. This format is used in a variety of southern states and in California. In California, the runoff is structured more like the Washington state open primary: If no candidate receives a majority, then the top finishers of each party proceed to the general election. If the top two finishers in a California special primary are from the same party, the runoff is between the first-place finisher and the best performer from the other party. In California, the runner-up of the majority party can be excluded from the runoff even if he or she outpolls the most successful candidates of the minority. The primary leader prevailed in every California runoff we examined.

The electoral system used did not relate significantly to party switches in special elections. Although open primary systems produced proportionally fewer switches than special elections held using party caucus nomination systems and special general elections, these differences were not statistically significant.

Table 6.2 Special Election Formats Used, 1982–1994

Format	States Using This format	Differs from Normal Format	Cases Using This Format (N/%)
Conventional	Maryland	No	21 (36.2)
(Primary and Election)	Michigan	No	
	Ohio	No	
	Connecticut[a]	No	
	Georgia[b]	No	
	Illinois	No	
	New York[c]	No	
	Tennessee	No	
	Alabama	No	
	Virginia[a]	No	
	Arizona	No	
	Massachusetts	No	
	Wisconsin	No	
	Oklahoma	No	
Party Caucus	Indiana	Yes	12 (20.6)
	Ohio	Yes	
	Colorado[a]	No	
	New York[b]	Yes	
	Wyoming[a]	No	
	Pennsylvania	Yes	
	Virginia[a]	No	
	Michigan	Yes	
	Kentucky	Yes	
Open Primary	Hawaii	Yes	1 (1.7)
Open Primary with Runoff	California	Yes	14 (24.1)
	Georgia[b]	Yes	
	Texas	Yes	
	Louisiana	No	
	Mississippi	Yes	
Held Concurrent with General Election			10 (17.2)

[a]State law or party rules allow use of either convention or primary to choose nominees.

[b]Governor has discretion to choose open primary/runoff or primary/runoff/general election format.

[c]New York has used both primaries and party caucuses to choose nominees.

Candidates for Special Elections

The history of special elections in the United States indicates that the party that has held the seat usually retains it, but when switches do occur, movement is usually away from the current president's party. Given the prevalence of Democratic seats among those vacated at midterm, the often abrupt departure of the incumbent, and short campaign cycle, we expect that Democratic candidates in special elections will be especially likely to include politically seasoned aspirants. Democratic down-ticket strength is readily evident in the fields of candidates who compete in special elections.

In special elections since 1982, the district's incumbent party has produced more candidates. In the thirty-two previously Democratic districts, twenty-one attracted three or more Democratic candidates, whereas in nine of sixteen previously Republican districts, only one Democrat sought the vacant office. Half of the thirty-two Democratic districts attracted three or more GOP aspirants, whereas half of the previously Republican districts had three or more; seven had just one GOP contender. In some instances, nomination rules that surround general elections limited candidate emergence. Information about other potential contenders is quite limited, especially in the districts using a caucus or party executive committee to choose candidates.

Democrats did run in greater numbers than Republicans. Of the 306 major-party candidates for special elections, 56.9 percent were Democrats. Far more often, experienced Democrats than experienced Republicans ran in special elections. As indicated in table 6.3, almost half of all Democrats contesting special elections had prior elective service, compared with only a quarter of Republicans, and the proportion of Democrats who were state legislators was ten points higher than among Republicans. For regular open seat elections during this period, Republican candidates had electoral experience in about 35 percent of cases, whereas Democrats had electoral experience just over 41 percent of the time (see chapter 3). Compared with regular open seat contests, special elections attract experienced Democratic candidates significantly more often (chi square = 3.365, p < .05, 1 d.f.) and significantly fewer Republican experienced candidates (chi square = 4.804, p < .05, 1 d.f.). In part, this reflects the natural tendency for better candidates to run on their party's home turf, and Democrats had held two-thirds of the vacated seats prior to special elections (Bond et al. 1997; see also chapter 3).

The distribution of electoral experience in special elections follows the patterns observed in the other open seats. State legislators are the most prevalent of experienced candidates for both parties, followed by local elected officials and then former members of Congress or statewide officials, who rarely contest these seats.

When we examine who wins special elections, the power of political experience once again shows through. Of forty-eight special election winners, thirty-three (68.8 percent) had previously held elective office. The distribution of experience was roughly proportional between Democratic and Republican winners. In addition, of the ten seats that changed parties in the special elections, seven were won by experienced candidates, and just over 72 percent of the districts retained by the district incumbent party had experienced defenders.

Table 6.3   Candidate Political Experience in Special Elections, 1982–1994

Experience	Republicans	Democrats
State Legislator	16.6	26.4
Former Congressman	> 1.0	1.7
Statewide Elected Official	—	3.4
Local Elected Official	7.5	17.2
Legislative Staffer	1.1	2.3
Lobbyist/Political Appointee	3.8	4.6
Total Percent with Elective Experience	25.0	48.8
N	132	174

Widows

Only five widows or widowers ran for the twenty-two special election open seats produced by the death of their incumbent spouse. One widow and the lone widower lost their special elections. After Gladys Noon Spellman (D-MD) was declared incapacitated and her seat vacant by the House of Representatives, her husband competed in a field of thirty-one candidates and finished second in the Democratic primary behind the eventual winner, State Senator Steny Hoyer, in 1981. The losing widow, Kathy McDonald, sought to succeed her husband, Larry (D-GA) who was killed in a Korean commercial jet shot down by the Soviets in 1983. Despite being the leading candidate in the open primary field, McDonald lost to state legislator Buddy Darden (D) in the runoff.

Jean Ashbrook, the widow of GOP Representative John Ashbrook (R-OH), ran to fill the remainder of her husband's term in 1981 with the promise of retiring after it was over. The fact that, subsequent to Ashbrook's death, the district was dismantled to accommodate the loss of seats by Ohio in reapportionment may have contributed both to Mrs. Ashbrook's decision as well as to the level of party opposition accorded her candidacy. Another widow, Cathy Long (D-LA), held her husband's seat for the balance of his term before retiring in 1986. The only widow to continue in Congress, Sala Burton (D-CA), served from 1983 until her own death in early 1987. All of the widows faced opposition. Only Mrs. Ashbrook faced a single opponent; the others faced at least four rivals and the widower faced a significant portion of metro Baltimore in his primary. In both instances in which the widow and widower lost, the seat was retained by the incumbent party.[10]

Women

Chapter 5 noted that many of the perceived barriers to female candidate success did not exist in open seat elections. In this section, we examine some of those same hypotheses in the context of special elections. Women made up a slightly larger share of the candidates in special elections than in other open seat contests. Of the 306 major party candidates in special elections, 43 were women (14.3 percent), compared with 191 women out of 1,502 candidates (12.7 percent) in other open seat contests, which is not a statistically significant difference. As indicated in table 6.4, these women less often came from the ranks of state legislators than their male counterparts but more often had local elective experience. Overall, women were as likely as men to have some form of elective experience, and more than twice as often, these women had other appointive or partisan experience in politics.

Women were far more successful than men in obtaining nominations in special elections. Of the forty-three women who competed in special elections, eighteen (41.8 percent) made it to a general election or runoff. By comparison, just over a quarter of men were in a similar position (see table 6.5). If the four widows who ran are excluded, the level of female nomination success is still ten points higher than that of males.

Women generally ran better than men across the board. As table 6.6 indicates, female candidates were far more likely to lead an initial primary and were slightly better at coming in second place. Almost three-quarters of women finished among the top three candidates in either an open primary or traditional primary, compared with just over half of their male opponents.

Special elections afforded opportunities for female electoral advancement. Ten of the eighteen women (55.6 percent) who were nominated won a seat in Congress, compared with 49.2 percent of the men. In three of these cases, the new congresswoman was a widow, and Susan Molinari (R-NY) was the daughter of the departed member of Congress. Overall, the women who ascended to the House in special elections were politically experienced candidates. Of the ten, half had previously held elective office, two were former party officials, and one had been the Democratic nominee for the U.S. Senate three years prior. Three of the eight losing women had held elective office.

Table 6.4   Gender and Political Experience in Special Elections, 1982–1994

Experience	Female	Male
State Legislator*	13.9	23.5
Former Member of Congress	2.3	1.1
Statewide Elected Official	4.7	1.5
Local Elected Official	18.6	12.2
Legislative Staffer	2.3	1.5
Lobbyist/Political Appointee	9.3	3.4
Total Percent with Elective Experience	39.5	38.4
N	43	263

Table 6.5 Gender and Nominations in Special Elections

	Female	Male
Candidates Running	43	263
Candidates Winning Nominations	18	67
Percent Winning Nominations	41.8	25.4

Note: "Nominations" includes winning an open primary outright, finishing in a position to run in a general runoff under an open system, and winning a special primary [or runoff] to compete in a special general election. *N* does not equal 96 (2 × 48 seats) because 8 nominations were decided in caucus, and 3 races were won outright in open primaries without runoffs, resulting in only 1 "nominee."

Compared with their male counterparts, women were more likely to secure nomination and to win election. Because of the small number of special elections held, these differences do not always meet conventional standards of statistical significance. However, the results of special elections do support our conclusions in chapter 5 about women in open seats: When disruptions of the normal political balance occur through redistricting or other episodic events, opportunities for female advancement are created. Although we cannot definitively conclude that women were advantaged by the sudden creation of open seats through death or retirement, there is no evidence that women run worse than men in special elections or that the systems of election present barriers to female advancement. Indeed, the opposite appears to be the case.

EXPLAINING SPECIAL ELECTION OUTCOMES

The initial examination of experience for open seat special elections indicated that experience preceded success across party lines and gender, echoing the findings about open seats in general from chapters 2 and 3. In

Table 6.6 Primary Position of Female and Male Candidates in Special Elections

Position	Female	Male
First	16 (37.2)	58 (22.1)
Second	9 (20.9)	45 (17.1)
Third	6 (13.9)	35 (13.3)
Fourth or Lower	12 (27.9)	125 (47.5)
Total Candidates	43	263

Note: Position totals will not equal 96 (2 × 48 seats) because of the use of open primaries, which pool all candidates regardless of party. Also, some states used caucuses or committees to nominate candidates.

the forty-eight special elections from 1982 to 1994, the incumbent party won 79.1 percent of cases. Republicans retained 75 percent of their vacated seats, whereas Democrats retained 80.1 percent of theirs. Overall, the GOP gained a net of two seats in the forty-eight special elections examined. This rate of partisan change is roughly equivalent to that of regular open seats for the same period. In the balance of this chapter, we test the out-party/national-party hypothesis and then the portability of the open seats model from chapter 2 to explain special election outcomes.

The Out-Party/National-Party Test

Table 6.7 presents three regression models to explain the president's party's performance in special elections. The first model is a simple bivariate regression estimate of the relationship between the president's party's vote and whether the outgoing incumbent was of the president's party. The second model controls for the party of the incumbent president (because the presidential party changed during the period under study) and the president's share of the district vote in the last election. The third model introduces controls for the political experience of the president's and opposition party's candidates as measured on the Krasno-Green index.

As the results in table 6.7 indicate, the prior control of the district goes far in explaining the vote share of the president's party. The prior-incumbency variable by itself explains 37 percent of the variance in the dependent variable and holds significance across two multivariate equations. When the GOP is in the White House, its candidates do better in special elections. Virtually all of the variance explained by the presidential control

Table 6.7   Regression Estimates of the President's Party's Performance in Special House Elections

Variable	I	II	III
President's Party Is Incumbent	18.71 (5.37)***	16.38 (4.39)***	16.37 (4.39)***
Republican President	—	9.86 (2.10)*	10.83 (2.27)**
President's Party % in Last Election	—	.30 (2.50)**	.25 (1.92)*
President's Party Experience	—	—	1.09 (1.36)+
Out-Party's Experience	—	—	−.49 (−.63)
Constant	36.00	13.02	12.68
Adjusted-R^2	.37	.46	.46
N = 46			

Note: Dependent variable is the president's party's candidate share of the special election vote. All variables are measured at the district level.

+p < .10, one-tailed test; *p < .05, one-tailed test; **p < .01, one-tailed test; ***p < .001, one-tailed test.

was absorbed in the constant. The second model shows that the president's party's candidates do better in districts in which the presidential ticket ran strongly in the past. Political experience indicators were significant at fairly liberal levels for the president's party and not at all for the out-party, as reported in the third model. This analysis of special elections confirms Sigelman's (1981) findings for elections prior to 1980: special elections tend to be vehicles of constancy. Contrary to the incumbent-government punishment hypothesis, the president's party does better in districts it previously held, and Republican candidates apparently did better when their party held the White House.

The Standard Open Seat Model

Having tested an incumbent-party/out-party model of special elections, we turn to an examination of whether the open seats model from chapter 2 can explain the vote in special elections. If special elections are distinct entities divorced from regular elections, then the candidate-constituency specific model from chapter 2 should fail. If these elections are indeed similar to regular open seat elections, then the case for ascribing significant national policy trends to them is undermined.

The dependent variable is the Republican candidate's percentage of the two-party vote.[11] The independent variables—candidate experience, campaign spending, racial characteristics, and the southern control—are coded in the same fashion as in chapter 2; coattails measures are not included for obvious reasons. Table 6.8 presents the model developed in stages similar to those employed in chapter 2. The first estimate is of the candidate-specific variables—spending and experience—on the vote. The second model adds controls for the racial and ethnic characteristics of the district and for region, thereby completing the model from chapter 2. The number of cases analyzed is fewer than the total number of special elections. Two cases are excluded because both candidates were from the same party, and three others are excluded because financial data could not be obtained for both candidates, leaving forty-three cases.

The results in table 6.8 indicate that the open seats model from chapter 2 does a good job of explaining the vote in special elections. The directions of the significant coefficients are consistent with the analysis of regular open seats. However, the impact of the spending and black-population controls are more pronounced than in regular open seats.

One variable that was significant in the open seats analysis but fails in this model is Democratic candidate experience. Democratic experience barely moves the needle when other factors are controlled, and the level of significance of the relationship is trivial. Recall that the frequency of experienced Democratic candidates in special elections is especially high; there-

Table 6.8   The Open Seats Model Tested on Special Elections

Variable	Candidate-Attributes Model	With Constituency Attributes	With Presidential Evaluation
Constant	42.43	47.55	46.67
Republican Experience	1.38 (1.62)+	1.41 (1.96)*	.96 (1.32)+
Democratic Experience	−.48 (−.51)	.01 (.02)	−.13 (−.18)
Republican Spending	2.89 (3.78)***	2.66 (4.05)***	2.78 (4.55)***
Democratic Spending	−2.48 (−3.27)***	−2.00 (−3.09)***	−2.09 (−3.48)***
Black Population	—	−.29 (−3.85)***	−.31 (−4.53)***
Hispanic Population	—	−.22 (−2.26)**	−.21 (−2.30)**
South	—	−1.22 (−.30)	—
Presidential Responsibility	—	—	.39 (1.64)+
Adjusted-R^2	.31	.54	.57
N = 43			

Note: Dependent variable is the Republican share of the two-party vote.
    +p < .10, one-tailed test; *p < .05, one-tailed test; **p < .01, one-tailed test; ***p < .001, one-tailed test.

fore, there is little variation in the measure, and it is not surprising that experience is insignificant. Tests of the model using the Jacobson measure of experience (chapter 2) produced the same result. Putting aside the lack of impact for Democratic experience, the model produced a remarkably good fit to the dependent variable, and the results are consistent with those observed in regular open seats.

To explore fully the applicability of the model, we reexamined it with an additional control. Earlier in this chapter, we tested the incumbent-party/out-party hypothesis on the results of special elections. That analysis indicated that there was some relationship between the incumbent presidential party, its prior performance, and the results of special elections. To test this hypothesis against the candidate-constituency model from chapter 2, we developed a measure of presidential responsibility. The measure is based on the presidential favorable evaluation at the time, according to the Gallup poll. In years in which the GOP holds the presidency, a presidential evaluation score is calculated by subtracting 50 from the score; under Democratic administrations, the score is calculated as 50 minus the Gallup approval score. A negative score indicates a net disadvantage in public opinion to the GOP; a positive score indicates a net advantage. As indicated by the estimates in the last column, the presidential responsibility score is significantly related at the .1 level to the vote in special elections and leaves the other predictors virtually unaltered.[12] The coefficient for Republican experience is smaller but is still in the correct direction and is significant at the .1 level. Although responsibility is not the overwhelming predictor of special election outcomes, it is important to understanding the votes at the margins.

Unlike in the analysis on other open seats, the candidate experience measures were overwhelmed by measures of national partisan tides. A partial explanation may be found in the work of Bond, Fleisher, and Talbert (1997). As noted in chapter 3, Bond and colleagues found that quality Democratic candidates tended to emerge in a greater range of districts, rather than following the partisan strength hypothesis. In special elections, experienced Democrats, who make up the vast bulk of out-party candidates analyzed, emerged with greater frequency than in regular open seat elections. The opportunities that these suddenly open seats afforded attracted experienced candidates, regardless of the partisan conditions (the relationship between the experience measures and the incumbent president's vote strength is negligible). In both parties, highly experienced candidates snared nominations at rates greater than in other open seats. The truncated campaign season produced by a special election heightens the edge enjoyed by officeholders. Public officials often have advantages in name recognition and fund-raising; in the course of a regular campaign, amateurs have a better chance of overcoming these handicaps than in the few weeks leading up to a special election. Therefore, the declining significance of experience is not surprising, simply because the variable is relatively constant as a result of a highly experienced pool of competitors.

CONCLUSION

Special elections are subject to many of the same influences as other open seat contests. In many ways, these contests illustrate the underlying contours of open seats that have been discussed throughout this volume. When partisan tides and the focus of a national campaign are laid aside, the effects of constituency attributes and spending are still evident and explain quite effectively the results of special elections. These attributes also represent the structural factors at the core of debates regarding representation and pluralism in the United States, which further underscores the relevance of the findings. Although the strong experience effects observed generally in open seats are not evident in special elections, the dominance of experienced candidates among the nominees and winners of special elections indicates their importance in special elections.

Sigelman (1981) argued that simply because special elections did not produce a great deal of partisan change was no reason to discount those elections as unimportant. As he stated,

> Even though the party identification of the winner does not often change as the result of a special election, the identity of the winner does. . . . Special elections are indeed special. In large measure, what makes them special in the sense of the outcomes they produce is the very same characteristic that proves their rai-

son d'être: the fact that the contested seat is open. Even beyond the inoperability factor, however, special elections are demonstrably different in some intriguing ways from general elections, both on-year and off-year. (1981, 585–6)

Special elections provide sudden, dramatic opportunities for change that make them interesting. Even though the media and voters often deem these races to be unimportant or uninteresting, they do attract fields of candidates that are as large and as broadly experienced as in the most hotly contested, high-profile open seat contest.

Of particular interest is the analysis of the role of women in special open seat elections. The conventional wisdom suggests that women would be disadvantaged in special elections, much as it would probably argue that women are disadvantaged by the electoral system in general. Special elections occur in relative isolation, often among less-interested or disinterested electorates, and have a very short campaign season (Sigelman 1981). To overcome those barriers requires the marshaling of political assets, connections, and money, which are often perceived to be less accessible to women (see chapter 5). On the other hand, to the extent that women fare better when seeking open seats than when opposing incumbents, women should do reasonably well in special elections.

In fact, when women run in by-elections, they are as or more successful than their male counterparts. Women more often find themselves positioned to compete in runoffs or general elections; they finish higher in primaries; and they generally win at higher rates than men. Of course, women still run in fewer numbers than men, although the discrepancies are no greater than for normally scheduled open seat elections. Still, when the normal political order is disrupted by a vacancy, the same effects observed as a result of redistricting and retirement were apparent in special elections. Women are able to exploit the opportunities afforded by these vacancies and increase their presence in Congress.

In the context of all open seats, special elections seem to be as vulnerable to the partisan tides, candidate spending, and constituency characteristics that structure other open seats outcomes. In that respect, then, special election outcomes that defy the conventional wisdom—changes in partisan control, for example—can be viewed as the product of normal electoral circumstances.

NOTES

1. The term "by-election" is normally used in reference to off-cycle elections for vacancies in the British parliament. When vacancies occur in the House of Commons, an election would be held "on the by" or in the interval between regular parliamentary elections.

2. The Little Congress was an organization of legislative staffers that mimicked the actual body in that it elected a speaker, organized committees, and debated significant issues. Johnson's exploits as Speaker of the Little Congress are detailed in Robert Caro's (1982) *The Years of Lyndon Johnson* and in Doris Kearns's (1976) *Lyndon Johnson and the American Dream*.

3. Johnson was entertaining the visiting NYA director from Kansas.

4. Although Roosevelt's court-packing scheme was not implemented, the reaction of the Supreme Court to the threat of packing and, perhaps, to the results of the Texas election indicate the referendum strategy did work. The Supreme Court was much more disposed to support New Deal legislation against constitutional challenge after 1937 than it had been before.

5. "Morphing" was a popular technique with the GOP challengers and open seat candidates in 1994. The Democratic opponent would be pictured on screen. As the voice-over linked the Democrat to the policies of the Clinton administration, the face of the Democratic candidate would transform into the face of Bill Clinton.

6. Tying an opponent to an unpopular political figure is not sufficient grounds to win a special election. The campaign in Kentucky tied Joe Prather convincingly to Bill Clinton and was indicative of a coming Republican electoral trend. Subsequent efforts in California to link Republican Tom Campbell to the unpopular Republican Speaker Newt Gingrich had little effect, as the GOP picked up the vacated seat of senior Democrat Norman Mineta in 1995.

7. That unique case occurred in 1986, when Neil Abercrombie (D-HA) was elected to fill the last three months of the term of Cecil Heftel, who resigned to become governor. Abercrombie won the special election to fill the seat but lost the regular primary held the same day for the regular term.

8. Arguably the 1989 resignation of two Democratic leaders was eclipsed by the departure in early 1999 of Speaker Newt Gingrich (R-GA) and his successor, Bob Livingston (R-LA). Gingrich announced his intention to resign coincident with his announcement that he would not seek reelection as Speaker. The decision not to stand for another term as Speaker came when Gingrich, facing a challenge from Livingston, found that he lacked support among House Republicans. GOP House members had soured on the hero of 1994, blaming him for their party's loss of five seats in 1998. Only once before in the twentieth century had the party not in control of the White House failed to gain House seats in a midterm election.

Livingston decided to leave the House before being selected Speaker when his extramarital affairs were revealed. In announcing his resignation amidst the House impeachment debate, Livingston urged President Clinton to follow the same course.

9. In Georgia, it is possible that four trips to the polls will be necessary because a general election runoff is required if no candidate polls at least 45 percent of the vote.

10. In 1998, two California widows held on to their husband's seats. Mary Bono (R) took almost two-thirds of the vote, and Lois Capps (D) outspent Tom Bordonaro (R) by almost two to one to retain the seat her husband had wrested from Republicans in 1996. Widow's luck did not persist into 1999, as George Brown's widow (D-CA), Marta, failed to win nomination for the remainder of her husband's term.

11. For conventional-model and strong-party systems, this variable is calculated as the Republican's percentage of the total vote for the Democratic and Republican nominees. In the open primary/runoff cases, it is that percentage in the runoff or of the top Democrat and top Republican if no runoff occurred. The two cases in which candidates from the same party appear in a runoff were deleted from the analysis.

12. The insignificant southern coefficient is dropped from the equation.

Chapter 7

Understanding the Past, Predicting the Future

Most studies about congressional elections agree that contests against incumbents are not competitive; this in turn makes the likelihood of changing Congress difficult. This book has lifted the veil of incumbency to examine the underlying face of congressional elections. We found that the presence of incumbents is not the only reason elections can be uncompetitive. For the most part, however, open seat elections are more competitive and are more closely linked to candidate and structural factors.

This chapter summarizes the results of the analyses presented in chapters 2 through 6. The findings are then considered in the broader context of electoral change in Congress and as they help explain the consequences of one popular, but quickly waning, reform of the 1990s, the term limits movement. Recent trends in open seats are discussed. Then we use our model to explore the potential for change in Congress by way of open seats in the 2000 elections, and discuss the potential safety or vulnerability of all congressional districts should those districts come open. We close with some thoughts about the underlying competitive structure of elections to "the people's house."

THE ORIGINS OF THE CONGRESSIONAL
CAREER IN OPEN SEATS

House elections are more competitive when seats are open, although open seats are not always highly competitive. The analysis in chapter 2 indicated that almost two-thirds of the members of Congress elected to open seats win a "safe" initial election. The literature on congressional elections leaves the impression that Members of Congress come to the chamber as the products of marginal wins, successful candidates who have barely survived highly competitive efforts. In a sense, that is true, because the margins in the open seats are narrow, compared with incumbent contests, but truly competitive elections are not the norm. The typical new legislator has a comfortable win but by less than the margin an incumbent can expect—a phenomenon dubbed the "retirement slump" (Alford and Brady 1993). Just over one-third—36.8 percent—of the 364 contested open seat races between 1982 and 1998 were won by less than 55 percent of the vote, whereas 26.4 percent were won with between 55 percent and 60 percent of the vote. Another 36.8 percent were won by candidates who attracted more than 60 percent of the vote. In contrast, from 1982 to 1996, an average of three-fourths of House incumbents polled more than 60 percent of the vote (Ornstein, Mann, and Malbin 1998, 68). Open seat winners survived in races that, although more competitive than the average incumbent race, were not usually as competitive as a race lost by an incumbent.

The outcomes in open seats are structured by the same candidate attributes associated with strong performances by challengers to incumbents. More experienced candidates and candidates who raise more money are more likely to win. Candidates who hold the advantage on both the experience and financial dimensions win more than 80 percent of the time. Open seats also tend to be won by the nominees of the party that has done well in the district in the past and when constituency characteristics favor that party.

The variation in competition observed in general elections for open seats was also evident in the primaries. No matter how safe or competitive a district in general elections, the preceding primary was usually competitive. Again, candidate attributes affect the competition. Candidates who had no primary challenge were usually highly experienced officeholders similar to those whom Gary Jacobson (1997) finds to be the best congressional challengers. However, experienced candidates who competed in contested primaries did not have significantly greater primary nomination percentages. In sum, at both the primary and general election levels, competition in open seats is frequent though not universal.

If new members of Congress run scared, then as Frank Lucas observed in chapter 2, paranoia is likely a product of more than the final vote percentage. Few new legislators avoided both primary and general election challengers. So in the end, the new legislators look back on a contest that, for a third of them, was narrowly won. The other two-thirds look back and see that they performed better than the conventional wisdom predicted, which would be a marginal win with less than 55 percent of the vote.

EXPLAINING REPUBLICAN FRUSTRATIONS

Republicans experienced great political frustration during the 1980s. Despite the presidential electoral successes of Ronald Reagan and George Bush,

Republicans never approached majority status in the U.S. House of Representatives. Some might consider this frustration moot, given the GOP reign as majority party beginning in 1995. An examination of the open seats promotes an understanding of how the GOP achieved majority status in 1994. Cutting through the proffered explanations for Republican frustration, such as incumbency advantage or southern bias, allows a clearer view of why Republicans finally took control of the House.

The electoral frustration of the Republican party did not stem from incumbency advantage or other systematic bias. Disproportionate Republican retirements and the inability of Republican congressional candidates to run as well as GOP presidential nominees in the open districts were more likely causes. The connection between national elections and congressional elections was incomplete, which frustrated Republican efforts to build a congressional majority on the back of the Reagan and Bush successes. Through 1992, Republicans ran behind the presidential normal vote in most open seats and usually ran behind the presidential candidate in presidential years. In 1994, GOP congressional candidates exceeded the normal vote for the first time in more than a decade as Newt Gingrich linked local elections to a national campaign.

Republicans had a smaller pool of quality candidates and suffered because of the weaker teams they fielded in the 1980s and early 1990s. Alan Ehrenhalt (1990) suggests that attractive Republican potential candidates had fewer motivations to enter electoral politics. If there are fewer potential quality candidates in a constituency, it stands to reason that there will be fewer quality candidates who run. Jacobson and Kernell (1983) argue that the candidate quality problem is a product of candidates' strategic planning. Incumbents scare off exceptional potential challengers; the more ambitious congressional aspirants wait for the seat to come open, even though, as noted above, they will likely face a competitive primary. The GOP faced quality-candidate problems even in the open seats because their nominees had held office less often than Democrats. These differences also characterized special elections.

Republicans, however, achieved parity in financing open seat candidates and have dominated private sector PAC contributions in recent years. Again, however, candidate quality helps determine receipts. PACs are most likely to invest in high-quality, experienced candidates and especially those who have already secured party money. During much of the 1980s, the GOP search for PAC money was checked by the tendency of corporate and trade PACs to hedge their bets and invest in Democrats as well as Republicans in open seats. Although business's heart might belong to the GOP, its head dictated sharing support with Democrats as long as they held the congressional majority and could dominate floor debates and committee deliberations. Labor PACs backed Democratic candidates for

Congress almost exclusively. Republicans had no major funding source whose partisan loyalty could compare with the undeviating support Democrats received from labor. However, since winning control of Congress, corporate and trade PAC money has followed its heart to the GOP.

When deciding whom to support, PACs seem to rely on candidate experience and information about the contested district's past political leanings. Money went disproportionately to candidates with political pedigrees and who were in districts that had supported the candidate's party in past presidential or congressional elections. The findings also suggest that PACs turn to the parties for guidance and give more generously to candidates who attract party money. Prior to 1994, there is also evidence that PAC cohorts may have hedged their bets at times, because when a PAC cohort supported an opponent, it reduced a candidate's take from that PAC.

OPEN SEATS AND REFORM: TERM LIMITS

Recognizing that changing public policy is facilitated by changing the personnel of Congress (Clausen 1973), some recent reform efforts have focused on the competitiveness of congressional elections. The most prominent proposal, term-limits, was based on both electoral competitive and institutional arguments. The electoral competitive argument assumed that the absence of incumbents made elections more competitive. Many Republicans seized on term limits as an instrument to bludgeon Democrats; in the wake of the change in majority, conservative rhetoric regarding term limits has tempered.[1] The institutional argument held that there is an arrogance of power that accompanies long-term incumbency; disrupting incumbents' careers would constrain this arrogance and make government more responsive.

This latter argument is beyond the scope of this study. The former argument, the contention that term limits would make elections more competitive, is valid but not as sweeping as advocates would hope. Clearly open seats are more competitive than incumbent elections. About a third of the open seat contests we studied are "marginal" contests, and the likelihood of a partisan switch is greater in the open seats.

Having a large number of open seats as a result of term limits introduces greater partisan volatility, even though the overall balance of Congress would not be dramatically altered. In the time period covered by this study, only in 1982 and 1994 did the swing of seats toward a party exceed twenty. However, for this same period, more than one-third of open seats changed party, and only in 1988 and 1992 did the proportion of open seats changing party fall below 20 percent. Even if partisan shifts do not favor one party, open seats promote partisan change at the district level. Term limits would not only introduce more new legislators in more districts, but those limits should also cause more voters to experience periodic changes in the partisan identity of their representative and therefore introduce a greater variety over time in the representative style and policy stands of a district's legislator.

GENDER AND THE OPEN SEAT CANDIDATE

The increase in female representatives in the early 1990s exceeded the most optimistic projections of growth made in the 1970s and 1980s. To no small extent, the election of large numbers of women stemmed from opportunities to run in districts without incumbents. Women do well in open seats and win under the same circumstances as men, namely by having money and prior political experience.

To exploit fully the opportunities afforded in open seats requires that women hold office and create political connections down ticket. Examination of the political advancement of women in Florida indicated that disrupting the incumbency advantage in the state legislature in 1982 facilitated the election of several congresswomen via open seats in 1992. The analysis of special elections provides further evidence that women run as well or better than men when vacancies occur. Future growth in female representation will require two changes in the role of women in open seat elections. First, far more women will have to run, and those candidacies will have to bring the kinds of political connections, fund-raising ability, and prior political experiences that are associated with success in general. Second, if the general goal of more women is to be accomplished, the effort to recruit and elect women through open seats will have to occur in both parties. Women succeeded in 1992 in no small part because they disproportionately ran as Democrats in districts with Democratic tendencies. In 1994, women did not make substantial gains because they ran disproportionately as Democrats in a year when Democrats were out of political favor.

Roughly half of all congressional districts come open during the decade between reapportionments. If women can win half the open seats in a given year while distributing female retirements in rough proportion to their share of seats entering each election, then the House can become roughly majority female within two decades. So long as the gender gap in the electorate favors Democrats, women may be more inclined to seek congressional office as Democrats. Future female gains will rely on the successes of the Democratic party unless this trend abates.

OPEN SEAT ELECTIONS SINCE 1994: BACK TO NORMAL?

Was 1994 an epic election, a departure from the past in the tradition of previous realigning elections? Or was it an aberration, a temporary departure from the status quo? Chapter 2 showed that the 1994 elections were largely an exercise in status quo politics. Only in the South, where anti-Democratic and anti-Clinton sentiment ran strongest, did a significant difference in the relationship between the predictors of open seat election outcomes and the vote in the open seats emerge (see also Gaddie 1995b). To determine whether 1994 ushered in a new era of congressional elections requires an examination of 1996 and 1998 elections.

The open seats model in chapter 2 identified money and political experience as the principal correlates of success in congressional elections. Candidates who have the advantage in both of these attributes are far more successful than candidates who lack money or prior political experience. Table 7.1 replicates the analysis from chapter 2 by examining Republican success in open seats in 1996 and 1998 while controlling for spending and prior political experience. For the 1996 to 1998 couplet, nominees of either party who held advantages in both spending and experience won at least 80 percent of the time outside the South and always down in Dixie. These levels of success are quite similar to those in the period of 1982 to 1992 (table 2.3), although nonsouthern Republicans did somewhat better when they held the advantage on one dimension in 1996 to 1998 than in 1982 to 1992. As with the earlier period, Republicans who lacked both advantages won at much lower rates in 1996 to 1998 than in 1994.

Open seats continued to be vehicles for partisan change after the 1994 watershed. In 1996 and 1998, more than 30 percent of open seats changed hands. Republicans had fewer successes in the 1996 to 1998 open seats than at the beginning of the decade. GOP candidates only won thirty-nine of eighty-two contested open seats in 1996 to 1998: ten of twenty-three in the South and twenty-nine of fifty-nine in the rest of the nation. The GOP had held forty of those seats entering the election so that Republicans had a net loss of one in open seats.

Why did the GOP not do better? Part of the explanation comes from the underlying partisan nature of the districts involved. In the 1980s and early 1990s, Republican congressional candidates consistently ran behind their party's presidential vote. In 1994, in a break with recent history, Republi-

Table 7.1   Experience, Spending, and Republican Electoral Success in Open Seats, 1996 and 1998

	Nonsouthern Seats		Southern Seats	
Republican Advantages	N	*GOP win (%)*	N	*GOP win (%)*
Spending and Experience	16	13 (81.3)	5	5 (100.0)
Spending or Experience	18	12 (66.7)	9	5 (55.6)
Neither Advantage	25	4 (16.0)	9	0 (0)

cans generally ran ahead of the normal vote and won 75 percent of the open seats. But in 1996 and 1998, especially outside the South, the seats that came open tended to be competitive or to lean Democratic. In the South, where Republicans ran stronger for president than elsewhere, the average normal vote for an open seat in 1996 (reported in table 7.2) was just under 51 percent; in the rest of the nation, it hovered below 50 percent. In 1998, only three open seats were in the South, and on average, they leaned Republican. The thirty nonsouthern open seats had an average normal two-party vote of only 44 percent Republican, indicating a weak GOP presidential baseline and therefore a potentially weak congressional vote.[2] Few districts inclined toward the GOP came open in 1998 and all but one Republican loss occurred in districts that voted Democratic in presidential elections.

How does the open seats model from chapter 2 perform when applied to the late 1990s? To ascertain the portability of the open seat model to post-1994 elections, we reestimated the model from table 2.8 using cases from 1996 and 1998. The coding of all variables is the same as indicated in chapter 2. The analysis presented in table 7.3 is as robust as in chapter 2, and all of the variables are in the same directions and attain similar levels of significance. The only difference is a heightened relationship between racial composition of the district and the GOP vote. Presidential coattails are still highly significant; however, the slope is slightly less steep than in the cases for 1982 to 1992, indicating a possible weakening of the presidential vote on the congressional vote (see Campbell 1997).

Given the marked similarities in open seats both before and after the 1994 election, we pooled all of the open seat elections from 1982 to 1998 and reestimated the regression equation. The results appear in table 7.4. The direction of the slopes in table 7.4 is similar to those reported for 1982 to 1992 in table 2.8, and every variable is significant using a one-tailed test. Republicans do better when they have more experience, spend more money, and run in districts in which GOP presidential nominees have made stronger showings. Republicans running in the South get larger shares of the vote than their colleagues elsewhere. The GOP vote share in

Table 7.2 "Natural Constituencies?" The Republican Presidential Normal Vote in the Open Seats in 1996 and 1998

	N	Mean	SD
1996			
South	20	50.76	7.61
Nonsouth	29	49.54	10.87
1998			
South	3	51.43	2.08
Nonsouth	30	44.17	10.79

Table 7.3   The Open Seat Model, 1996

Model	b	t
Intercept	32.577	
Republican Candidate Experience	.840	2.211**
Democratic Candidate Experience	−.825	−2.195**
Republican Candidate Spending ($100K)	.865	4.723***
Democratic Candidate Spending ($100K)	−.751	−3.771***
Black Population	−.295	−4.702***
Hispanic Population	−.186	−3.263***
South	2.270	1.255
Presidential Coattails	.405	4.088***
Year 1996	16.232	3.340***
Adjusted-R^2	.75	
N	82	

**p < .01, one-tailed test; ***p < .001, one-tailed test.

open seat contests is lower when Democrats have more experience and spend more money. Concentrations of blacks and Hispanics also disadvantage Republican nominees. The interaction term from table 2.11, created by multiplying Democratic experience times South times 1994, indicates that Republicans did better in the South in that critical year even when running against seasoned Democrats. Slopes in tables 7.4 and 2.8 are generally about the same size, although the impact of GOP spending (.81) is less than for the earlier period (1.11). The dichotomous regional variable, the one predictor not significant for 1982 to 1992, is 50 percent larger in table 7.4. The dummy variable for 1994 indicates that when other factors are held constant, a Republican polled almost 6 percentage points more of the vote in 1994, which provides additional evidence of the unique nature of the "Gingrich revolution."

We are now prepared to examine whether the 1994 election constituted a major shift in open seat voting. The indicators of electoral success might have changed, especially in regard to the candidate quality and the South. In fact, the open seat model from before 1994 does an excellent job of explaining open seat congressional elections after 1994. Post-1994 congressional elections appear to have returned to the patterns of behavior exhibited before 1994, albeit with a slight muting of the influence of candidate spending. The unique nature of the 1994 election and the lack of change in the behavior of the predictive model since then suggest that 1994 was an episodic deviation from a continuing status quo.

The model for 1996 to 1998 was also estimated with controls for candidate gender. Gender was not a significant indicator of open seat outcomes; however, some trends in female competition emerged that may suggest prob-

Table 7.4   The Open Seat Model, 1984–1996

Model	b	t
Constant	50.23	
Republican Candidate Experience	1.36	6.87***
Democratic Candidate Experience	−1.44	−6.89***
Republican Candidate Spending ($100K)	.81	7.33***
Democratic Candidate Spending ($100K)	−.71	−7.37***
Black Population	−.27	−9.63***
Hispanic Population	−.15	−5.10***
South	1.51	1.66*
Presidential Coattails	.41	6.58***
Year 1984	−21.40	−5.26***
Year 1988	−20.77	−5.62***
Year 1992	−13.96	−5.68***
Year 1994	5.94	4.87***
Year 1996	−17.52	−5.79***
Democratic Experience × South × Year 1994	1.20	2.33**
Adjusted-R^2	.72	
N	364	

Note: The dependent variable is the Republican candidate's share of the major two-party vote.
$*p < .05$, one-tailed test; $**p < .01$, one-tailed test; $***p < .001$, one-tailed test.

lems for increased female presence in Congress. After 1992, women ran in open seats at rates roughly comparable to the previous decade, but they have fared less well in open seat contests since the "Year of the Woman." Women won 46 percent of the contests in which they were nominated. The fact that more than two-thirds of women who were nominated were Democrats tells at least part of the story, for in a period that did not particularly advantage Democrats in congressional elections, women ran disproportionately as Democrats. The fact that these women were generally equally funded and more politically experienced than male nominees of both parties indicates that some aspect of partisanship contributed to the relatively poor showing of women candidates after 1992.

LOOKING TO THE FUTURE

We looked to the past and have presented explanations for the behavior of congressional elections in the absence of incumbents. Now we extend our work beyond the data to consider what the future might look like in open U.S. House elections.

This is a reasonable, if not necessary, extension of the work. Political scientists study elections for two reasons: (1) to ascertain the broader meaning of elections, that is, to understand the reasons behind the outcomes; and (2) to predict the outcomes of future elections. The use of regression analysis is helpful in both tasks. When explaining outcomes, the ability to identify and measure potentially significant variables allows estimates of arithmetic relationships between explanations and outcomes. If the earlier models prove to be especially robust, we then can take data on those same variables, apply them to future cases, and generate "estimates" or "best guesses" as to future outcomes.

Our models are robust and, given the right information, can generate accurate predictions. If prior to an election, we knew the political experience and the amount of spending by open seat candidates and had a good idea of what the presidential vote would be in a district, the results from the regression model in table 7.4 could be used to estimate the vote in a district. The prediction would not be perfect, though it should be close. Using the model from this study to forecast the 2000 open seat elections is difficult. At the time of this writing (winter 2000), not all open seats are known, and nominees and expenditures are uncertain. Nor have the presidential standard-bearers been selected, to say nothing of the potential coattails those candidates might provide. Therefore, measures of variables such as candidate experience or spending advantage are impossible. However, the application of a variation of the model from chapter 2 will generate estimates of the competitiveness of districts, should they come open.

Gaddie and McCollum (1998) made the first effort to extend the open seat model to generate vote forecasts. They developed a district-specific measure of incumbency advantage and posited that the incumbency advantage was simply the vote for the incumbent, minus the expected vote in the district, were it open.[3] This assertion is also at the heart of the Alford and Brady (1989) and Gelman and King (1991) measures of the incumbency advantage, which are not generated for individual congressional districts but which use as a basis for estimation the open seat vote. In taking an advanced look at the congressional elections of 2000, we will apply the first part of their technique to derive a predicted vote in a congressional district in the absence of an incumbent.

The model used by Gaddie and McCollum varies slightly from the open seat model presented in chapter 2. Their measure of experience is the dichotomous term used by Jacobson (1990) indicating whether the candidate had previously held public office. Another difference is that they measure spending using a dichotomous variable, which was coded 1 if the Republican spent more money or 0 if the Democrat held the spending advantage.[4] A third difference is that instead of using a measure of presidential coattails, they used a measure of the presidential normal vote in the district to account for national electoral influences.

Their analysis, based on data from 1988 to 1996, produced highly accurate projections for 1996 and 1998 open seat elections. As indicated in figure 7.1, there is a close correlation between the expected vote based on the technique described above and the actual vote outcomes (for thirty-three open seats in 1998, adjusted-R^2 = .86). Absent any actual data on candidate spending or experience, the model correctly forecast the partisan outcome in seventy-five of eighty-three cases across the two elections.

We replicate their analysis with some slight variations, using data from the longer 1982 to 1998 time period. This model, which appears in table 7.5, is slightly less successful in explaining variance in the Republican vote share (adjusted-R^2 = .67) than the model in table 7.4 (adjusted-R^2 = .72). Because the use of dichotomous measures of spending and experience allowed Gaddie and McCollum to generate more accurate predicted vote outcomes, we retain their specification to make predictions to the year 2000. Our rationale will become apparent when we describe how they deal with missing data for candidate experience and spending by generating likely predictions of candidate experience and predictions of which party would likely have the spending advantage.[5]

To generate vote predictions for districts in 2000 requires values for each independent variable that can be multiplied by the regression coefficient to generate a predicted value of the district vote. At the district level, data on black and Hispanic population, the South, and the year controls are available. Missing are data on who will have the spending advantage and whether the Republican or Democratic candidates have prior office-holding experience. All of these variables exert a strong influence on the vote share; to make an accurate estimation requires the development of estimates of experience, spending advantage, and coattails to complete our prediction.

Gaddie and McCollum address this problem by developing estimates of the likelihood that experienced candidates emerge in each district and by estimating the probability that a Republican will have the spending advantage. They then take the probability that a GOP candidate is experienced (a figure necessarily bounded by 0 and 1) and substitute it into the data set as a value for political experience. Similar estimations and substitutions are made for the Democrat's experience and for the spending advantage. This technique and estimation of the spending and experience factors are discussed at length in the appendix.

The following information is needed to compute the expected GOP vote in a district, based on these conditions: (1) political experience and spending advantage that reflect the likely tendencies of the district; (2) district GOP presidential vote that is 4 percentage points higher than the normal vote for the 1992 to 1996 elections (in other words, a national GOP presidential vote of 50 percent); (3) year 2000 election variable = average of the

Figure 7.1 Plotting the Predicted and Actual Vote in the Open Seats, 1996 and 1998

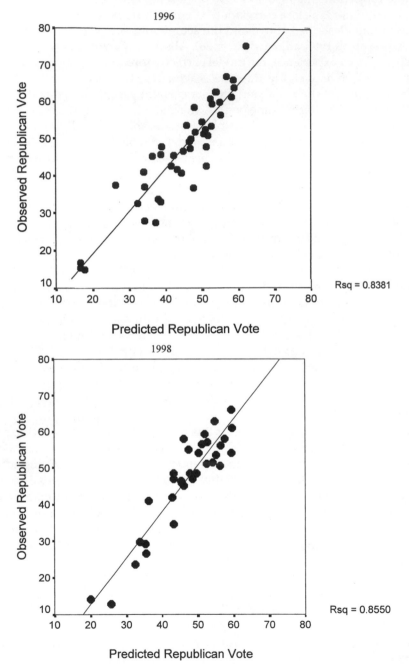

Source: Gaddie and McCollum (1998).

Table 7.5   The Gaddie and McCollum Forecast Model, Using Data from 1984 to 1996

Model	b	t
Intercept	46.863	
Republican Candidate Experience	3.95	4.68***
Democratic Candidate Experience	−4.02	−4.85***
Republican Spending Advantage	7.29	8.46***
Black Population	−.29	−9.82***
Hispanic Population	−.18	−5.55***
South	2.87	3.07**
Presidential Coattails	.39	5.74***
Year 1984	−20.38	−4.57***
Year 1988	−19.64	−4.84***
Year 1992	−14.06	−5.23***
Year 1994	6.97	5.92***
Year 1996	−16.42	−4.91***
Adjusted-R^2	.67	
N	364	

$**p < .01$, one-tailed test; $***p < .001$, one-tailed test.

presidential election year variables from 1984 to 1996 cumulative; and (4) data on racial and ethnic composition of the district and whether the district is in the South. Using hypothetical data for experience and spending, along with actual district demographics, produces an expected GOP vote for each district. As an example, suppose that the probability of a Republican experienced candidate = .70, whereas the probability of an experienced Democratic candidate = .33 and the probability of the Republican holding the spending advantage = .60. Assume that the expected presidential coattail influence is equal to the normal vote, and in this district, that number = 52. The average for the presidential election year control is −17.63. The district is in the Midwest, so South = 0. The district is 10 percent black and 5 percent Hispanic. The expected GOP vote for the district is therefore

$$46.863 + 3.95(.70) - 4.02(.33) + 7.29(.60) - .29(10.00) - .18(5.00) + 2.87(0.00) + .39(52.00) + -17.63(1.00) = 51.525$$

percent of the vote in the hypothetical district. This technique is used to generate open seat forecasts for the 2000 elections. The forecasts for all 412 districts for which we have complete data appear in the appendix. Table 7.6 presents the expected Republican vote in the twenty-seven districts in which incumbents have indicated their intention of moving on, either because of retirement or the pursuit of progressive ambition, as of January 15, 2000.

Table 7.6 Seats at Risk? Vacancies and Expected Outcomes for 2000

Incumbent/CD	Reason for Departure	1998 GOP Vote	Exp. GOP Vote, 2000	P(Flip)[a]	Evans-Novak
Archer, R, TX-7	Retiring	94.0[c]	[b]		Sure GOP
Barrett, R, NE-3	Retiring	100.0[c]	[b]		Sure GOP
Bateman, R, VA-1	Retiring	78.0	56.43	.19	?
Campbell, R, CA-15	Running for Senate	61.0	44.92	.76	Leaning GOP
Canady, R, FL-12	Retiring	100.0[c]	55.16	.24	Sure GOP
Chenoweth, R, ID-1	Retiring	55.0	60.16	.08	Sure GOP
Clay, D, MO-1	Retiring	27.0	20.25	.01	Sure Dem.
Coburn, R, OK-2	Retiring	58.0	48.95	.56	Leaning GOP
Ewing, R, IL-15	Retiring	62.0	50.87	.46	Probable GOP
Fowler, R, FL-4	Retiring	100.0[c]	61.14	.06	?
Franks, R, NJ-7	Running for Senate	53.0	48.73	.57	Leaning GOP
Goodling, R, PA-19	Retiring	68.0	59.98	.08	Sure GOP
Hill, R, MT-AL	Retiring	53.0	51.94	.39	Leaning Dem.
Kasich, R, OH-12	Retiring	67.0	45.57	.73	Leaning GOP
Klink, D, PA-4	Running for Senate	36.0	47.41	.36	Leaning Dem.
McCollum, R, FL-8	Running for Senate	66.0	58.71	.11	Sure GOP
McIntosh, R, IN-2	Running for Governor	61.0	56.07	.20	Sure GOP
Metcalf,R, WA-2	Retiring	55.0	50.23	.49	Leaning Dem.
Packard, R, CA-48	Retiring	77.0	58.95	.11	Sure GOP
Pickett, D, VA-2	Retiring	0.0[c]	52.90	.66	?
Porter, R, IL-10	Retiring	100.0[c]	50.37	.48	Leaning Dem.
Salmon, R, AZ-1	Retiring	64.0	53.60	.31	Sure GOP
Sanford, R, SC-1	Retiring	92.0[c]	57.73	.14	Sure GOP
Stabenow, D, MI-8	Running for Senate	42.0	47.83	.38	Leaning GOP
Talent, R, MO-2	Running for Governor	71.0	55.93	.18	Probable GOP
Weygand, D, RI-2	Running for Senate	25.0	40.66	.10	Probable Dem.
Wise, D, WV-2	Running for Governor	26.0	49.81	.49	Leaning Dem.

[a]Probability that the seat will change parties.
[b]Expected vote not computed due to missing data in district.
[c]No major party opponent.

Initial projections regarding twenty-seven seats expected to come open in 2000 indicate a level of competitiveness similar to that observed for open seats in the 1980s and 1990s; however, the balance of retirements is skewed toward the GOP. Just six of the twenty-seven vacated seats are held by Democrats so that, initially, the Republicans are over-exposed in the open seats. Should the GOP win open seats at the rate they did in the 1980s and early 1990s, Democrats could expect to win fourteen open seats for a net gain of eight, which is more than enough switches to produce a narrow Democratic majority in the House, assuming that there are no incumbent defeats or they are equally distributed across both parties.

But are these seats really at risk? If we take the difference between the expected vote generated by the technique illustrated in the equation above and 50 percent, and then divide by the standard error of the regression, we can generate a probability that the actual GOP vote will be less than 50 percent. For districts with retiring Republican incumbents, this is the probability the district will flip to the other party; for Democratic incumbent districts, 1 minus this probability is the likelihood of a flip occurring to the other party.

The expected vote generated in table 7.6 predicts that Republicans will poll more than 55 percent of the two-party vote in ten of the twenty-one districts they currently hold. Republicans are predicted to win narrower margins in Arizona's First District, Washington's Second District, Illinois's Tenth District, Illinois's Fifteenth District, and Montana. In Oklahoma's Second District, where Tom Coburn is honoring his pledge to serve only three terms, the expected GOP vote is just below 49 percent, while in California's Fifteenth District, New Jersey's Seventh District, and Ohio's Twelfth District, the likelihood is greater that the district will flip to the Democrats than stay with the GOP. Missouri's First District and Rhode Island's Second District should remain safely Democratic, and Democrats are predicted to get about 52 percent of the vote in Michigan's Eighth District and Pennsylvania's Fourth District. West Virginia's Second District, which Bob Wise (D) is expected to vacate to run for governor, is projected as a dead heat with the Republican coming up short. The second-to-last column in table 7.6 reports that the likelihood of a change in partisan control is above .25 in thirteen of twenty-seven districts, nine of which are held by Republicans. If every district in which the probability of partisan change ≥.25 actually changed hands, Democrats would win eleven of twenty-seven open seats, for a net gain of five seats in the House. In five districts, four currently held by Republicans, the probability of a flip exceeds .5. Should the out party win each of these districts, Democrats would emerge with a net gain of three.

Various political observers also make predictions about the likely outcome in congressional contests. Washington, D.C., columnists and talk show personalities Rowland Evans and Robert Novak are among those who carefully track political developments and make projections beginning well in advance of the elections. The final column of table 7.6 includes the Evans and Novak assessments made in the fall of 1999, almost exactly one year before the election. Evans and Novak factor the identity and backgrounds of potential candidates into their evaluations. For the most part, Evans and Novak and we agree on the likely outcomes in open seats in the autumn of 2000. Every instance in which there is disagreement, Evans and Novak have identified the district as leaning toward one party—acknowledgment of a more fluid situation than in those districts that they identify as "probable" for a party and far more competitive than those labeled as "sure" for a party. With the exception of California's Fifteenth District, these are districts in which our projections indicate competitiveness, with the anticipated Republican vote between 45 and 55 percent.[6] Of the eight disagreements, five involve districts in which we estimate a Democratic victory, that is, the expected GOP vote is less than 50 percent, but which Evans and Novak see as leaning Republican (CA-15, OK-2, NJ-7, OH-12, and MI-8). In another three districts, we estimate that a Republican will poll more than 50 percent of the vote, whereas Evans and Novak see a Democratic advantage (MT-at large, WA-2, and IL-10). It will be interesting to see whether Evans and Novak, with their knowledge of possible candidates and consideration of the impact of particular candidacies, are more successful in this exercise than we are.

If most districts are projected to be retained by the party that currently holds them, even if they come open, where are the best targets of opportunity and the targets of futility? In table 7.7, we go beyond the districts that currently open in 2000 and identify the thirty most competitive districts and the fifteen safest districts for each party, should those districts not have an incumbent come filing time. The safest Democratic districts tend to be in the urban northeast, with the top four in New York City and those ranked fifth and sixth on the south side of Chicago. The only supersafe seats west of the Mississippi are in Los Angeles. All of the safest Democratic districts had minority legislators in the 106th Congress, with New York's Sixteenth District being predominately Hispanic, whereas the other fourteen districts had African American legislators. None of the fifteen safest Democratic districts are in the South. That none of the South's majority–minority districts ranked among the Democrats' safest underscores David Lublin's (1997) observation that outside the South, large numbers of liberals who are neither black nor Hispanic live in close proximity to minorities and can be used for drawing Democratic districts. In the South, creating Democratic districts is more dependent on the availability of minorities.

The safest GOP districts, by contrast, are spread across seven southern states and include Georgia's Sixth District, which former Speaker Newt Gingrich represented. Two districts are in Utah, whereas the remaining three are in the Midwest and include Dan Burton's Indiana Sixth District, the safest GOP district. However, because Republicans lack a constituency that matches the 90 percent loyalty that African American voters give Democrats, the safest GOP districts would give the majority party about two-thirds of the vote in an open seat—well below what Democrats could expect in their safest constituencies.

The most competitive districts are spread across the nation. Eight of the thirty (27 percent) are down South, which is roughly proportional to the

Table 7.7 Safest and Most Competitive Districts When Open

District	% GOP	District	% GOP
Safest Democratic Districts		*30 Most Competitive Districts*	
NY-11	6.64	WA-3	49.41
NY-16	8.35	OH-18	49.42
NY-15	8.69	FL-22	49.42
NY-10	9.71	GA-1	49.51
IL-1	10.78	PA-13	49.56
IL-2	11.06	PA-15	49.56
MI-15	11.29	WI-4	49.59
MI-14	11.75	NY-1	49.61
CA-35	12.31	CA-41	49.63
MD-7	12.57	GA-3	49.79
IL-7	13.21	WV-2	49.81
PA-2	13.67	NY-3	49.85
NY-6	13.90	OR-5	49.87
NJ-10	14.65	CT-5	49.94
CA-32	15.48	MI-1	49.96
		KY-6	50.00
Safest Republican Districts		FL-10	50.05
IN-6	67.79	FL-5	50.05
AL-6	67.67	NY-19	50.13
TX-19	67.43	NY-24	50.18
TX-21	66.71	WA-2	50.23
NC-2	66.07	MI-6	50.27
GA-6	66.06	PA-11	50.28
NC-10	66.02	IL-10	50.37
UT-1	65.90	MO-8	50.38
UT-3	65.33	MS-1	50.55
OH-2	64.50	MN-1	50.55
NC-6	64.44	FL-21	50.64
FL-1	64.05	MD-1	50.64
TN-1	63.91	TX-12	50.80
KS-1	63.88		
VA-7	63.75		

Note: A complete list of district competitiveness when open appears in the appendix.

region's share of the nation's population. Many are suburban districts that are adjacent to old centers of Democratic strength—a northern urban area or a rural southern region. All have at least a 45 percent chance of going to the out party, should they come open. The most balanced district in the nation, according to the model, is the Sixth Congressional District of Kentucky, in which each party is projected to get exactly 50 percent of the vote. In 1998, this district elected Republican Ernie Fletcher with 53 percent of the vote when the seat came open as former incumbent Scotty Baesler became the Democratic nominee for the U.S. Senate.[7]

Republicans have more at risk in the most competitive districts as they currently hold twenty of the seats. Until Michael Forbes (New York's First District) switched parties in July 1999, only nine of the thirty seats had Democratic incumbents. (Party switching may pay a marginal benefit to Forbes because the projected open seat vote is 49.6 percent for the GOP.) Republicans currently occupy seven of the seats in which the projected GOP vote is below 50 percent, whereas Democrats fill two seats in which the projected GOP vote exceeds 50 percent.

In 1998, three of these seats were open, and Brian Baird (D-WA) won as projected in table 7.7 with a 55 percent majority, replacing Republican Senate nominee Linda Smith. In Pennsylvania's Fifteenth District, Pat Toomey (R) also took 55 percent of the vote, about five points above what table 7.7 predicts. Toomey, Baird, and Fletcher each replaced a member of the opposite party—strong evidence of the competitive nature of these districts.

Another district (Pennsylvania's Thirteenth District) experienced a change in 1998 as Joseph Hoeffel (D) turned the tables after losing by eighty-four votes in 1996. As additional evidence of how competitive this district was during the 1990s, it is the same one in which Marjorie Margolies-Mezvinsky (D) lost 49 to 45 percent in 1994 after casting the decisive vote for President Clinton's 1993 budget proposal. Jon Fox, who was the Republican nominee in this district in each election from 1992 to 1998, got 49 percent of the vote in three contests, winning twice when minor party candidates opened the way for a plurality win before slipping to 47 percent in 1998. We estimate the GOP vote share in this district at 49.56 percent.

Although 1998 results in some districts reinforce the presence of competitiveness identified in table 7.7, elsewhere the power of incumbency is all too obvious. Georgia's First and Third Districts, along with Florida's Fifth, Tenth, and Twenty-second and Illinois's Tenth District, were won by the only major party candidate on the ballot.[8] Republicans hold all of these except for the three in Florida, which suggests that should these districts not have an incumbent in 2000, Democrats might well concentrate on them as they seek to regain a House majority. The two Georgia districts might be particularly likely to attract Democratic attention because with black populations in excess of 24 percent, they have a sizable base vote for the party.

PLAYING NOSTRADAMUS

It is fitting, at the beginning of a new millennium, to play prognosticator or seer. The vision we seek to conjure is: "What would the House look like if every seat came open in 2000?" Political scientists are hesitant to make forecasts beyond the confines of a morning coffee or a happy hour beer. Efforts at forecasting often prove accurate but can go awry. Despite our own wariness at looking to the future, we have examined scenarios to give readers a look at the likely tendencies of all the congressional districts in the United States, should they come open. In the forecasts, only one value varied from equation to equation: the value of presidential coattails. In all of the equations, the values of the other independent variables are the same as described in the appendix, and district-level results for all of the scenarios appear in the appendix. These forecasts are useful. First, they serve as a validity check on the open seat model; if these very early forecasts are accurate, they reinforce our contention that the expected open seat vote is a good indicator of the partisan tendency of the district. Second, these estimates, subject to variations in the expected value of presidential coattails, help identify which districts are more (or less) competitive and which districts might be more vulnerable to changes in national political tides.

We present five scenarios: (1) even division, in which the Republican two-party vote for all districts averages 50 percent; (2) marginal Democratic win, in which the average Republican two-party vote is 47 percent; (3) marginal Republican win, in which the average Republican two-party vote is 53 percent; (4) landslide Democratic win, in which the average Republican two-party vote is 43 percent; and (5) landslide Republican win, in which the average Republican two-party vote is 57 percent.

The district presidential vote was computed based on the "normal" presidential vote for each district for 1992 to 1996. The average normal vote for the Republican party is 45.44 percent. To adjust the vote in each district, we subtracted 45.44 from the national GOP vote specified in the five scenarios and then added the product to the GOP normal vote in each district to obtain an estimated presidential vote for 2000.[9]

Baseline Scenario: Even Division

What would a completely open-seat congressional election look like if the presidential parties were evenly matched? According to the data, it would probably produce a Democratic House of Representatives. The point estimates, results of which appear in the third column of table 7.8, indicate that, should they all come open, Democrats would be favored in 236 of the 412 districts analyzed (57.3 percent) and Republicans favored in 176 districts. Approximately 150 districts are partisan "battlegrounds" that have at least a one-in-four probability of going either way. This baseline estimate, which was also the basis for discussion of tables 7.6 and 7.7, indicates that, despite 1994, the basic tendency of the House of Representatives is toward a Democratic majority.

Why is this the case? First, Democrats have more "safer" districts than the Republicans. Applying David Mayhew's (1974) definition of a "safe" district—winner takes more than 55 percent of the vote—then more than 60 percent of the congressional districts in the United States are effectively safe even in the absence of an incumbent. Of those "one-party" districts, three-fifths are safe for the Democrats. The Democratic districts isolated from the partisan tides of American politics are in historically Democratic urban areas, and many have large minority populations. As James Campbell (1996) has observed, these are also lower-turnout districts that cost less in time and effort for Democrats to win and retain. Of the remaining 159 districts that are more closely in play, Democrats are slightly advantaged in 53 percent of the marginal, battleground districts.

A second reason for the projected Democratic majority is that the party is more likely to produce experienced candidates. According to Gaddie and McCollum (1998), the average probability of an experienced Democrat emerging in an open seat is .49, whereas for the Republicans, it is .42. In most districts, the probability of an experienced Democrat emerging is greater than that of an experienced Republican. Third, an "even" presidential performance advantages the Democratic party. With the exception of 1994, Republican open seat candidates have run behind the two-party normal vote in their district. In 1996 and 1998, they came closer to equaling the normal vote than in the 1980s, but the GOP normal vote in the 1990s was lower than in the 1980s. It takes an exceptional presidential performance to pull additional congressional districts over to the Republican congressional column.

Table 7.8   U.S. House Election Outcomes, under Different Scenarios

Type of District	Scenario				
	Democratic Landslide	Democratic Marginal	Even Division	Republican Marginal	Republican Landslide
Safe Democrat	186	166	151	134	117
Marginal Democrat	94	91	85	72	63
Marginal Republican	71	75	74	91	91
Safe Republican	61	80	102	115	141
GOP Average Vote	43.6	45.2	46.3	47.5	49.1
% GOP Seats	32.0	37.6	42.7	50.0	56.3

Republican Marginal Win

The 2000 race may be closely divided. But what if the Republican presidential nominee wins a clear majority, say by a 53 to 47 percent margin? What would the balance of Congress look like?

Under a 53 to 47 percent GOP marginal win, the value of coattails increases across all districts by 3 percentage points from the baseline scenario. Such an across-the-board increase is unlikely but, given that this is a scenario, it is the most easily explained and interpreted change to consider. A shift of 3 points toward the Republicans would increase the GOP congressional vote by 1.16 points. Although this does not seem like much, it is sufficient to shift 30 congressional districts into the Republican column, resulting in an even split of the 412 districts should they all be open. The first column of table 7.9 identifies the districts predicted to shift to the GOP should its nominee win the presidency narrowly in 2000. A comparison of the most competitive districts in table 7.7 and the GOP marginal win column of table 7.9 shows that districts in table 7.7 with an expected GOP vote below 50.01 are now projected as GOP wins. Only five of the Republican pickups are in the South, and another nine are out West, with the remaining sixteen located in the Midwest and on the East Coast. That only five additional GOP seats are predicted from the South indicates the scope of Republican gains during the 1990s in an environment that separated blacks and whites so as to create minority districts alongside heavily white ones likely to elect Republicans.

Democratic Marginal Win

To contrast against the Republican marginal win scenario, we estimated outcomes under a marginal 53 to 47 percent Democratic presidential victory. Under this scenario, the shift in the vote is the same size as a result of increased presidential coattails—1.16 points—but the shift is to the Democrats. In the absence of incumbency, Republicans would win only 155 seats, or 37.5 percent. This also approximates the observed Republican equilibrium of seats throughout most of the past half-century (Sprague 1980). From the baseline of an even division, twenty-one seats would shift away from the GOP under this scenario, as opposed to the thirty-seat Republican gain in the previous scenario. One-third of the switching districts reported in the third column of table 7.9 are in the South, with four in Florida alone (Fifth, Tenth, Eighteenth, and Twenty-first districts).[10] Only five of the switching districts were west of the Mississippi River and outside the South.

Republican Landslide

What if the Republicans stimulate an eight-year itch in the electorate so irritating that the GOP nominee wins a staggering victory? Although such

Table 7.9 Switching Districts in Marginal and Landslide Elections

Switch to Republican in		Switch to Democratic in	
Marginal Win	*Landslide*[a]	*Marginal Win*	*Landslide*
AZ-5	AL-3	CO-3	AL-1
CA-3	CA-10	FL-5	AL-5
CA-41	CA-11	FL-10	AZ-6
CA-43	CA-22	FL-18	CA-28
CT-5	CA-36	FL-21	CA-52
CT-6	IA-2	IA-4	IN-3
FL-22	IA-3	IL-10	IN-8
GA-1	IL-3	IL-15	KS-3
GA-3	IL-19	MD-1	KY-5
GA-8	KY-3	MI-6	MI-7
IL-20	MI-8	MN-1	MI-10
KY-6	MI-12	MN-2	MN-3
MI-1	MI-16	MO-8	MN-7
MO-6	MO-3	MS-1	MT-1
NC-7	NC-8	NY-13	NJ-12
NY-1	NJ-3	NY-19	OH-6
NY-3	NJ-7	NY-24	OH-19
OH-13	NY-25	PA-11	OK-6
OH-18	OH-10	TX-11	PA-8
OK-2	PA-4	TX-12	TN-3
OK-3	PA-12	WA-2	TN-6
OR-4	TX-1		TX-14
OR-5	VA-5		WA-8
PA-13	WI-1		
PA-15	WI-3		
PA-21	WI-7		
WA-1			
WA-3			
WI-4			
WV-2			

[a]All of the "marginal" district flips also occur with landslides.

an outcome is not likely, landslides must be considered, and they are often the source of tremendous changes in the composition of Congress. Republicans argued that, absent legislative incumbency, Ronald Reagan's landslide victory could have given them a House majority in the early 1980s. To test the impact of a landslide, we set the GOP presidential vote to an average of 57 percent, which would boost the GOP congressional vote from the baseline scenario by 2.71 points.

The GOP landslide scenario shifts fifty-six open seats to the GOP over the baseline and an additional twenty-six seats over the marginal GOP win. Republicans would have a clear majority of the House, 232 of the 412 seats analyzed (56.3 percent of seats). Of the gains above and beyond those predicted by the marginal GOP win scenario, four seats are in the South and another four are in California; most are in the Midwest and Northeast.

Democratic Landslide

Under open-seat conditions, a Democratic landslide produces a House of Representatives that harkens back to the era of the New Deal. If the Democratic presidential nominee were to win 57 percent of the vote, the model estimates a 280 to 132 Democratic majority (32 percent Republican seats). A total of forty-four Republican-leaning districts switch to the Democrats, including twenty-three districts that did not flip in the marginal Democratic scenario. Of those twenty-three new flips in the last column of table 7.9, five are in the South and five are out West (excluding Texas).

"Swingers" and "Kickers"

What does this application reveal about congressional elections? It indicates that both parties have stable bases that are not disrupted by partisan tides. Even under extreme conditions of landslide victories, the parties remain viable, even without their incumbents.

With the elimination of incumbents, most of the volatility in American congressional elections is confined to about one hundred districts, or just under one-quarter of all seats. Indeed, the districts most likely to change hands with minor shifts in the national tides—the "swingers"—only constitute 51 of 412 districts examined. Over half of the swingers are located in the Midwest and Northeast, and about a fifth are in the South and trans-Mississippi West, respectively. Eight of the twelve southern swingers are in Florida and Georgia.

The remaining districts that change hands in landslides kick over only when more extreme partisan tides are present. These districts—the "kickers"—are a bonus to a party that has a landslide election. Again, only about half of the kickers are in the South or West; most are in the Midwest and Northeast.

Most districts potentially vulnerable to partisan tides when open are in the Midwest and Northeast, especially in the industrial and older suburban districts. These are districts that, fifty years ago, would have been bedrock Republican districts. Now, after four decades of economic restructuring and emigration, they are highly competitive. Only 20 percent of southern and western districts were swingers or kickers, compared with 30 percent of midwestern and northeastern districts. This is especially interesting, given that the battle for president has been waged in the last two elections in the old industrial Midwest. Despite the increase in competition in the South and the large number of district shifts in that region since 1990 (an additional thirty-two GOP seats), the districts in which congressional control is likely to be determined are in a part of the nation that is consistently losing political clout in the aggregate.

CONCLUSION

At the beginning of this volume, we set out to trace the dynamic of congressional elections by looking underneath the veneer of incumbency and observing the latent competition that exists in congressional constituencies. It was our intention to identify the significant factors that influence congressional elections in the absence of incumbents and then use those factors to understand the extent to which congressional elections are competitive. The results of this study indicate that the speculation of Goidel and Shields (1994) is accurate: there is not as much competition in open seats as is often assumed. However, the open seats are more competitive than the incumbent contests, and, in turn, they are also more volatile, producing greater partisan change and enhancing the influence of national electoral tides on the balance of seats in Congress. At the margins, these elections are influenced by the same constituency and candidate factors that are also important to those who challenge incumbents.

On another level, our projections of the vote in congressional districts indicate that there is a disjunction in American politics that disadvantages the Republican party. According to our estimated district outcomes, the Republican party requires a convincing presidential victory to swing an all-open-seat Congress to the Republican column. The bias in the tendencies of the districts might be a product of the models or the cases analyzed; however, the predictive validity of our model indicates otherwise. The House tends to the Democratic party, under circumstances that indicate even competition for president at the national level. Twenty years ago, political scientist John Sprague (1980) speculated that the sustained Democratic majority in the House was a product of biases in safe seats, as a result possibly of redistricting or incumbency advantages that favored the Democrats. Starting from an even division of the House in 1930, Sprague demonstrated that the party system moved inexorably toward an equilibrium that was dominated by the Democrats holding more than 60 percent of seats. Our equilibrium presidential election projection indicates a 58 percent Democratic majority; much of the bias that Sprague uncovered is in fact the product of the underlying competitiveness of the districts in general, with an enhancing influence by incumbency on the side.

NOTES

1. Several legislators initially elected in 1994 after promising to limit their service to six years, recanted.

2. This proposition is borne out by an examination of the relationship between the district normal vote and the GOP congressional vote for the 1996 and 1998 elections. In both years, the GOP vote share in the open seats tracks closely with the normal vote. The normal vote for president is lower in 1996 and 1998 than at any point in our analysis; therefore, a weaker Republican performance in the open seats was likely.

3. Gaddie and McCollum argue that the incumbency advantage is the difference between the incumbent's actual vote in a district and what the incumbent's party would receive were the seat open. This is the same logic as behind Alford and Brady's "surge–slump" measure of incumbency advantage. Gaddie and McCollum extend the application of surge–slump by estimating an "expected" open seat vote for every district.

4. Gaddie and McCollum found that the dummy-variable indicator of spending advantage did not reduce the fit of the model to open seat election outcomes nor did it temporize or otherwise influence the slopes of the other predictive variables.

5. They produced an "estimated" value of the expected experience of the Republican and Democratic candidates by first estimating the likelihood that an experienced Democrat or Republican would emerge in an open seat, using a model similar to that of Bond, Fleisher, and Talbert (1997). The values of the predictor variables for experience are then entered into the equation to produce probabilities that experienced candidates emerge for each party in the district. Those probabilities are bounded by 0 and 1 and are then entered as the value of experience for the respective parties in each district, should the district come open. A similar process is used to estimate whether the Republican has the spending advantage.

6. The expected Republican vote in California's Fifteenth District (44.92) is just below the 45 percent threshold.

7. Baesler lost his Senate bid by fewer than ten thousand votes, the narrowest margin in 1998 Senate elections. It is rumored that he will try to regain his House seat in 2000.

8. Karen Thurman (D) won her fourth term in Florida's Fifth District, facing only a candidate of the Reform Party. That Thurman lost a third of the vote to the minor party candidate suggests that had a Republican come forward, the GOP nominee might have been competitive. In her initial election in what was then a newly drawn district, Thurman beat a Republican by a 49 to 43 percent margin. In the other five districts, the incumbent faced no general election challenge in winning reelection in 1998.

9. For the Even Division scenario, the adjustment was +4.56; for Marginal Republican Win, +7.56; for Marginal Democratic Win, +1.56; for Landslide Republican Win, +11.56; and for Landslide Democratic Win, −2.44.

10. Florida's Fifth District has been held by Democrat Karen Thurman since its creation in 1992. This points out that projections from models do not fully match reality. The relative strengths of competing candidates as measured on dimensions such as experience and fund-raising can generate outcomes at variance with the model's predictions.

Appendix

Forecasting the Open Seat Vote

How competitive is a district, absent the incumbent? What is the district's partisan tendency? How does a contest with an incumbent differ from the estimated level of competition were the district open? Gaddie and McCollum (1998) assumed that knowledge about the partisanship of a district, absent the incumbent, would help measure the incumbency advantage. This assumption rested on extensive prior political science research, especially the work of John Alford and David Brady (1989) on surge–slump analysis, and of Andrew Gelman and Gary King (1991), who sought to ascertain the aggregate value of incumbency for all incumbents in a given year. Both teams of scholars approached the notion of measuring the incumbency advantage as a value that was different from an open seat vote. To extend the measurement of the incumbency advantage, Gaddie and McCollum seek to develop expected votes in districts, given the absence of an incumbent and based on the likely tendencies of the district in terms of spending and candidate experience.

How does one translate the research on open seat elections into a viable measure of incumbency advantage? As we showed in chapter 2, there is sufficient research on the structure of open seat elections that indicates that those races are structured by constituency, partisan, and candidate attributes, especially campaign finance and political experience. Research on open seat elections in the 1980s and 1990s found that national political tides also structured competition (Flemming 1995; Abramowitz 1991b; Theilemann 1990). These findings reflect Jacobson's (1990, 1997a) findings about congressional elections involving incumbents: money, experience, and favorable constituencies structured election outcomes. These are very robust models, typically explaining between 60 percent and 80 percent of the variation in open seat election outcomes.

Gaddie and McCollum gathered data on open seat elections from 1988 to 1996 and then estimated a regression equation for competition for those districts. The parameters of the open seat model were then used to generate election results for every congressional district, subject to variations in the political and constituency factors that affect election outcomes. The difference between the estimated partisan vote in the absence of incumbency and the actual electoral outcome with the incumbent present indicates the magnitude of the incumbency advantage.

THE OPEN SEAT MODEL

The open-seats model was used to estimate the results of all open-seat contests between 1988 and 1996. The model incorporated the experience measures for both candidates (dichotomous variables indicating whether the candidate had held prior elective office; see also Jacobson 1990, and Bond, Fleisher, and Talbert 1997) and an indication of which candidate had the spending advantage (a dichotomous variable coded 1 if the GOP candidate had the advantage, 0 otherwise), as well as a normal vote control for the baseline partisanship of the district and controls for the black and Hispanic populations in the district (see Gaddie 1995a; Bond, Fleisher, and Talbert 1997). Because the data set incorporates elections from multiple years, a series of year-shift control variables were included for the years 1988, 1990, 1992, and 1994.

The results of the analysis appear in table A.1. Candidate attributes (experience and spending advantage) and constituency factors (e.g., partisan history and racial composition) are significantly related to electoral outcomes. The model was robust, explaining three-quarters of the variance in the GOP share of the two-party vote.

We will not elaborate here on the interpretation of the coefficients; it is sufficient to note that the results are entirely consistent with prior findings on open-seat contests. However, controlling for the spending advantage with a dichotomy has not detracted from the fit of the model, the significance of holding the spending advantage, or the slopes and significance of the other coefficients. In table A.1, we also present a model that uses the net Republican spending advantage (Republican spending minus Democratic spending) to control the effect of spending on open seats; all other specified variables are coded in the same manner as specified in model I. An examination of the two regression equations in table A.1 reveals that they are virtually identical, except that the slope and standard error for the spending advantage have changed in response to the change in the metric of the variable. These are effectively identical models, except that one has an operationalization of candidate spending for which we can easily generate values for our predictions.

The open seat model is effective in explaining and predicting the outcomes of elections without incumbents. However, the design of the model relies in part on having knowledge of candidate experience and financial advantage.

Incumbents stifle quality challengers. In the absence of incumbents, where do the candidates come from? What is the balance of financial quality? One solution to the problem of developing a measure for candidate experience and partisan funding advantage is to hold the effects of candidate experience and spending constant; that is, to assume that there is no spending advantage and that the level of experience is the same for all candidates or to assume spending and experience effects based on the null case for observed open seats. These are unrealistic constructions of open seat races. As we noted in chapters 3 and 4, most open seat races since 1982 feature candidates with unequal experience, and relatively few feature candidates who spend approximately equal amounts of money. Neutralizing the effects of those variables necessarily creates inaccurate estimates of the "unbiased" vote and reduces the prediction largely to a function of the normal vote and constituency attributes. Gaddie and McCollum instead generated "best estimates" of the expected experience of both parties' candidates and of the direction of the spending advantage. The estimated experience and spending figures for each district were then multiplied by the appropriate regression coefficients to facilitate the generation of an estimated level of competition absent incumbents.

Table A.1   Gaddie and McCollum's Estimates of Open Seat Election Outcomes, 1988–1994

Variables	I		II	
	b	SE_b	b	SE_b
Intercept	21.95	3.45***	23.08	3.46***
Republican Spending Advantage[a]	2.84	1.06**	.36	.10***
Democratic Political Experience	−3.25	.98***	−3.25	.98***
Republican Political Experience	3.47	.99***	3.60	.98***
Percent Black Population	−.14	.04***	−.14	.04***
Percent Hispanic Population	−.09	.04*	−.09	.04***
Normal GOP Vote (President)	.56	.06***	.57	.06***
1988 Year Control	−7.05	1.82***	−7.22	1.81***
1990 Year Control	−6.23	1.60***	−6.03	1.59***
1992 Year Control	−4.66	1.30***	−4.54	1.30***
1994 Year Control	5.75	1.33***	5.86	1.31***
R^2	.74		.75	
Adjusted-R^2	.73		.74	
SE	6.50		6.45	

Note: Dependent variable is the Republican candidate two-party vote at the district level; $N = 221$.

[a]In the first model the spending advantage is coded 1 if the Republican has the spending advantage, 0 otherwise. In the second model the spending advantage is spending by the Republican, minus spending by the Democrat, in $100,000 of 1996 dollars.

*p < .05, two-tailed test; **p < .01, two-tailed test; ***p < .001, two-tailed test.

Bond, Fleisher, and Talbert (1997) dealt directly with the problem of the emergence of experienced open seat candidates. Their model, which considered district partisanship (the normal vote and the incumbent's party), national factors (presidential approval and the state of the economy; see also Jacobson 1992), and the timing of the incumbent retirement, found that only district partisanship factors structured experienced candidate emergence. Related research by Canon (1990) found that experienced challenger emergence was tied to the size and partisan balance in the pool of potential quality candidates. In the absence of incumbents, the probability of winning is affected by the perceived partisan balance of the constituency. Districts that favor a party will most likely attract a quality challenger *as a result of favorable odds.* In addition, when there is a larger pool of experienced candidates, an experienced candidate should emerge, though a largely Republican pool may be less likely to produce an experienced Democrat, especially compared with a heavily Democratic pool.

Gaddie and McCollum translated this knowledge into a simulation of candidate experience by estimating the likelihood of the emergence of an experienced candidate using logistic regression. This technique generated coefficients that reflect the potential for an increase or decrease in the probability of getting the outcome of interest (a value of 1). Logistic regression therefore could be used to generate probabilities of an experienced candidate emerging for each congressional district. Those probabilities became a substitute for whether a hypothetical candidate in a district was experienced or not: the probability of an experienced candidate emerging in a particular district.[1] The substitution of probabilities will help us generate predictions that are based on the tendency of the district toward or away from having experienced nominees and thereby serves as a more conservative estimate of the impact of experience. The results of the logistic regressions appear in table A.2. The model does well in predicting the emergence of experienced candidates: about 70 percent of cases are correctly predicted for both Democrats and Republicans, and the proportional reduction in error over the null prediction is substantial.

A similar data problem with the spending advantage was overcome using the same technique. The financing of congressional elections is interactive and dynamic: the financial quality of one candidate depends on that of the other, especially in open seats (cf., Box-Steffensmeier 1996 on the dynamic and interactive nature of candidate fund-raising and spending). Recall that the regression in table A.1, with the dichotomous term for financial advantage, was also estimated with a companion regression using a linear (net advantage) spending variable. There was no difference in the fit of the model, slopes of other variables, or the significance of the two measures. The dichotomy was just as effective a measure for predicting outcomes, and the ability to predict who has the financial advantage

Table A.2   Logistic Regression Estimates of Experienced Candidate
Emergence

	Democratic Experience		Republican Experience	
Variable	b	SE_b	b	SE_b
Constant	3.5631	1.4579*	.0523	.0203**
Normal GOP Vote (President)	−.0653	.0215**	−.0091	.0051
Experienced Candidate Pool	.0128	.0064*	−.0022	.0139
GOP Pool Share	−.0210	.0139	.0490	.1639
Incumbent's Party	−.4103	.1662*	−.0825	.0216***
Percent Black Population	.0160	.0167	−.0210	.0139
Percent Hispanic Population	−.0093	.0141	−.4508	.6227
1988 Year Control	2.0674	.6797**	.3941	.5738
1990 Year Control	1.0453	.5687	.3845	.4592
1992 Year Control	1.7434	.4666**	.0113	.4515
1994 Year Control	.5011	.4529	−1.6667	1.3221
Correct Prediction	71.0%		69.7%	
Null Prediction	61.9%		50.2%	
PRE	23.9%		39.6%	
−2 Log-Likelihood	242.48		245.51	

Note: Dependent variable is a dichotomous variable coded 1 if a candidate has office-holding experience, 0 otherwise; $N = 221$.
*$p < .05$, two-tailed test; **$p < .01$, two-tailed test; ***$p < .001$, two-tailed test.

was not hindered by dynamic interactive effects. Gaddie and McCollum again use logistic regression to generate a probability, in this instance the probability of a Republican having the spending advantage in an open seat contest.

This equation did an excellent job of predicting the spending advantage (see table A.3). More than three-quarters of cases are correctly predicted, and the proportional reduction in error is 45.7 percent. Most of the equation's explanatory power is derived from the normal vote measure. Again, we are less concerned with explaining why someone has the spending advantage; the probability that the GOP has the spending advantage is our principal concern. Now we can also generate probabilities of Republican spending at the district level that are constrained by the boundaries of our spending advantage variable. In effect, we have changed dichotomous variables into bounded continuous variables.

The use of dummy variables for experience and spending means that the slope coefficients represent intercept shifts based on presence/absence of these attributes. Based on the logits, we can generate probabilities of those attributes being present, and those probabilities are necessarily bounded by 0 and 1, like the dummy variables themselves. We can introduce those probabilities into the equations to generate our predicted values of Y,

Table A.3   **Logistic Regression Estimates of the Republican Spending Advantage**

Variable	b	SE_b
Constant	−9.7710	1.6672***
Normal GOP Vote (President)	.1868	.0304***
Incumbent's Party	.1449	.1760
Percent Black Population	−.0263	.0219
Percent Hispanic Population	.0088	.0171
1988 Year Control	−1.6918	.7033*
1990 Year Control	−1.0097	.5944
1992 Year Control	−1.4046	.5075**
1994 Year Control	.9517	.4924*
Correct Prediction	77.0%	
Null Prediction	57.7%	
PRE	45.7%	
−2 Log-Likelihood	214.33	

Note: Dependent variable is a dichotomous variable coded 1 if the Republican candidate has a spending advantage, 0 otherwise; $N = 221$.
*p < .05, two-tailed test; **p < .01, two-tailed test; ***p < .001, two-tailed test.

reflecting the *tendency* of that district to produce experienced Democrats or Republicans and its tendency to produce a GOP spending advantage. The information constraint (previously described) for generating predicted values of the two-party vote using the open-seats model has now been removed.

The results of such an application appear in table A.1; in table A.4, we take the regression estimates from table 7.5 in the last chapter and use Gaddie and McCollum's estimates of spending advantage and candidate experience, along with the estimated size of the presidential coattails influence in each district (described in chapter 7), to generate a series of expected election outcomes for congressional districts in the United States, should they come open in 2000.

**Table A.4 District Level Vote Projections for Five Scenarios Assuming
Complete Open Seats**

District Vote Projections for 2000
(Assuming the seat is open)

Each column represents the district-level results for one of the scenarios
described in chapter 7. The last column is the probability that the GOP
retains a seat, based on the point-estimated vote from scenario A.

Scenario A: Perfect division of the presidential vote at 50%
Scenario B: Marginal GOP win (53%–47%)
Scenario C: Marginal Democratic win (47%–53%)
Scenario D: Landslide GOP win (57%–43%)
Scenario E: Landslide Democratic win (43%–57%)

STATE	CD	A	B	C	D	E	P(R)[a]
AK	1	58.90	60.06	57.74	61.61	56.19	.89
AL	1	51.78	52.94	50.62	54.49	49.07	.59
AL	2	55.24	56.41	54.08	57.95	52.54	.76
AL	3	48.78	49.94	47.62	51.49	46.07	.43
AL	4	55.95	57.11	54.79	58.66	53.24	.79
AL	5	51.69	52.85	50.53	54.40	48.98	.59
AL	6	67.67	68.83	66.51	70.38	64.96	.99
AL	7	19.95	21.11	18.79	22.66	17.24	.99
AR	1	39.55	40.71	38.39	42.26	36.84	.08
AR	2	41.66	42.82	40.50	44.37	38.95	.12
AR	3	56.18	57.34	55.02	58.89	53.47	.80
AR	4	36.73	37.89	35.57	39.44	34.02	.04
AZ	1	53.60	54.76	52.44	56.31	50.89	.69
AZ	2	31.46	32.62	30.30	34.17	28.75	.01
AZ	3	56.29	57.45	55.13	59.00	53.58	.81
AZ	4	57.26	58.42	56.10	59.97	54.55	.84
AZ	5	49.27	50.43	48.11	51.98	46.56	.46
AZ	6	51.88	53.05	50.72	54.59	49.18	.59
CA	1	44.52	45.68	43.36	47.23	41.81	.23
CA	2	57.76	58.92	56.60	60.47	55.05	.85
CA	3	48.92	50.09	47.76	51.63	46.22	.44
CA	4	58.05	59.22	56.89	60.76	55.35	.86
CA	5	37.74	38.90	36.58	40.45	35.03	.05
CA	6	39.70	40.86	38.54	42.41	36.99	.07
CA	7	31.60	32.76	30.44	34.31	28.89	.01
CA	8	27.76	28.92	26.60	30.47	25.05	.01
CA	9	21.41	22.58	20.25	24.12	18.71	.01
CA	10	48.49	49.65	47.33	51.20	45.78	.42
CA	11	48.44	49.61	47.28	51.15	45.74	.41
CA	12	37.42	38.58	36.26	40.13	34.71	.04

continued

Table A.4 Continued

District Vote Projections for 2000
(Assuming the seat is open)

Each column represents the district-level results for one of the scenarios described in chapter 7. The last column is the probability that the GOP retains a seat, based on the point-estimated vote from scenario A.

Scenario A: Perfect division of the presidential vote at 50%
Scenario B: Marginal GOP win (53%–47%)
Scenario C: Marginal Democratic win (47%–53%)
Scenario D: Landslide GOP win (57%–43%)
Scenario E: Landslide Democratic win (43%–57%)

STATE	CD	A	B	C	D	E	P(R)[a]
CA	13	35.88	37.04	34.72	38.59	33.17	.02
CA	14	39.04	40.21	37.88	41.75	36.34	.07
CA	15	44.92	46.08	43.76	47.63	42.21	.24
CA	16	34.23	35.39	33.07	36.94	31.52	.01
CA	17	36.73	37.89	35.57	39.44	34.02	.04
CA	18	47.10	48.26	45.94	49.81	44.39	.35
CA	19	53.73	54.90	52.57	56.44	51.03	.70
CA	20	37.08	38.25	35.92	39.79	34.38	.04
CA	21	57.95	59.11	56.79	60.66	55.24	.86
CA	22	47.56	48.73	46.40	50.27	44.86	.37
CA	23	46.98	48.14	45.82	49.69	44.27	.34
CA	24	43.61	44.77	42.45	46.32	40.90	.19
CA	25	52.71	53.87	51.55	55.42	50.00	.65
CA	26	28.88	30.05	27.72	31.59	26.18	.01
CA	27	46.27	47.43	45.11	48.98	43.56	.30
CA	28	51.70	52.87	50.54	54.41	49.00	.59
CA	29	35.06	36.22	33.90	37.77	32.35	.01
CA	30	26.42	27.58	25.26	29.13	23.71	.01
CA	31	31.82	32.98	30.66	34.53	29.11	.01
CA	32	15.48	16.64	14.32	18.19	12.77	.01
CA	33	20.52	21.69	19.36	23.23	17.82	.01
CA	34	31.37	32.53	30.21	34.08	28.66	.01
CA	35	12.31	13.47	11.15	15.02	9.60	.01
CA	36	47.30	48.46	46.14	50.01	44.59	.36
CA	37	15.75	16.91	14.59	18.46	13.04	.01
CA	38	41.20	42.36	40.04	43.91	38.49	.11
CA	39	54.25	55.41	53.09	56.96	51.54	.72
CA	40	54.01	55.17	52.85	56.72	51.30	.71
CA	41	49.63	50.79	48.47	52.34	46.92	.49
CA	42	36.78	37.94	35.62	39.49	34.07	.03
CA	43	49.05	50.21	47.89	51.76	46.34	.45

Table A.4 Continued

District Vote Projections for 2000
(Assuming the seat is open)
Each column represents the district-level results for one of the scenarios described in chapter 7. The last column is the probability that the GOP retains a seat, based on the point-estimated vote from scenario A.
Scenario A: Perfect division of the presidential vote at 50%
Scenario B: Marginal GOP win (53%–47%)
Scenario C: Marginal Democratic win (47%–53%)
Scenario D: Landslide GOP win (57%–43%)
Scenario E: Landslide Democratic win (43%–57%)

STATE	CD	A	B	C	D	E	P(R)[a]
CA	44	46.98	48.15	45.82	49.69	44.28	.34
CA	45	57.62	58.78	56.46	60.33	54.91	.85
CA	46	43.12	44.29	41.96	45.83	40.42	.18
CA	47	59.64	60.80	58.48	62.35	56.93	.91
CA	48	58.95	60.11	57.79	61.66	56.24	.89
CA	49	45.84	47.01	44.68	48.55	43.14	.29
CA	50	32.13	33.29	30.97	34.84	29.42	.01
CA	51	57.24	58.40	56.08	59.95	54.53	.84
CA	52	52.32	53.48	51.16	55.03	49.61	.62
CO	1	33.99	35.15	32.83	36.70	31.28	.01
CO	2	46.31	47.47	45.15	49.02	43.60	.69
CO	3	50.82	51.98	49.66	53.53	48.11	.54
CO	4	54.50	55.66	53.34	57.21	51.79	.72
CO	5	61.81	62.97	60.65	64.52	59.10	.94
CO	6	54.19	55.36	53.03	56.90	51.49	.72
CT	1	36.61	37.77	35.45	39.32	33.90	.04
CT	2	43.70	44.87	42.54	46.41	41.00	.19
CT	3	40.50	41.66	39.34	43.21	37.79	.10
CT	4	44.65	45.81	43.49	47.36	41.94	.23
CT	5	49.94	51.11	48.78	52.65	47.24	.50
CT	6	48.89	50.05	47.73	51.60	46.18	.45
DE	1	41.73	42.90	40.57	44.44	39.03	.13
FL	1	64.05	65.21	62.89	66.76	61.34	.97
FL	2	46.07	47.24	44.91	48.78	43.37	.29
FL	3	35.02	36.18	33.86	37.73	32.31	.02
FL	4	61.14	62.30	59.98	63.85	58.43	.94
FL	5	50.05	51.21	48.89	52.76	47.34	.50
FL	6	62.01	63.17	60.85	64.72	59.30	.95
FL	7	58.84	60.00	57.68	61.55	56.13	.89
FL	8	58.71	59.88	57.55	61.42	56.01	.89

continued

Table A.4 Continued

District Vote Projections for 2000
(Assuming the seat is open)

Each column represents the district-level results for one of the scenarios described in chapter 7. The last column is the probability that the GOP retains a seat, based on the point-estimated vote from scenario A.

Scenario A: Perfect division of the presidential vote at 50%

Scenario B: Marginal GOP win (53%–47%)

Scenario C: Marginal Democratic win (47%–53%)

Scenario D: Landslide GOP win (57%–43%)

Scenario E: Landslide Democratic win (43%–57%)

STATE	CD	A	B	C	D	E	P(R)[a]
FL	9	57.79	58.95	56.63	60.50	55.08	.86
FL	10	50.05	51.21	48.89	52.76	47.34	.50
FL	11	44.32	45.48	43.16	47.03	41.61	.22
FL	12	55.16	56.32	54.00	57.87	52.45	.76
FL	13	57.96	59.13	56.80	60.67	55.26	.86
FL	14	61.22	62.38	60.06	63.93	58.51	.94
FL	15	58.96	60.12	57.80	61.67	56.25	.89
FL	16	55.16	56.32	54.00	57.87	52.45	.76
FL	17	15.80	16.97	14.64	18.51	13.10	.01
FL	18	51.06	52.22	49.90	53.77	48.35	.55
FL	19	43.73	44.89	42.57	46.44	41.02	.20
FL	20	44.65	45.81	43.49	47.36	41.94	.23
FL	21	50.64	51.80	49.48	53.35	47.93	.53
FL	22	49.42	50.58	48.26	52.13	46.71	.47
FL	23	22.96	24.12	21.80	25.67	20.25	.01
GA	1	49.51	50.67	48.35	52.22	46.80	.47
GA	2	39.73	40.89	38.57	42.44	37.02	.08
GA	3	49.79	50.95	48.63	52.50	47.08	.49
GA	4	33.08	34.24	31.92	35.79	30.37	.01
GA	5	18.74	19.90	17.58	21.45	16.03	.01
GA	6	66.06	67.22	64.90	68.77	63.35	.99
GA	7	58.85	60.01	57.69	61.56	56.14	.89
GA	8	48.98	50.15	47.82	51.69	46.28	.45
GA	9	55.23	56.39	54.07	57.94	52.52	.77
GA	10	41.79	42.95	40.63	44.50	39.08	.87
GA	11	53.46	54.62	52.30	56.17	50.75	.68
HI	1	44.51	45.67	43.35	47.22	41.80	.22
HI	2	42.23	43.39	41.07	44.94	39.52	.14
IA	1	47.19	48.35	46.03	49.90	44.48	.35
IA	2	48.30	49.46	47.14	51.01	45.59	.41
IA	3	48.54	49.70	47.38	51.25	45.83	.43

Table A.4 Continued

District Vote Projections for 2000
(Assuming the seat is open)
Each column represents the district-level results for one of the scenarios described in chapter 7. The last column is the probability that the GOP retains a seat, based on the point-estimated vote from scenario A.
Scenario A: Perfect division of the presidential vote at 50%
Scenario B: Marginal GOP win (53%–47%)
Scenario C: Marginal Democratic win (47%–53%)
Scenario D: Landslide GOP win (57%–43%)
Scenario E: Landslide Democratic win (43%–57%)

STATE	CD	A	B	C	D	E	P(R)[a]
IA	4	50.89	52.06	49.73	53.60	48.19	.54
IA	5	55.53	56.69	54.37	58.24	52.82	.78
ID	1	60.16	61.32	59.00	62.87	57.45	.92
ID	2	62.33	63.50	61.17	65.04	59.63	.96
IL	1	10.78	11.94	9.62	13.49	8.07	.01
IL	2	11.06	12.22	9.90	13.77	8.35	.01
IL	3	47.93	49.09	46.77	50.64	45.22	.41
IL	4	23.02	24.18	21.86	25.73	20.31	.01
IL	5	41.59	42.75	40.43	44.30	38.88	.12
IL	6	58.52	59.68	57.36	61.23	55.81	.08
IL	7	13.21	14.38	12.05	15.92	10.51	.01
IL	8	59.49	60.65	58.33	62.20	56.78	.90
IL	9	34.62	35.78	33.46	37.33	31.91	.02
IL	10	50.37	51.54	49.21	53.08	47.67	.52
IL	11	45.65	46.82	44.49	48.36	42.95	.27
IL	12	38.04	39.21	36.88	40.75	35.34	.05
IL	13	59.15	60.32	57.99	61.86	56.45	.89
IL	14	55.97	57.13	54.81	58.68	53.26	.79
IL	15	50.87	52.03	49.71	53.58	48.16	.54
IL	16	55.00	56.16	53.84	57.71	52.29	.75
IL	17	46.94	48.11	45.78	49.65	44.24	.34
IL	18	53.31	54.47	52.15	56.02	50.60	.68
IL	19	47.72	48.88	46.56	50.43	45.01	.37
IL	20	48.92	50.08	47.76	51.63	46.21	.44
IN	1	34.95	36.12	33.79	37.66	32.25	.02
IN	2	56.07	57.23	54.91	58.78	53.36	.80
IN	3	52.41	53.57	51.25	55.12	49.70	.62
IN	4	59.79	60.95	58.63	62.50	57.08	.91
IN	5	60.85	62.01	59.69	63.56	58.14	.93
IN	6	67.79	68.96	66.63	70.50	65.09	.99

continued

Table A.4 Continued

District Vote Projections for 2000
(Assuming the seat is open)
Each column represents the district-level results for one of the scenarios described in chapter 7. The last column is the probability that the GOP retains a seat, based on the point-estimated vote from scenario A.
Scenario A: Perfect division of the presidential vote at 50%
Scenario B: Marginal GOP win (53%–47%)
Scenario C: Marginal Democratic win (47%–53%)
Scenario D: Landslide GOP win (57%–43%)
Scenario E: Landslide Democratic win (43%–57%)

STATE	CD	A	B	C	D	E	P(R)[a]
IN	7	61.37	62.54	60.21	64.08	58.67	.94
IN	8	52.49	53.65	51.33	55.20	49.78	.63
IN	9	52.77	53.94	51.61	55.48	50.07	.65
IN	10	36.40	37.56	35.24	39.11	33.69	.03
KS	1	63.88	65.04	62.72	66.59	61.17	.97
KS	2	54.03	55.19	52.87	56.74	51.32	.71
KS	3	51.90	53.06	50.74	54.61	49.19	.60
KS	4	57.64	58.80	56.48	60.35	54.93	.85
KY	1	48.45	49.61	47.29	51.16	45.74	.42
KY	2	55.24	56.40	54.08	57.95	52.53	.77
KY	3	41.60	42.76	40.44	44.31	38.89	.12
KY	4	57.01	58.17	55.85	59.72	54.30	.83
KY	5	51.89	53.06	50.73	54.60	49.19	.60
KY	6	50.00	51.16	48.84	52.71	47.29	.50
LA	1	—	—	—	—	—	
LA	2	19.19	20.35	18.03	21.90	16.48	.01
LA	3	—	—	—	—	—	
LA	4	—	—	—	—	—	
LA	5	—	—	—	—	—	
LA	6	—	—	—	—	—	
LA	7	—	—	—	—	—	
MA	1	40.56	41.72	39.40	43.27	37.85	.10
MA	2	39.93	41.09	38.77	42.64	37.22	.08
MA	3	42.88	44.04	41.72	45.59	40.17	.16
MA	4	40.54	41.70	39.38	43.25	37.83	.10
MA	5	43.23	44.39	42.07	45.94	40.52	.17
MA	6	43.73	44.89	42.57	46.44	41.02	.19
MA	7	41.06	42.23	39.90	43.77	38.36	.21
MA	8	26.69	27.85	25.53	29.40	23.98	.01
MA	9	39.99	41.15	38.83	42.70	37.28	.08
MA	10	45.38	46.54	44.22	48.09	42.67	.26

Table A.4 Continued

District Vote Projections for 2000
(Assuming the seat is open)
Each column represents the district-level results for one of the scenarios
described in chapter 7. The last column is the probability that the GOP
retains a seat, based on the point-estimated vote from scenario A.
Scenario A: Perfect division of the presidential vote at 50%
Scenario B: Marginal GOP win (53%–47%)
Scenario C: Marginal Democratic win (47%–53%)
Scenario D: Landslide GOP win (57%–43%)
Scenario E: Landslide Democratic win (43%–57%)

STATE	CD	A	B	C	D	E	P(R)[a]
MD	1	50.64	51.81	49.48	53.35	47.94	.53
MD	2	56.43	57.60	55.27	59.14	53.73	.81
MD	3	37.74	38.91	36.58	40.45	35.04	.05
MD	4	16.40	17.56	15.24	19.11	13.69	.01
MD	5	41.91	43.08	40.75	44.62	39.21	.13
MD	6	59.28	60.44	58.12	61.99	56.57	.90
MD	7	12.57	13.73	11.41	15.28	9.86	.01
MD	8	42.81	43.98	41.65	45.52	40.11	.16
ME	1	45.32	46.48	44.16	48.03	42.61	.26
ME	2	44.67	45.83	43.51	47.38	41.96	.23
MI	1	49.96	51.12	48.80	52.67	47.25	.49
MI	2	57.78	58.95	56.62	60.49	55.08	.86
MI	3	57.95	59.11	56.79	60.66	55.24	.86
MI	4	53.03	54.19	51.87	55.74	50.32	.66
MI	5	43.44	44.60	42.28	46.15	40.73	.18
MI	6	50.27	51.44	49.11	52.98	47.57	.52
MI	7	51.81	52.97	50.65	54.52	49.10	.60
MI	8	47.83	48.99	46.67	50.54	45.12	.49
MI	9	41.10	42.26	39.94	43.81	38.39	.11
MI	10	52.54	53.70	51.38	55.25	49.83	.63
MI	11	55.53	56.69	54.37	58.24	52.82	.78
MI	12	48.61	49.77	47.45	51.32	45.90	.43
MI	13	41.59	42.75	40.43	44.30	38.88	.12
MI	14	11.75	12.91	10.59	14.46	9.04	.01
MI	15	11.29	12.45	10.13	14.00	8.58	.01
MI	16	47.37	48.53	46.21	50.08	44.66	.36
MN	1	50.55	51.71	49.39	53.26	47.84	.53
MN	2	50.84	52.00	49.68	53.55	48.13	.55
MN	3	52.31	53.48	51.15	55.02	49.61	.62
MN	4	41.22	42.38	40.06	43.93	38.51	.11

continued

Table A.4 Continued

District Vote Projections for 2000
(Assuming the seat is open)
Each column represents the district-level results for one of the scenarios
described in chapter 7. The last column is the probability that the GOP
retains a seat, based on the point-estimated vote from scenario A.
Scenario A: Perfect division of the presidential vote at 50%
Scenario B: Marginal GOP win (53%–47%)
Scenario C: Marginal Democratic win (47%–53%)
Scenario D: Landslide GOP win (57%–43%)
Scenario E: Landslide Democratic win (43%–57%)

STATE	CD	A	B	C	D	E	P(R)[a]
MN	5	36.67	37.83	35.51	39.38	33.96	.03
MN	6	47.17	48.33	46.01	49.88	44.46	.35
MN	7	51.62	52.78	50.46	54.33	48.91	.59
MN	8	43.99	45.15	42.83	46.70	41.28	.21
MO	1	20.25	21.42	19.09	22.96	17.55	.01
MO	2	55.93	57.09	54.77	58.64	53.22	.21
MO	3	47.48	48.64	46.32	50.19	44.77	.36
MO	4	53.50	54.67	52.34	56.21	50.80	.69
MO	5	34.27	35.43	33.11	36.98	31.56	.02
MO	6	49.28	50.44	48.12	51.99	46.57	.46
MO	7	59.46	60.62	58.30	62.17	56.75	.90
MO	8	50.38	51.54	49.22	53.09	47.67	.52
MO	9	37.55	38.71	36.39	40.26	34.84	.05
MS	1	50.55	51.71	49.39	53.26	47.84	.53
MS	2	26.17	27.33	25.01	28.88	23.46	.01
MS	3	53.85	55.01	52.69	56.56	51.14	.70
MS	4	42.82	43.98	41.66	45.53	40.11	.16
MS	5	56.92	58.08	55.76	59.63	54.21	.83
MT	1	51.94	53.11	50.78	54.65	49.24	.61
NC	1	26.21	27.37	25.05	28.92	23.50	.01
NC	2	66.07	67.24	64.91	68.78	63.37	.99
NC	3	53.34	54.50	52.18	56.05	50.63	.68
NC	4	45.53	46.69	44.37	48.24	42.82	.27
NC	5	53.78	54.94	52.62	56.49	51.07	.70
NC	6	64.44	65.61	63.28	67.15	61.74	.98
NC	7	49.02	50.18	47.86	51.73	46.31	.44
NC	8	48.39	49.55	47.23	51.10	45.68	.41
NC	9	62.23	63.39	61.07	64.94	59.52	.95
NC	10	66.02	67.18	64.86	68.73	63.31	.99
NC	11	55.67	56.83	54.51	58.38	52.96	.79
NC	12	23.90	25.06	22.74	26.61	21.19	.01

Table A.4 Continued

District Vote Projections for 2000
(Assuming the seat is open)
Each column represents the district-level results for one of the scenarios
described in chapter 7. The last column is the probability that the GOP
retains a seat, based on the point-estimated vote from scenario A.
Scenario A: Perfect division of the presidential vote at 50%
Scenario B: Marginal GOP win (53%–47%)
Scenario C: Marginal Democratic win (47%–53%)
Scenario D: Landslide GOP win (57%–43%)
Scenario E: Landslide Democratic win (43%–57%)

STATE	CD	A	B	C	D	E	P(R)ᵃ
ND	1	55.86	57.02	54.70	58.57	53.15	.79
NE	1	—	—	—	—	—	
NE	2	—	—	—	—	—	
NE	3	—	—	—	—	—	
NH	1	—	—	—	—	—	
NH	2	47.23	48.39	46.07	49.94	44.52	.35
NJ	1	37.37	38.53	36.21	40.08	34.66	.04
NJ	2	44.18	45.35	43.02	46.89	41.48	.21
NJ	3	48.75	49.91	47.59	51.46	46.04	.43
NJ	4	46.53	47.70	45.37	49.24	43.83	.32
NJ	5	59.08	60.24	57.92	61.79	56.37	.89
NJ	6	42.89	44.05	41.73	45.60	40.18	.16
NJ	7	48.73	49.89	47.57	51.44	46.02	.43
NJ	8	40.24	41.40	39.08	42.95	37.53	.09
NJ	9	42.47	43.63	41.31	45.18	39.76	.15
NJ	10	14.65	15.81	13.49	17.36	11.94	.01
NJ	11	59.30	60.46	58.14	62.01	56.59	.90
NJ	12	52.08	53.24	50.92	54.79	49.37	.61
NJ	13	30.12	31.28	28.96	32.83	27.41	.01
NM	1	43.86	45.02	42.70	46.57	41.15	.20
NM	2	45.94	47.10	44.78	48.65	43.23	.29
NM	3	41.00	42.16	39.84	43.71	38.29	.11
NV	1	42.22	43.38	41.06	44.93	39.51	.14
NV	2	55.25	56.42	54.09	57.96	52.55	.76
NY	1	49.61	50.77	48.45	52.32	46.90	.48
NY	2	44.74	45.90	43.58	47.45	42.03	.23
NY	3	49.85	51.01	48.69	52.56	47.14	.49
NY	4	40.63	41.79	39.47	43.34	37.92	.10
NY	5	42.76	43.92	41.60	45.47	40.05	.16
NY	6	13.90	15.06	12.74	16.61	11.19	.01

continued

Table A.4 Continued

District Vote Projections for 2000
(Assuming the seat is open)
Each column represents the district-level results for one of the scenarios described in chapter 7. The last column is the probability that the GOP retains a seat, based on the point-estimated vote from scenario A.
Scenario A: Perfect division of the presidential vote at 50%
Scenario B: Marginal GOP win (53%–47%)
Scenario C: Marginal Democratic win (47%–53%)
Scenario D: Landslide GOP win (57%–43%)
Scenario E: Landslide Democratic win (43%–57%)

STATE	CD	A	B	C	D	E	P(R)[a]
NY	7	35.02	36.18	33.86	37.73	32.31	.02
NY	8	29.83	30.99	28.67	32.54	27.12	.01
NY	9	40.07	41.23	38.91	42.78	37.36	.08
NY	10	9.71	10.87	8.55	12.42	7.00	.01
NY	11	6.64	7.81	5.48	9.35	3.94	.01
NY	12	25.12	26.28	23.96	27.83	22.41	.01
NY	13	50.96	52.13	49.80	53.67	48.26	.55
NY	14	34.88	36.04	33.72	37.59	32.17	.02
NY	15	8.69	9.85	7.53	11.40	5.98	.01
NY	16	8.35	9.51	7.19	11.06	5.64	.01
NY	17	16.09	17.25	14.93	18.80	13.38	.01
NY	18	42.69	43.85	41.53	45.40	39.98	.15
NY	19	50.13	51.30	48.97	52.84	47.43	.51
NY	20	46.17	47.33	45.01	48.88	43.46	.30
NY	21	42.66	43.82	41.50	45.37	39.95	.15
NY	22	54.26	55.43	53.10	56.97	51.56	.72
NY	23	52.84	54.00	51.68	55.55	50.13	.65
NY	24	50.18	51.34	49.02	52.89	47.47	.51
NY	25	47.87	49.03	46.71	50.58	45.16	.39
NY	26	44.90	46.06	43.74	47.61	42.19	.24
NY	27	56.11	57.27	54.95	58.82	53.40	.80
NY	28	42.16	43.33	41.00	44.87	39.46	.14
NY	29	45.95	47.11	44.79	48.66	43.24	.29
NY	30	37.86	39.02	36.70	40.57	35.15	.05
NY	31	55.01	56.17	53.85	57.72	52.30	.75
OH	1	45.28	46.44	44.12	47.99	42.57	.26
OH	2	64.50	65.67	63.34	67.21	61.80	.98
OH	3	44.25	45.41	43.09	46.96	41.54	.21
OH	4	59.83	60.99	58.67	62.54	57.12	.91
OH	5	56.67	57.83	55.51	59.38	53.96	.82
OH	6	52.38	53.54	51.22	55.09	49.67	.62

Table A.4 Continued

District Vote Projections for 2000
(Assuming the seat is open)
Each column represents the district-level results for one of the scenarios described in chapter 7. The last column is the probability that the GOP retains a seat, based on the point-estimated vote from scenario A.
Scenario A: Perfect division of the presidential vote at 50%
Scenario B: Marginal GOP win (53%–47%)
Scenario C: Marginal Democratic win (47%–53%)
Scenario D: Landslide GOP win (57%–43%)
Scenario E: Landslide Democratic win (43%–57%)

STATE	CD	A	B	C	D	E	P(R)ª
OH	7	57.47	58.64	56.32	60.19	54.77	.85
OH	8	61.66	62.82	60.50	64.37	58.95	.95
OH	9	41.58	42.74	40.42	44.29	38.87	.12
OH	10	47.91	49.07	46.75	50.62	45.20	.39
OH	11	16.50	17.66	15.34	19.21	13.79	.01
OH	12	45.52	46.69	44.36	48.23	42.82	.27
OH	13	49.32	50.48	48.16	52.03	46.61	.46
OH	14	42.10	43.26	40.94	44.81	39.39	.14
OH	15	56.22	57.38	55.06	58.93	53.51	.80
OH	16	53.36	54.52	52.20	56.07	50.65	.68
OH	17	39.30	40.47	38.14	42.01	36.60	.07
OH	18	49.42	50.58	48.26	52.13	46.71	.47
OH	19	51.54	52.70	50.38	54.25	48.83	.58
OK	1	58.48	59.64	57.32	61.19	55.77	.88
OK	2	48.95	50.11	47.79	51.66	46.24	.44
OK	3	49.07	50.23	47.91	51.78	46.36	.45
OK	4	55.27	56.43	54.11	57.98	52.56	.77
OK	5	63.36	64.53	62.20	66.07	60.66	.97
OK	6	52.18	53.34	51.02	54.89	49.47	.62
OR	1	47.26	48.42	46.10	49.97	44.55	.35
OR	2	57.04	58.20	55.88	59.75	54.33	.84
OR	3	39.94	41.10	38.78	42.65	37.23	.08
OR	4	49.32	50.48	48.16	52.03	46.61	.47
OR	5	49.87	51.03	48.71	52.58	47.16	.49
PA	1	16.83	17.99	15.67	19.54	14.12	.01
PA	2	13.67	14.83	12.51	16.38	10.96	.01
PA	3	40.76	41.93	39.60	43.47	38.06	.10
PA	4	47.41	48.57	46.25	50.12	44.70	.36
PA	5	57.56	58.72	56.40	60.27	54.85	.85
PA	6	54.53	55.69	53.37	57.24	51.82	.74

continued

Table A.4 Continued

District Vote Projections for 2000
(Assuming the seat is open)
Each column represents the district-level results for one of the scenarios described in chapter 7. The last column is the probability that the GOP retains a seat, based on the point-estimated vote from scenario A.
Scenario A: Perfect division of the presidential vote at 50%
Scenario B: Marginal GOP win (53%–47%)
Scenario C: Marginal Democratic win (47%–53%)
Scenario D: Landslide GOP win (57%–43%)
Scenario E: Landslide Democratic win (43%–57%)

STATE	CD	A	B	C	D	E	P(R)[a]
PA	7	54.30	55.46	53.14	57.01	51.59	.73
PA	8	52.59	53.75	51.43	55.30	49.88	.64
PA	9	61.82	62.98	60.66	64.53	59.11	.95
PA	10	55.13	56.29	53.97	57.84	52.42	.76
PA	11	50.28	51.44	49.12	52.99	47.57	.51
PA	12	48.67	49.83	47.51	51.38	45.96	.43
PA	13	49.56	50.72	48.40	52.27	46.85	.48
PA	14	36.23	37.39	35.07	38.94	33.52	.03
PA	15	49.56	50.73	48.40	52.27	46.86	.48
PA	16	59.90	61.07	58.74	62.61	57.20	.91
PA	17	59.78	60.94	58.62	62.49	57.07	.91
PA	18	43.47	44.63	42.31	46.18	40.76	.18
PA	19	59.98	61.15	58.82	62.69	57.28	.92
PA	20	45.42	46.58	44.26	48.13	42.71	.27
PA	21	48.95	50.11	47.79	51.66	46.24	.44
RI	1	39.65	40.81	38.49	42.36	36.94	.08
RI	2	40.66	41.82	39.50	43.37	37.95	.10
SC	1	57.73	58.90	56.57	60.44	55.03	.86
SC	2	53.43	54.59	52.27	56.14	50.72	.68
SC	3	55.83	56.99	54.67	58.54	53.12	.79
SC	4	58.05	59.21	56.89	60.76	55.34	.87
SC	5	44.08	45.24	42.92	46.79	41.37	.21
SC	6	24.62	25.78	23.46	27.33	21.91	.01
SD	1	54.69	55.85	53.53	57.40	51.98	.74
TN	1	63.91	65.07	62.75	66.62	61.20	.97
TN	2	58.25	59.41	57.09	60.96	55.54	.87
TN	3	52.67	53.84	51.51	55.38	49.97	.64
TN	4	53.85	55.02	52.69	56.56	51.15	.70
TN	5	41.10	42.26	39.94	43.81	38.39	.11
TN	6	52.31	53.47	51.15	55.02	49.60	.63
TN	7	57.58	58.74	56.42	60.29	54.87	.85

Table A.4 Continued

District Vote Projections for 2000
(Assuming the seat is open)
Each column represents the district-level results for one of the scenarios described in chapter 7. The last column is the probability that the GOP retains a seat, based on the point-estimated vote from scenario A.
Scenario A: Perfect division of the presidential vote at 50%
Scenario B: Marginal GOP win (53%–47%)
Scenario C: Marginal Democratic win (47%–53%)
Scenario D: Landslide GOP win (57%–43%)
Scenario E: Landslide Democratic win (43%–57%)

STATE	CD	A	B	C	D	E	P(R)[a]
TN	8	45.48	46.65	44.32	48.19	42.78	.27
TN	9	24.50	25.66	23.34	27.21	21.79	.01
TX	1	48.48	49.64	47.32	51.19	45.77	.42
TX	2	46.53	47.70	45.37	49.24	43.83	.32
TX	3	—	—	—	—	—	
TX	4	61.10	62.26	59.94	63.81	58.39	.93
TX	5	—	—	—	—	—	
TX	6	—	—	—	—	—	
TX	7	—	—	—	—	—	
TX	8	—	—	—	—	—	
TX	9	—	—	—	—	—	
TX	10	42.22	43.38	41.06	44.93	39.51	.14
TX	11	50.90	52.06	49.74	53.61	48.19	.55
TX	12	50.80	51.96	49.64	53.51	48.09	.54
TX	13	56.05	57.21	54.89	58.76	53.34	.80
TX	14	52.03	53.19	50.87	54.74	49.32	.61
TX	15	34.23	35.39	33.07	36.94	31.52	.02
TX	16	33.94	35.11	32.78	36.65	31.24	.01
TX	17	56.29	57.45	55.13	59.00	53.58	.81
TX	18	—	—	—	—	—	
TX	19	67.43	68.59	66.27	70.14	64.72	.99
TX	20	36.03	37.19	34.87	38.74	33.32	.05
TX	21	66.71	67.88	65.55	69.42	64.01	.99
TX	22	—	—	—	—	—	
TX	23	44.35	45.51	43.19	47.06	41.64	.22
TX	24	—	—	—	—	—	
TX	25	—	—	—	—	—	
TX	26	—	—	—	—	—	
TX	27	37.81	38.97	36.65	40.52	35.10	.05
TX	28	32.50	33.67	31.34	35.21	29.80	.01

continued

Table A.4 Continued

District Vote Projections for 2000
(Assuming the seat is open)
Each column represents the district-level results for one of the scenarios described in chapter 7. The last column is the probability that the GOP retains a seat, based on the point-estimated vote from scenario A.
Scenario A: Perfect division of the presidential vote at 50%
Scenario B: Marginal GOP win (53%–47%)
Scenario C: Marginal Democratic win (47%–53%)
Scenario D: Landslide GOP win (57%–43%)
Scenario E: Landslide Democratic win (43%–57%)

STATE	*CD*	*A*	*B*	*C*	*D*	*E*	*P(R)*[a]
TX	29	—	—	—	—	—	
TX	30	—	—	—	—	—	
UT	1	65.90	67.06	64.74	68.61	63.19	.99
UT	2	57.44	58.60	56.28	60.15	54.73	.85
UT	3	65.33	66.49	64.17	68.04	62.62	.98
VA	1	56.43	57.59	55.27	59.14	53.72	.81
VA	2	52.90	54.06	51.74	55.61	50.19	.66
VA	3	21.39	22.55	20.23	24.10	18.68	.01
VA	4	44.71	45.87	43.55	47.42	42.00	.23
VA	5	48.29	49.45	47.13	51.00	45.58	.41
VA	6	58.16	59.32	57.00	60.87	55.45	.87
VA	7	63.75	64.91	62.59	66.46	61.04	.97
VA	8	44.01	45.17	42.85	46.72	41.30	.21
VA	9	54.45	55.61	53.29	57.16	51.74	.73
VA	10	62.51	63.67	61.35	65.22	59.80	.05
VA	11	52.88	54.04	51.72	55.59	50.17	.65
VT	1	43.24	44.40	42.08	45.95	40.53	.28
WA	1	48.96	50.12	47.80	51.67	46.25	.56
WA	2	50.23	51.39	49.07	52.94	47.52	.51
WA	3	49.41	50.57	48.25	52.12	46.70	.47
WA	4	55.84	57.00	54.68	58.55	53.13	.79
WA	5	53.14	54.30	51.98	55.85	50.43	.67
WA	6	45.37	46.53	44.21	48.08	42.66	.27
WA	7	33.29	34.45	32.13	36.00	30.58	.01
WA	8	51.48	52.64	50.32	54.19	48.77	.58
WA	9	45.15	46.31	43.99	47.86	42.44	.26
WI	1	48.55	49.71	47.39	51.26	45.84	.43
WI	2	45.74	46.91	44.58	48.45	43.04	.28
WI	3	47.33	48.49	46.17	50.04	44.62	.36
WI	4	49.59	50.75	48.43	52.30	46.88	.48
WI	5	30.21	31.37	29.05	32.92	27.50	.01

Table A.4 Continued

District Vote Projections for 2000
(Assuming the seat is open)

Each column represents the district-level results for one of the scenarios described in chapter 7. The last column is the probability that the GOP retains a seat, based on the point-estimated vote from scenario A.

Scenario A: Perfect division of the presidential vote at 50%
Scenario B: Marginal GOP win (53%–47%)
Scenario C: Marginal Democratic win (47%–53%)
Scenario D: Landslide GOP win (57%–43%)
Scenario E: Landslide Democratic win (43%–57%)

STATE	CD	A	B	C	D	E	P(R)[a]
WI	6	55.17	56.34	54.01	57.88	52.47	.76
WI	7	48.14	49.30	46.98	50.85	45.43	.40
WI	8	53.32	54.48	52.16	56.03	50.61	.67
WI	9	62.16	63.32	61.00	64.87	59.45	.04
WV	1	46.87	48.03	45.71	49.58	44.16	.34
WV	2	49.81	50.97	48.65	52.52	47.10	.49
WV	3	41.91	43.07	40.75	44.62	39.20	.14
WY	1	57.21	58.37	56.05	59.92	54.50	.84

[a]The probability that a district will be won by the Republican candidate is calculated by subtracting 50 from the expected vote under scenario A, and then dividing the remainder by the standard error of the regression equation for open seats in chapter 7. The resulting number is interpreted as a z-score on the normal distribution table, and the probability of that z-score occurring is added to .50 for positive scores, and subtracted from .50 for negative scores, to compute the probability.

NOTE

1. Logistic regression coefficients can be translated into probabilities by a simple arithmetic exercise. The maximum likelihood estimates (coefficients) indicate whether the variable is related to increasing odds of an outcome occurring (positive MLEs) or decreasing odds of an outcome occurring (negative MLEs). To obtain the probability of an event of interest occurring for a particular case, one need only multiply the relevant MLEs by the values of the variables they are associated with, then add those products together, much as in generating predicted values from OLS coefficients. After that step is completed, the next step is to translate those log odds into a probability. This is accomplished by performing the following translation:

$$P_{Y=1} = e^{L_P}/(1 + e^{L_P})$$

Where L_p = the log odds (the product of the summed MLEs multiplied by the values for the given case); e = Euler's Constant, which is always set to 2.71828. The product of this equation, always bounded by 0 and 1, represents the probability of obtaining a "1" value (see Cole, 1996, 262–265).

Methodological Sources

A variety of methodologies have been applied in the course of this study. Although many noncited influences often play into the development of research designs and the implementation of same, such as experience or a cruel teacher, several published resources contributed to the decision to use certain tools in this research. All quantitative analyses were conducted using SPSS/Windows 9.0. Errors in application or interpretation reside with the investigator.

Achen, C. H. 1982. *Interpreting and Using Regression.* Beverly Hills, Calif.: Sage.

Aldrich, J. H., and F. E. Nelson. 1984. *Linear Probability, Logit, and Probit Modeling.* Beverly Hills, Calif.: Sage.

Demaris, A. 1992. *Logit Modeling: Practical Applications.* Beverly Hills, Calif.: Sage.

Easton, D. 1965. *A Framework for Political Analysis.* Englewood Cliffs, N.J.: Prentice-Hall.

Fenno, Richard F. 1990. *Watching Politicians: Essays on Participant Observtion.* Berkeley, Calif.: IGS Press.

Gale, D. 1960. *The Theory of Linear Economic Models.* Chicago: Chicago Press.

Lewis-Beck, Michael. 1980. *Applied Regression: An Introduction.* Beverly Hills, Calif.: Sage.

Mohr, L. B. 1988. *Impact Analysis for Program Evaluation.* Chicago: Dorsey Press.

Pindyck, R. S., and D. L. Rubenfeld. 1976. *Econometric Models and Economic Forecasts.* New York: McGraw-Hill.

Sayres, L. W. 1989. *Pooled Time Series Analysis.* Beverly Hills, Calif.: Sage.

Stimson, J. T. 1985. "Regression in Space and Time: A Statistical Essay," *American Journal of Political Science* 29:914–947.

References

Abel, Douglas D., and Bruce I. Oppenheimer. 1994. "Candidate Emergence in a Majority Hispanic District: The 29th District in Texas," in Thomas A. Kazee, ed., *Who Runs for Congress?* Washington, D.C.: Congressional Quarterly Press.

Abramowitz, Alan I. 1983. "Partisan Redistricting and the 1982 Congressional Elections," *Journal of Politics* 45:767–770.

———. 1989. "Campaign Spending in U.S. Senate Elections," *Legislative Studies Quarterly* 14:487–507.

———. 1991a. "Open Seat Elections to the U.S. House of Representatives." Paper presented at the annual meeting of the Southern Political Science Association, Tampa, Fla.

———. 1991b. "Incumbency, Campaign Spending, and the Decline of Competition in U.S. House Elections," *Journal of Politics* 53:34–57.

Aistrup, Joseph A. 1990. "Republican Contestation of U.S. State Senate Elections in the South," *Legislative Studies Quarterly* 15:227–245.

———. 1995. "Southern Republican Subnational Advancement: The Redistricting Explanation," *American Review of Politics* 16:15–32.

———. 1996. *The Southern Strategy Revisited.* Lexington: University Press of Kentucky.

Aistrup, Joseph A., and Ronald Keith Gaddie. 1999. "Candidate Recruitment and the New Southern Party System." Paper presented at the annual meeting of the Southern Political Science Association, Savannah, Ga., November 3–6.

Alexander, Herbert E. 1984. *Parties and PACs: Relationships and Inter-relationships.* Los Angeles: Citizens Research Foundation.

Alford, John, and David Brady. 1989. "Personal and Partisan Advantage in U.S. Congressional Elections, 1846–1986," in Lawrence C. Dodd and Bruce I. Oppenheimer, eds., *Congress Reconsidered*, 4th ed. Washington, D.C.: Congressional Quarterly Press.

Alford, John, and John R. Hibbing. 1981. "Increased Incumbency Advantage in the House," *Journal of Politics* 43:1042–1061.

Alford, John, Holly Teeters, Daniel S. Ward, and Rick K. Wilson. 1994. "Overdraft: The Political Cost of Congressional Malfeasance," *Journal of Politics* 56:788–801.

Alston, Chuck. 1992a. "Big Money Slips Back into Government," *Congressional Quarterly Weekly Report* 50 (March 7):591.

———. 1992b. "Campaign Finance Bills Compared," *Congressional Quarterly Weekly Report* 50 (February 9):489–495.

219

Anderson, Kristi, and Stuart J. Thorson. 1984. "Congressional Turnover and the Election of Women," *Western Political Quarterly* 37:143–156.

Austin, Clint. Interview with authors, March 18, 1999.

Balz, Daniel J., and Ronald Brownstein. 1996. *Storming the Gates: Protest Politics and the Republican Revival*. Boston: Little, Brown.

Barber, James David. 1965. *The Lawmakers: Recruitment and Adaptation to Legislative Life*. New Haven: Yale University Press.

Barone, Michael, and Grant Ujifusa. 1975, 1977, 1979, 1981, 1983, 1985, 1987, 1989, 1991, 1993, 1995, 1997, 1999. *The Almanac of American Politics*. Washington, D.C.: National Journal.

Bauer, Monica, and John R. Hibbing. 1989. "Which Incumbents Lose in House Elections: A Response to Jacobson's 'The Marginals Never Vanished,'" *American Journal of Political Science* 33:262–272.

Bednar, Nancy L., and Allen D. Hertzke. 1995. "The Christian Right and Republican Realignment in Oklahoma." *PS: Political Science & Politics* 28:11–15.

Bianco, William T. 1984. "Strategic Decisions on Candidacy in U.S. Congressional Elections," *Legislative Studies Quarterly* 9:351–364.

Black, Earl, and Merle Black. 1987. *Politics and Society in the South*. Cambridge, Mass.: Harvard University Press.

Bledsoe, Timothy, and Mary Herring. 1990. "Victims of Circumstances: Women in Pursuit of Political Office," *American Political Science Review* 84:213–223.

Bond, Jon R., Cary Covington, and Richard Fleisher. 1985. "Explaining Challenger Quality in Congressional Elections," *Journal of Politics* 47:510–529.

Bond, Jon R., Richard Fleisher, and Jeffrey C. Talbert. 1997. "The Experience Factor in Open Seat Congressional Elections, 1976–1994," *Political Research Quarterly* 50:281–299.

Born, Richard. 1984. "Reassessing the Decline of Presidential Coattails: U.S. House Elections from 1952–1980," *Journal of Politics* 46:60–79.

Box-Steffensmeier, Janet. 1996. "A Dynamic Analysis of the Role of War Chests in Campaign Strategy," *American Journal of Political Science* 40:352–371.

Bullock, Charles S., III. 1975. "Redistricting and Congressional Stability," *Journal of Politics* 37:568–575.

———. 1983. "The Effects of Redistricting on Black Representation in Southern Legislatures." Paper presented at the annual meeting of the American Political Science Association, Chicago.

———. 1995a. "The Impact of Changing the Racial Composition of Congressional Districts on Legislators' Roll Call Behavior," *American Politics Quarterly* 23:141–158.

———. 1995b. "Winners and Losers in the Latest Round of Redistricting," *Emory Law Journal* 44:943–977.

Bullock, Charles S., III, and Ronald Keith Gaddie. 1993. "Changing from Multi-Member to Single-Member Districts: Partisan, Racial, and Gender Impacts," *State and Local Government Review* 25:155–163.

Bullock, Charles S., III, and Patricia Lee Findley Heys. 1972. "Recruitment of Women for Congress," *Western Political Quarterly* 25:416–423.

Bullock, Charles S. III., and Mark Rozell. 1998. *The New Politics of the Old South*. Lanham, Md: Rowman & Littlefield.

Bullock, Charles S., III, and Michael A Scicchitano. 1982. "Senate Defections and Re-Elections," *American Politics Quarterly* 10:477–488.

Bullock, Charles S., III, and David J. Shafer. 1998. "Party Targeting and Electoral Success," *Legislative Studies Quarterly* 22:573–84.

Burrell, Barbara C. 1994. *A Woman's Place Is in the House: Campaigning for Congress in the Feminist Era*. Ann Arbor: University of Michigan Press.

Butler, David, and Denis Kavanaugh. 1981. *The British General Election of 1979*. London: Macmillan.

Cain, Bruce E. 1984. *The Reapportionment Puzzle*. Berkeley: University of California Press.

Cain, Bruce E., John A. Ferejohn, and Morris P. Fiorina. 1984. "The Constituency Service Basis of the Personal Vote for U.S. Representatives and British Members of Parliament," *American Political Science Review* 78:110–125.

———. 1987. *The Personal Vote: Constituency Service and Electoral Independence*. Cambridge, Mass.: Harvard University Press.

Campagna Janet, and Bernard Grofman. 1990. "Party Control and Partisan Bias in 1980s Congressional Redistricting." *The Journal of Politics* 52:1242–57.

Campbell, Angus. 1966. "Surge and Decline: A Study of Electoral Change," in Angus Campbell, Philip E. Converse, Warren E. Miller, and Donald E. Stokes. *Elections and the Political Order*. New York: Wiley.

Campbell, James E. 1986. "Presidential Coattails and Midterm Losses in State Legislative Elections," *American Political Science Review* 80:45–64.

———. 1996. *Cheap Seats: The Democratic Party's Advantage in U.S. House Elections*. Columbus: Ohio State University Press.

———. 1997. *The Presidential Pulse of Congressional Elections*. 2nd ed. Lexington: University Press of Kentucky.

Campbell, James E., and Joe A. Sumners. 1990. "Presidential Coattails in Senate Elections," *American Political Science Review* 84:513–524.

Canon, Bradley C. 1978. "Factionalism in the South: A Revisitation of V.O. Key and a Test of Theory," *American Journal of Political Science* 22:833–48.

Canon, David T. 1990. *Actors, Athletes, and Astronauts: Political Amateurs in the United States Congress*. Chicago: University of Chicago Press.

———. 1993. "Sacrificial Lambs or Strategic Politicians? Political Amateurs in U.S. House Elections," *American Journal of Political Science* 37:1119–1141.

Caro, Robert. 1982. *The Years of Lyndon Johnson: The Path to Power*. New York: Knopf.

Carroll, Kathleen M. 1983. "The Age Difference Between Men and Women Politicians," *Social Science Quarterly* 64:332–339.

Carroll, Susan J. 1985. "Political Elites and Sex Differences in Political Ambition: A Reconsideration," *Journal of Politics* 47:1231–1243.

Chubb, John. 1988. "Institution, the Economy, and the Dynamics of State Elections," *American Political Science Review* 82:133–154.

Clausen, Aage R. 1973. *How Congressmen Decide: A Policy Focus*. New York: St. Martin's Press.

Collie, Melissa P. 1981. "Incumbency, Electoral Safety, and Turnover in the House of Representatives, 1952–76," *American Political Science Review* 75:119–131.

Cover, Albert D. 1977. "One Good Term Deserves Another: The Advantage of Incumbency in Congressional Elections," *American Journal of Political Science* 21:523–541.

Darcy, R., and James R. Choike. 1986. "A Formal Analysis of Legislative Turnover:

Women Candidates and Legislative Representation," *American Journal of Political Science* 30:237–255.

Darcy, R., and Charles D. Hadley. 1988. "Black Women in Politics: The Puzzle of Success," *Social Science Quarterly* 69:629–645.

Denzau, Arthur, and Michael C. Munger. 1986. "Legislators and Interest Groups: How Unorganized Interests Get Represented," *American Political Science Review* 80:89–106.

Dewar, Helen. 1991. "Trouble Fielding a Team: For Want of Candidates, the GOP Could Lose Big in '92," *Washington Post Weekly Edition*, August 19–25:12.

Dimock, Michael A., and Gary C. Jacobson. 1995. "Checks and Choices: The House Bank Scandal's Impact on Voters in 1992," *Journal of Politics* 57:1143–1159.

Downs, Anthony. 1957. *An Economic Theory of Democracy*. New York: Harper-Collins.

Duverger, Maurice. 1954. *Political Parties: Their Organization and Activity in the Modern State*. New York: Wiley.

Ehrenhalt, Alan. 1983. *Politics in America*. Washington, D.C.: CQ Press.

———. 1991. *The United States of Ambition*. New York: Times Books.

Erikson, Robert S. 1972. "Malapportionment, Gerrymandering, and Party Fortunes in Congressional Elections," *American Political Science Review* 66:1234–1245.

———. 1976. "Is There Such a Thing as a Safe Seat?" *Polity* 8:623–632.

Feigert, Frank B., and Pippa Norris. 1990. "Do By-Elections Constitute Referenda? A Four-Country Comparison," *Legislative Studies Quarterly* 15:183–200.

Fenno, Richard F. 1978. *Home Style*. Boston: Little, Brown.

———. 1982. *The United States Senate: A Bicameral Perspective*. Washington, D.C.: American Enterprise Institute.

———. 1996. *U.S. Senators on the Campaign Trail*. Norman: University of Oklahoma Press.

———. 1991. *When Incumbency Fails: The Senate Career of Mark Andrews*. Washington, D.C.: CQ Press.

Ferejohn, John A. 1977. "On the Decline of Competition in Congressional Elections," *American Political Science Review* 71:166–76.

Flemming, Gregory H. 1995. "Presidential Coattails in Open Seat Elections," *Legislative Studies Quarterly* 20:197–211.

Fowler, Linda L. 1993. *Candidates, Congress, and the American Democracy*. Ann Arbor: University of Michigan Press.

Fowler, Linda L., and Robert D. McClure. 1989. *Political Ambition: Who Decides to Run for Congress*. New Haven: Yale University Press.

Gaddie, Ronald Keith. 1995a. "Is There an Inherent Democratic Party Advantage in U.S. House Elections? Evidence from the Open Seats," *Social Science Quarterly* 76:203–212.

———. 1995b. "Negating the Democratic Advantage in Open Seat Congressional Elections—A Research Update," *Social Science Quarterly* 75:673–680.

———. 1995c. "Investing in the Future: Economic Political Action Committee Contributions to Open Seat House Candidates," *American Politics Quarterly* 23:339–354.

———. 1996. "Pragmatism and the Corporate Shift: An Alternative Perspective," *Social Science Quarterly* 77:924–928.

————. 1997. "Congressional Seat Swings: Revisiting Exposure in House Elections," *Political Research Quarterly* 50:675–686.

Gaddie, Ronald Keith, and Lesli E. McCollum. 1998. "Estimating the Incumbent Advantage: A New Approach to an Old Problem." Paper presented at the annual meeting of the Southwestern Political Science Association, Corpus Christi, Tex.

————. 2000. "Money and the Incumbency Advantage in U.S. House Elections," in Joseph P. Zimmerman and Wilma Rule, eds., *The U.S. House of Representatives: Remodel or Rebuild?* Westport, Conn.: Praeger.

Gaddie, Ronald Keith, and Jonathan D. Mott. 1998. "The 1996 Open Seat Congressional Elections," *Social Science Quarterly* 79:444–454.

Gaddie, Ronald Keith, Jonathan D. Mott, and Shad D. Satterthwaite. 1999. "Partisan Dimensions to Corporate Realignment in Congressional Campaign Finance," *Public Integrity* 4:6–43.

Gaddie, Ronald Keith, and James L. Regens. 1997. "Economic PAC Allocations in Open Seat Senate Elections," *American Politics Quarterly* 25:347–362.

Gilmour, John B., and Paul Rothstein. 1993. "Early Republican Retirement: A Cause of Democratic Dominance in the House of Representatives," *Legislative Studies Quarterly* 18:345–365.

Gelman, Andrew, and Gary King. 1990. "Estimating Incumbency Advantage Without Bias," *American Journal of Political Science* 34:1142–1165.

Gertzog, Irwin N. 1979. "Changing Patterns of Female Recruitment to the U.S. House of Representatives," *Legislative Studies Quarterly* 6:429–445.

Glaser, James A. 1996. *Race, Campaign Politics, and the Realignment in the South*. New Haven: Yale University Press.

Goidel, Robert K., and Todd G. Shields. 1994. "The Vanishing Marginals, the Bandwagon, and the Mass Media," *Journal of Politics* 56:802–810.

Green, Donald Philip, and Jonathan S. Krasno. 1988. "Salvation for the Spendthrift Incumbent: Reestimating the Effects of Campaign Spending in House Elections," *American Journal of Political Science,* 32:884–907.

Grier, Kevin B., and Michael C. Munger. 1991. "Committee Assignments, Constituent Preferences, and Campaign Contributions," *Economic Inquiry* 29:24–43.

————. 1993. "Comparing Interest Group PAC Contributions to House and Senate Incumbents, 1980–1986," *Journal of Politics* 55:615–643.

Grier, Kevin B., Michael C. Munger, and G. Torrent. 1990. "Allocation Patterns of PAC Monies: The Case of the U.S. Senate," *Public Choice* 67:111–28.

Herrnson, Paul S. 1995. *Congressional Elections: Campaigning at Home and in Washington*. Washington, D.C.: CQ Press.

Hibbing, John R. 1982. "Voluntary Retirement from the U.S. House: The Costs of Congressional Service," *Legislative Studies Quarterly* 7:57–74.

Hotelling, H. 1929. "Stability in Competition," *Economic Journal* 39:41–57.

Huckshorn, Robert J., and Robert C. Spencer. 1971. *The Politics of Defeat: Campaigning for Congress*. Amherst: University of Massachusetts Press.

Jackson, Brooks. 1990. *Honest Graft: Big Money and the American Political Process*. Washington, D.C.: Farragut Publishing Company.

Jacobson, Gary C. 1978. "The Effects of Campaign Spending in Congressional Elections," *American Political Science Review* 72:769–783.

————. 1980. *Money in Congressional Elections*. New Haven: Yale University Press.

————. 1985. "Money and Votes Reconsidered: Congressional Elections, 1972–1982," *Public Choice* 47:7–62.

————. 1987. "The Marginals Never Vanished: Incumbency and Competition in Elections to the U.S. House of Representatives," *American Journal of Political Science* 31:126–141.

————. 1989. "Parties and PACs in Congressional Elections," in Lawrence C. Dodd and Bruce I. Oppenheimer, eds., *Congress Reconsidered*, 4th ed. Washington, D.C.: CQ Press.

————. 1990. *The Electoral Origins of Divided Government: Competition in U.S. House Elections, 1946–1988*. Boulder, Colo.: Westview Press.

————. 1997. *The Politics of Congressional Elections*, 4th ed. New York: Harper-Collins.

Jacobson, Gary C., and Samuel Kernell. 1982. "Strategy and Choice in the 1982 Congressional Elections," *PS* 14 (Summer):423–430.

————. 1983. *Strategy and Choice in Congressional Elections*. New Haven: Yale University Press.

Jacobson, Gary C., and Michael A. Dimock. 1994. "Checking Out: The Effects of Bank Overdrafts on the 1992 House Elections," *American Journal of Political Science* 38:601–624.

Jones, Charles O. 1981. "New Directions in U.S. Congressional Research: A Review Article," *Legislative Studies Quarterly* 6:455–468.

Kazee, Thomas A. 1994. *Who Runs for Congress? Ambition, Context, and Candidate Emergence*. Washington, D.C.: Congressional Quarterly Press.

Kearns, Doris. 1976. *Lyndon Johnson and the American Dream*. New York: St. Martin's.

Key, V. O. 1949. *Southern Politics in State and Nation*. New York: Knopf.

Krasno, Jonathan S,. and Donald Phillip Green. 1988. "Preempting Quality Challengers in House Elections," *Journal of Politics* 50:920–936.

Lamis, Alexander. 1988. *The Two-Party South Expanded Edition*. New York: Oxford University Press.

Leyden, Kevin M., and Stephen A. Borrelli. 1994. "An Investment In Goodwill: Party Contributions and Party Unity Among U.S. House Members in the 1980s," *American Politics Quarterly* 22:421–452.

Lineberry, Robert L., John E. Sinclair, Lawrence C. Dodd, and Alan M. Sager. 1976. "The Case of the Wrangling Professors: The Twenty-First District of Texas," in Alan L. Clem, ed., *The Making of Congressmen: Seven Campaigns of 1974*. North Scituate, Mass.: Duxbury Press.

Lublin, David I. 1997. "The Election of African Americans and Latinos to the U.S. House of Representatives, 1972–1994," *American Politics Quarterly* 25:269–286.

————. 1998. *The Paradox of Representation: Racial Gerrymandering and Minority Interests in Congress*. Princeton, N.J.: Princeton University Press.

Mann, Thomas E., and Raymond E. Wolfinger. 1980. "Candidates and Parties in Congressional Elections," *American Political Science Review* 74:616–632.

Mayhew, David R. 1966. *Party Loyalty Among Congressmen: The Difference Between Democrats and Republicans, 1947–1962*. Cambridge, Mass.: Harvard University Press.

————. 1974a. "Congressional Elections: The Case of the Vanishing Marginals," *Polity* 6:295–317.

————. 1974b. *Congress: The Electoral Connection*. New Haven: Yale University Press.

Miller, Warren E., and Donald E. Stokes. 1963. "Constituency Influence in Congress," *American Political Science Review* 57:45–57.

Moore, Michael C., and John R. Hibbing. 1992. "Is Serving in Congress Fun Again? Voluntary Retirements from the House since the 1970s," *American Journal of Political Science* 36:824–828.

Mondak, Jeffrey J. 1994. "Presidential Coattails and Open Seats," *American Politics Quarterly* 21:307–319.

Mughan, Anthony. 1986. "Toward a Political Explanation of Government Vote Losses in Midterm By-Elections," *American Political Science Review* 80:761–775.

Niemi, Richard G., and Laura R. Winsky. 1992. "The Persistence of Partisan Redistricting Effects in Congressional Elections in the 1970s and 1980s." *The Journal of Politics* 54:565–72.

Norris, Pippa, and Frank B. Feigert. 1989. "Government and Third-Party Performance in Mid-Term By-Elections: The Canadian, British and Australian Experience," *Electoral Studies* 8:11–130.

Ornstein, Norman J., Thomas E. Mann, and Michael J. Malbin. 1998. *Vital Statistics on Congress 1997–1998*. Washington, D.C.: Congressional Quarterly Books.

————. 1988. *Vital Statistics on Congress 1987–1988*. Washington, D.C.: Congressional Quarterly Books

Overby, L. Marvin, Beth M. Henschen, Michael H. Walsh, and Julie Strauss. 1992. "Courting Constituency? An Analysis of the Senate Confirmation Vote on Justice Clarence Thomas," *American Political Science Review* 86:997–1003.

Parker, Glenn R. 1992a. *Institutional Change, Discretion, and the Making of Modern Congress: An Economic Interpretation*. Ann Arbor: University of Michigan Press.

————. 1992b. "The Distribution of Honoraria Income in the U.S. Congress: Who Gets Rents in Legislatures and Why?" *Public Choice* 73:167–181.

————. 1994. *Institutional Discretion and the Creation of Modern Congress*. Ann Arbor: University of Michigan Press.

Paul, Chris, and Al Wilhite. 1990. "Efficient Rent-Seeking Under Varying Cost Structures," *Public Choice* 64:279–290.

Petrocik, John R., and Scott W. Desposato. 1998. "The Partisan Consequences of Majority–Minority Redistricting in the South, 1992 and 1994," *The Journal of Politics* 60:613–633.

Pollock, James K. 1941. "British By-Elections between the Wars," *American Political Science Review* 35:519–528.

Posner, Richard A. 1986. *An Economic Analysis of Law*, 3rd ed. Boston: Little, Brown and Company.

Price, H. David. 1957. *Negro Politics in the South: A Chapter in Florida History*. New York: New York University Press.

Pritchard, Anita. 1992a. "Strategic Considerations in the Decision to Challenge a State Legislative Incumbent," *Legislative Studies Quarterly* 17:381–394.

————. 1992b. "Changes in Electoral Structure and the Success of Women Candidates: The Case of Florida," *Social Science Quarterly* 73:62–70.

Regens, James L., Euel W. Elliott, and Ronald Keith Gaddie. 1991. "Regulatory Costs, Committee Jurisdictions, and Corporate PAC Contributions," *Social Science Quarterly* 72:751–760.

Regens, James L., and Ronald Keith Gaddie. 1995. *The Economic Realities of Political Reform: Elections and the United States Senate.* New York: Cambridge University Press.

Regens, James L., Ronald Keith Gaddie, and Brad Lockerbie. 1995. "The Electoral Consequences of Voting to Declare War," *The Journal of Conflict Resolution* 39:168–182.

Robeck, Bruce W. 1982. "State Legislator Candidacies for the U.S. House: Prospects for Success," *Legislative Studies Quarterly* 7:507–514.

Sabato, Larry J. 1985. *PAC Power: Inside the World of Political Action Committees.* New York: W.W. Norton.

Schwab, Larry. 1985. "The Impact of 1980 Reapportionment in the United States," *Political Geography Quarterly* 4:141–158.

Sigelman, Lee. 1981. "Special Elections to the U.S. House: Some Descriptive Generalizations," *Legislative Studies Quarterly* 6:577–588.

Sinclair, Barbara. 1989. *The Transformation of the U.S. Senate.* Baltimore, Md.: Johns Hopkins University Press.

Smist, Frank J., Jr., and John P. Meiers. 1995. "Buying and Selling an Open Seat for Congress: A Case Study of the 1994 Race to Succeed Alan Wheat in Missouri's Fifth District." Paper presented at the annual meeting of the Southern Political Science Association, Tampa, Fla.

Sorauf, Frank J. 1988. *Money in American Elections.* Glenview, Ill.: Scott, Foresman.

Sorauf, Frank J., and Scott A. Wilson. 1992. "Campaigns and Money: A Changing Role for the Political Parties?" in Sandy Maisel, ed., *The Parties Respond: Changes in the American Party System.* Boulder, Colo.: Westview Press.

Sprague, John. 1981. "One-Party Dominance in Legislatures," *Legislative Studies Quarterly* 6:259–285.

Squire, Peverill. 1991. "Preemptive Fund-raising and Challenger Profile in Senate Elections," *Journal of Politics* 53:1150–1164.

Stambough, Stephen J., and Gregory R. Thorson. 1995. "Anti-Incumbency and the 1992 Elections: The Changing Face of Presidential Coattails," *Journal of Politics* 57:210–220.

Stanley, Harold W. 1992. "Southern Republicans in Congress: Have They Fallen and They Can't Get Up?" *Social Science Quarterly* 73:136–140.

Stanley, Harold W., and Richard G. Niemi, 1993. *Vital Statistics on American Politics*, 4th ed. Washington, D.C.: Congresional Quarterly Books.

Stigler, George J. "The Theory of Economic Regulation," *Bell Journal of Economics and Management Science* 2:137–146.

Stokes, Donald E. 1967. "Parties and the Nationalization of Electoral Forces," in William Chambers and Walter Dean Burnham, eds., *The American Party Systems: Stages of Political Development.* New York: Oxford University Press.

Studlar, Donley T., and Lee Sigelman. 1987. "Special Elections: A Comparative Perspective," *British Journal of Political Science* 17:247–256.

Su, Tie-ting, Alan Neustadtl, and Dan Clawson. 1995. "Business and the Conservative Shift: Corporate PAC Contributions, 1976–1986," *Social Science Quarterly* 76:20–40.

Swain, Carol M. 1995. *Black Faces, Black Interests: The Representation of African Americans in Congress.* Cambridge, Mass.: Harvard University Press.

Theilemann, Gregory S. 1992. "The Rise and Stall of Southern Republicans in Congress," *Social Science Quarterly* 72:123–135.

———. 1991. "Stalled Realignment: Southern Congressional Elections in the 1980s." Unpublished manuscript.

Thomas, Sue. 1994. *How Women Legislate.* New York: Oxford University Press.

Tufte, Edward. 1975. "Determinants of the Outcomes of Midterm Congressional Elections," *American Political Science Review* 69:812–826.

Uhlaner, Carole Jean, and Kay Lehman Schlozman. 1986. "Candidate Gender and Congressional Campaign Receipts," *Journal of Politics* 48:30–50.

Volgy, Thomas J., John E. Schwarz, and Hildy Gottleib. 1986. "Female Representation and the Quest for Resources: Feminist Activism and Electoral Success," *Social Science Quarterly* 67:156–168.

Wetherell, T.K. 1991. "Florida Takes the Big Money Out of Political Campaigns." *State Legislatures* August: 44.

Wilcox, Clyde. 1987. "Timing of Strategic Decisions: Candidacy Decisions in 1982 and 1984," *Legislative Studies Quarterly* 12:565–572.

Wilcox, Clyde, and Bob Biersack. 1990. "Research Update: The Timing of Candidacy Decisions in the House, 1982–1988," *Legislative Studies Quarterly* 15:115–126.

Wilhite, Allen, and John Thielmann. 1986. "Women, Blacks, and PAC Discrimination," *Social Science Quarterly* 67:283–298.

Wright, John R. 1989. "PAC Contributions, Lobbying, and Representation," *Journal of Politics* 51:713–729.

Index

Abramowitz, Alan I., 4, 20, 28, 97, 111
access/influence paradigm, 109
advertising, television, 72–73
African Americans. *See* blacks
Aistrup, Joseph A., 29
Alabama, 31
Alford, John, 8, 193n3, 197
Almanac of American Politics, 155
Anderson, Kristi, 130
anti-Democratic sentiment, 174
anti-incumbent sentiment, 3
anti-president sentiment, 3, 46–48, 153, 167nn5–6, 174
apportionment, 152
Arizona, 182–83
Arkansas, 69–71, 84n10
Ashbrook, Jean, 159
Ashbrook, John, 159
Ashcroft, John, 83n3
Aspin, Les, 153

Baesler, Scotty, 186, 193n7
Baird, Brian, 186
Baker v. Carr, 25
Barbour, Haley, 123
Barca, Peter, 153
Barr, Bob, 73
Becker, Daniel, 72
Bennett, Charles, 133
Bethune, Ed, 69
Bianco, William T., 53, 76
Biersak, Bob, 53

bipartisanship: Coelho's strategy, 121; PAC contributions, 110, 111–13, 121
blacks, 184; ability to raise money, 98; as candidates, 54–55; experience factor in contests, 78; fund-raising, 103–4, 128n5; Georgia redistricting and, 72; as legislators, 7, 12n6; majority-black districts, 74, 103–4, 128n5, 133; open seat election models, 42–43, 199–200; racial composition and election outcomes, 48–49; redistricting and, 29–34, 50–51n4, 72; Republican electoral success and, 30–34, 45–46; support of Democrats, 29–30; as voting bloc, 43
Bolling, Richard, 54
Bond, Jon R., 76–78, 97, 98, 165, 193n5, 200
Bono, Mary, 167n10
Bordonaro, Tom, 167n10
Born, Richard, 39
Box-Steffensmeier, Janet, 99
Brady, David, 8, 193n3, 197
Brown, Corrine, 133, 134
Brown, Marta, 167n10
Buchanan, James D., 150
Buckley v. Valeo, 87
Buckley, William F., 135
Bullock, Charles S., III, 29, 150
Burton, Phil, 28
Burton Plan, 28, 29, 50n3

About the Authors

Ronald Keith Gaddie is associate professor of political science at the University of Oklahoma. He is author or coauthor of a half dozen books, including *The Economic Realities of Political Reform: Elections and the U.S. Senate* (Cambridge University Press, 1995), *David Duke and the Politics of Race in the South* (Vanderbilt University Press, 1995), and *Regulating Wetlands Protection: Environmental Federalism and the States* (SUNY Press, 2000), and journal articles on campaign finance, legislative elections, southern politics, and environmental policy. He is also faculty consultant to the University of Oklahoma Public Opinion Learning Laboratory, and serves on the editorial board of *Social Science Quarterly*.

 Charles S. Bullock, III, is Richard B. Russell Professor of Political Science at the University of Georgia. He is the author or coauthor of over a dozen books, including *The New Politics of the Old South* (Rowman & Littlefield, 1998), *David Duke and the Politics of Race in the South* (Vanderbilt University Press, 1995), and *Runoff Elections in the United States* (University of North Carolina Press, 1992), and journal articles on topics such as race politics, southern politics, legislative process, and policy implementation. He is a former president of the Southern Political Science Association (1986), and is a member of the editorial boards of *The Journal of Politics* and *Social Science Quarterly*.